LANGUAGE AND COGNITION:
A DEVELOPMENTAL PERSPECTIVE

edited by

ESTHER DROMI

Tel Aviv University, Israel

Human Development, Volume 5

The Tel Aviv Workshop in Human Development

Sidney Strauss, Series Editor

ABLEX PUBLISHING CORPORATION
NORWOOD, NEW JERSEY

Printed in the United States of America.

Library of Congress Cataloging-in-Publication Data

Language and cogntion : a developmental perspective / edited by
  Esther Dromi.
      p.   cm. — (Human development series ; v. 5)
    Includes bibliographical references and index.
    ISBN 0-89391-682-X
    1. Language acquisition.   2. Cognition in children.   I. Dromi,
  Esther.   II. Series: Human development (Norwood, N.J.) ; v. 5.
  P118.L2558   1992
  401'.93 — dc20   92-12020
                                                          CIP

Ablex Publishing Corporation
355 Chestnut Street
Norwood, New Jersey 07648

To Udi and Keren

Contents

Acknowledgments

I would like to express my gratitude to Professor Sidney Strauss, the head of the Human Development and Education Unit at the School of Education of Tel Aviv University, for encouraging me to undertake the exciting challenge of organizing the Fifth Annual Workshop of the Unit, and subsequently editing this volume. Thanks are also extended to the workshop participants for creating such a stimulating intellectual meeting, and for contributing to the wonderful warm atmosphere during our days of discussion. I truly appreciate their cooperation and responsiveness throughout the long process of preparing the manuscripts of chapters. Finally, my heartfelt thanks go out to my husband and daughter, for their love, constant support and involvement, and sincere interest in my academic life.

Human Development: Preface to the Series

Sidney Strauss
Series Editor

This book series is the product of annual workshops held by the Unit of Human Development and Education in the School of Education at Tel Aviv University. Whenever a new publication comes out, the person responsible for it feels compelled to answer the question: Why a new X (journal, book, book series)? I do not feel exonerated from asking and answering that question. The purpose of the series is to address topics of theory, as well as conceptual and methodological issues that reflect the diversity and complexity of human development. It aims to address four needs in our field, as they relate to edited books.

There are few attempts to deal with important developmental phenomena in a concentrated manner in most of the book series in our field. They generally contain a collection of chapters or unrelated topics. There is a need to have leading experts present their views about relatively circumscribed issues. Our books will be organized around a topic where contributors write chapters that fit into a larger picture the editor will be illuminating.

A second need in our field is to have more interdisciplinary work. We generally read books written by developmental psychologists for developmental psychologists. Restricting inquiry to the psychological realm promotes a rather narrow view of human development. The view of man as a biological entity and cultural producer and consumer as well as a psychological being has been deeply neglected, and an element that will characterize our books is the inclusion of representatives of intellectual disciplines to discuss topics we believe to be of importance for our field.

Most work in developmental psychology is published in English and written by Americans. Much of the Western and Eastern European work is unknown to the vast majority of developmental psychologists, and the same can be said with more emphasis for work being done in Latin America, Asia, and Africa. Whenever possible, we will bring leading intellectual figures from these continents to contribute to our deliberations.

The fourth need is to attend to the applied parts of developmental psychology. Some of the later books will revolve around issues relating developmental psychology and education. We chose this out of the conviction that educational issues force one to face the depth of human complexity and its development in ways that traditional academic developmental psychology often turns away from.

The topics for the books are chosen with an eye towards directions our field is taking or we think should be taking. In some instances we will have a book about a topic that has been discussed in the literature and is ripe for a summary or stocktaking. In other instances the book will be around a topic that has not been discussed at all or has only begun to be written about. In still other cases the book will be about a topic that was once a subject of inquiry and then dropped. We will publish a book around that topic if we believe it should be resurrected because of developments in the field.

The support given by Ablex Publishing Corporation, the Tel Aviv University Committee for Conferences, and different heads of the School of Education (Rina Shapira and Shimon Reshef) have made the workshops and this book series possible, and their support is gratefully acknowledged. This is especially so in light of the financial hardships in the publishing field and in Israel. Continuing support of this series is a welcome sign that despite economic adversity, there is a commitment to the intellectual pursuits that are of interest to us all.

It is the hope of the members of the Unit of Human Development and Education that this series will reflect the lively and stimulating workshops that have been held at Tel Aviv University, and that the community of developmental psychologists will find interest in the issues discussed in these pages.

Sidney Strauss
Ramat Hasharon
August 1985

Introduction

Language and Cognition:
A Developmental Perspective*

Esther Dromi

Tel-Aviv University

The frustration confronted by many psycholinguists with regard to the interrelationships between language, cognition, and development has been well described in a metaphor by Campbell (1988), who stated that to explore this unclear and misunderstood relationship means "to enter a very dark forest indeed! It is not so much the question of not being able to see the wood for the trees: one cannot even see the trees" (1988, p. 30).

With a partial understanding of the fascinating problem at hand, on the basis of the existing literature which I shall explore in this introduction, a workshop was organized at Tel-Aviv University in December 1987 around the theme "Language and Cognition: A Developmental Perspective." This volume presents the thoughts and study of the group of psychologists and psycholinguists who were invited to discuss this relationship from their own varying perspectives. We intentionally invited scholars who study a variety of acquisition topics, among subjects in different age groups, by applying a range of research methodologies. We were well aware that these scientists conduct research within differing theoretical frameworks, and the participants were selected not for their commitment to a specific view with regard to the meeting's theme, but rather because their work which touches upon this theme lies in the forefront of contemporary scientific work in child language acquisition. By introducing a specific theme to the meeting, we hoped that each of the participants would address unique aspects of the complex, ambiguous, and thought-provoking issue.

In this introduction, I will attempt to present the state-of-the-art theoretical and empirical orientations utilized as explanatory models for the central theme addressed in this book. I will then detail, within my synopsis of this volume, the elements in each chapter which relate to the interrelations between cognition and language.

* The author wishes to thank Dee B. Ankonina for her most helpful editorial assistance. Address for correspondence: Dr. Esther Dromi School of Education Tel Aviv University, Ramat Aviv Tel-Aviv, Israel 69978.

Linguistic and Cognitive Correlates: A Review

The interrelations between language, cognition, and development have always been a matter of considerable interest to philosophers, psychologists, and psycholinguists (see historical reviews in Bowerman, 1978, and Cromer, 1974, 1976). The 1970s and early 1980s can be characterized as "blooming decades" with respect to the number of publications on the nature of the linkage between cognitive development and language acquisition and on the possible directions of influence between these two domains of human functioning. Whereas earlier studies (e.g., Watson, 1924; Luria, 1961; Whorf, 1956) stressed the heavy dependence of cognitive development on language, several alternative models during the recent era were proposed and investigated, emphasizing the independent status of cognitive functioning, the important role of cognition as a facilitator of language development, and the bidirectional interrelations between language and cognition in development. (A presentation of alternative hypothetical models depicting relationships between language and cognition appear in Bates, Benigni, Bretherton, Camaioni, & Volterra, 1977, and in Rice & Kemper, 1984.)

According to the "strong cognitive hypothesis" which dominated during the early 1970s (e.g., Cromer, 1976; Bloom, 1973; Sinclair de Zwart, 1971, 1973; Macnamara, 1972), well-defined conceptual notions serve as a prerequisite condition for acquiring the linguistic devices to encode them (see Sugarman, 1983, for an illuminating discussion of the logical distinctions among antecedent, precursor, and prerequisite behaviors). These researchers particularly accentuated that the strong effect of cognition on language is particularly true with regard to those aspects of language which express meanings. Bloom (1973), for example, has argued that full mastery of object permanence is mandatory prior to the establishment of consistent meanings and the identification of the lexical spurt. Cromer (1976) has also noted that prior to the acquisition of conventional linguistic devices for expressing complex temporal notions (e.g., the notion expressed by present perfect forms), children lexicalize such ideas by terms such as "yet," "now," and so on, which convey the underlying meaning in the absence of more developed syntactic capability. Cromer suggests that underlying concepts are well-established before children learn the formal linguistic means to encode them.

A number of direct attempts to study the relations between linguistic and cognitive developments during the second year of life were published during the late 1970s (e.g., Bates, 1979; Corrigan, 1976; Bloom, Lifter, & Broughton, 1981; Gopnik, 1982, 1984; McCune-Nicolich, 1981). These investigations failed to reveal unidirectional links between general measures of early language (e.g., MLU, emergence of first words, or vocabulary size) and subjects' performance on measurable cognitive tasks.

The lack of empirical evidence for strong developmental links between children's linguistic and nonlinguistic achievements has been explained at two different levels. Some researchers have claimed that only very specific kinds of relations exist between linguistic behaviors and cognitive developments, whereas other researchers have questioned the very use of correlational cross-sectional studies as a means for detecting links between language and cognition.

Bates (1979; Bates et al., 1977) proposed that very specific relations between language and cognition are rooted in the "homologue" explanation. According to this position, both cognition and language are derived from a common, deeper underlying system of operations and structures. Therefore, positive correlations between linguistic and cognitive functions are identified not at the general level, but rather between *within*-stage cognitive tasks and *specific* language attainments.

Corrigan (1978, 1979) and Fischer and Corrigan (1981) have argued that subject age, sample size, and type of cross-sectional experimental testing situation strongly determine the nature of results and introduce biases which mask the true synchrony across tasks in development. Bloom, Lifter and Broughton (1985) also pinpointed the weakness of correlational studies, claiming their insufficiency as tools to assess the complex relationships between language and thought. Cognitive developmental scales (e.g., Uzgiris & Hunt, 1975) can be viewed as suitable only to serve as superficial, convenient indices of general cognitive development. Such measures are not sensitive enough to document dynamic, gradual developmental processes, which may be revealed only by close examination through longitudinal, detailed studies of changes in linguistic and nonlinguistic behaviors over time in individual subjects.

The position that language and cognition are sets of specific skills (Fischer, 1980), and that the two are interrelated in localized, task-dependent linkages, has recently been supported by Gopnik and Meltzoff (1985, 1986). In cross-sectional and longitudinal studies, these researchers investigated the language-cognition relations in 15- to 21-month-old children. Their conclusions highlighted two specific, dissociable connections between the two domains in this period. One correlation was identified between the acquisition of disappearance words (e.g., "gone") and the solution of object-concept Task Level 14 (Uzgiris & Hunt, 1975). A separate relation was revealed between the acquisition of success/failure words (e.g., "no," "Oh-oh," "there") and the solution of means-end Task Levels 10–12 (Uzgiris & Hunt, 1975). According to Gopnik and Meltzoff, these relations appear stronger than more general relations between linguistic and cognitive developments in the one-word stage, and moreover, seem stronger than the relations between the two kinds of cognitive or semantic developments themselves. The authors' cross-sectional as well as longitudinal analyses demonstrated that such relations involve the concurrent emergence of cognitive and semantic attainments, suggesting that semantic and cognitive processes are closely intertwined (see Bowerman, 1978, for a similar claim).

Another area which was extensively studied during the late 1970s and early 1980s consisted of the correspondence between the development of the child's capacity for pretend play and the development of representational and informative speech (e.g., McCune-Nicolich, 1977; Veneziano, 1981; Bates, 1979). Such studies reported a close temporal proximity between children's ability to produce these two behaviors. This correspondence was explained as manifesting the child's more general underlying cognitive ability to represent reality and act upon it, to mentally go back in time, and to consider others' states and intentions.

From the above summary of active research during the last two decades, the following conclusion can be drawn: The present-day understanding of the interesting, complex interrelationships between language and cognition is limited, partial, and still very vague. Available results indicate that at least during some developmental stages, such linkages are interactional and specific. Therefore, initial unidirectional linear models for explaining the language-cognition links have failed to accurately capture them (Rice & Kemper, 1984). Not all of the constructs that require close investigation have yet been identified, and very little is known about linguistic and nonlinguistic linkages beyond the early stages of language development. Moreover, the methodologies and research tools for studying this link do not seem to be fully developed.

As will become clear from the following review of the different chapters, the workshop participants who contributed to the present book do not define their work within the conceptualization of cognition and language as separate entities. This fact represents the view shared by our guests that language and cognition are not in fact independent constructs that influence each other in one direction or another. A lot of discussion was devoted to linguistic matters, and assumptions on the relevance of research findings to cognitive matters were often only implicitly made. At the same time, however, in many of the chapters in this collection, cognitive issues are thoroughly discussed, such as the general representational capacities of children, their categorization abilities, the relationship between production, comprehension, and general information processing abilities, and the role of constraints in establishing meaning.

I assume that the present publication reflects a shift in the way psycholinguists today examine the correspondence between language and cognition. As pointed out by one of the active participants in the workshop: "There are two different types of cognition which have been used here in this workshop (and elsewhere). In one sense, linguistics is part of language capacity, that is part of the cognitive capacities of human beings; in another sense there is language on one hand and cognition on the other" (A. Kasher, personal communication, December 1987). The chapters in this collection mainly address the former issues related to the child's developing language capacity as related to a set of general cognitive developments.

In the following section of this introduction, the major themes of each chapter are highlighted as a general content guide for the interested reader.

A Synopsis of the Book

The subject matter discussed in this volume covers a wide range of research areas. Chapters are organized in chronological order with respect to subjects' ages or levels of linguistic functioning, from infancy through adulthood. The opening chapter in the book is unique for a number of reasons: (a) its theoretical rather than empirical orientation; (b) its focus on questions related to infants' cognitive development during the first year of life and before productive language emerges; and (c) its critique of Piaget's developmental theory. The deep problems that Sugarman raises challenge the mere possibility of constructing models to explain the concept of development and to formulate explanatory theories on the basis of descriptions of overt behaviors.

Sugarman introduces Piaget's developmental theory as the most comprehensive attempt to attribute the development of mental life to a continuous process of self-generation, or construction of successive stages. Each stage is constructed on the basis of the previous one and leads to the next, more developed stage. Piaget proposes that all of intelligence develops out of the action of mere reflexes at birth, and that all the qualities associated with purposeful activities (e.g., intentionality, subjective experience of space, time, object, causality) arise gradually through babies' exercise of their initial reflexive capabilities.

On the basis of extensive analyses of Piaget's original claims and empirical evidence, primarily with regard to two developmental transitions during the sensorimotor stage, Sugarman concludes that even if all of Piaget's empirical observations were accurate, his theory could not explain how intelligence develops. The theory's circularity is its main flaw, whereby *the mental states upon which Piaget relies to explain observed shifts in infants' overt behaviors must be presupposed for the theory to explain them*. The two transitions that Sugarman examines in detail consist of: (a) the coordination of action in different modalities (i.e., looking and reaching), yielding the conceptual construction of a unified object (Stage II of S/M development), and (b) the motivation for acting, which involves separating the doing from its anticipated result, which in turn involves generating the unambiguous distinction between means and ends (Stage IV in S/M development).

Sugarman argues that the gap she identified in Piaget's theory is not going to be closed by additional demonstrations of infants' early capacities. This gap, in her opinion, is a logical one: "One always ends up having to presuppose the development in question, or else give it up. . . . That babies may innately turn toward a sound they hear, for example, rather than developing this coordination, does not imply that babies perceive a unified object that can be both seen and heard" (p. 22).

Toward the end of her thought-provoking chapter, Sugarman suggests that in order to clarify the problem of what is innate versus what really develops throughout the human life span, future research should be directed toward the identification of developmental primitives, so that psychologists will be able to delimit the class of innate capacities. Although she represents a clear developmental position, Sugarman's suggestion surprisingly fits the direction of research reported by Markman (Chapter 3) and Carey (Chapter 4), who deal with postulated innate constraints and their implications for meaning acquisition.

Chapters 2, 3, and 4 in the book concern the intriguing question of how young children acquire the conventional meanings of words. This question is intimately related to the understanding of the complex relationships among conceptual, linguistic and social factors that underlie language development. Dromi (Chapter 2), describing in great detail the course of lexical development throughout the one-word stage, reviews diary data of several researchers who conducted intensive case-study research with children at the outset of productive speech. The author focuses on the establishment of reference and its correspondence with cognitive functions such as symbolic representation, categorization, and classification.

The detailed description of early lexical development presented by Dromi is organized at three distinct levels of analysis. At the outset, Dromi provides figures on the quantitative characteristics of the one-word stage (i.e., the number of lexical terms learned by children, the rate of acquisition, and the shape of the accumulation curve). The second level of analysis, regarding classification of words' distribution in different categories of reference, is related to the underlying contents that early words encode and to their category membership (e.g., object words, action words, social words, attributes, etc.). Dromi's third level of analysis, that of the level of word extension, represents the scope of word use as it changes over time. The analysis of word extension was selected as a heuristic for comparing children's and adults' word usage in order to determine to what extent children's early productions are conventional.

All of Dromi's analyses are dynamic in the sense of observing and coding changes in the manner a word is uttered by the subject over time. This approach is highly revealing of developmental changes that must be attributed to the child's growing cognitive and linguistic capacities. Dromi's findings strongly indicate that children do not enter into the language acquisition task fully equipped with universal grammatical distinctions and with clearly defined semantic/conceptual categories. Throughout the one-word stage, the child's linguistic system undergoes major structural changes, gradually becoming more differentiated, more symbolic, and conventional. Dromi hypothesizes that the course of meaning acquisition reflects the course of the general conceptual developments that take place during the sensorimotor period. In her opinion, the child becomes a proficient word learner only after altering her initial strategy of embedding words in schematic representations of everyday situations to a much more mature strategy of attaching words to well-defined underlying concepts.

   In the concluding sections of her chapter, Dromi discusses some contributing factors other than the purely cognitive ones, that might determine the initial mapping of a new word and the path it takes toward conventional meaning. Dromi particularly addresses the important role of input conditions with regard to both its linguistic and contextual components. She contrasts the acquisition of nominal terms with that of predicate terms, and concludes that verbs are mapped by the child more effectively than nouns since they are modeled and embedded within syntactic frames. This claim is further elaborated by Niagles, Gleitman, and Gleitman (Chapter 5) who test the viability of their syntactic bootstrapping hypothesis regarding somewhat older children at a more developed syntactic level. Another issue which is of concern to Dromi is that of the role of linguistic constraints as a means to guide and accelerate lexical learning. Dromi argues that extension data do not provide a straightforward answer to the question of whether hypothesized constraints are innate or acquired. Furthermore, evidence on production fails to clarify whether such constraints are linguistic or cognitive. On the basis of her finding that children become much more effective and successful word learners during the second half of the one-word stage, Dromi concludes that lexical learning is far more constrained toward the end of the stage than it was during its beginning.

   Markman's and Carey's chapters report on sets of experiments designed to test the role of constraints (be they linguistic or cognitive) in limiting the kind of initial hypotheses that children induce in learning new words. Markman reviews evidence for two specific constraints that have been proposed in the literature: the taxonomic and whole object constraint, and the constraint of mutual exclusivity. In her concern with the rapid and quite efficient process of lexical learning by young children, Markman (Chapter 3) vividly describes her own brilliant, well-manipulated sequence of related experiments (each study emerging from the results and conclusions of the previous one) on the application of these constraints in the initial mapping of new words. In the laboratory condition, when children are asked to match a label with an unfamiliar object, they (a) assume that the new word selects a whole object, and (b) hypothesize that if the object is familiar the word must select another object that belongs to the same superordinate category. Markman argues that there is a qualitative difference between children's classification behavior with and without linguistic cues. In the absence of a verbal label, young children often classify items thematically, but when hearing a new word children are induced to look for categorical relationships instead of thematic ones. According to Markman the taxonomic assumption is honored by children from the age of 18 months, a finding which suggests its fundamental role in lexical learning. Markman speculates that the lexical spurt observed during the second half of the one-word stage (see Dromi, Chapter 2) overtly manifests the emergence of the taxonomic constraint.

   The assumption of mutual exclusivity is defined by Markman as observing the notion that each object has only one label to denote it. Thus, "a single object cannot be a cow and a bird or a cow and a dresser or a chair and a table" (p. 16). Markman reviews several studies by Markman and Wachtel (1988), Golinkoff, Hirsh Pasek, Lavallee, and Baduini (1985), and Hutchinson (1986) in which this hypothesis was tested and confirmed. In these studies, children were presented with two objects, one with a known label and the other without. When a new label was introduced, children always assumed it referred to the unknown object. A modification of the experimental condition revealed that when a novel label is introduced in the presence of one object that already has a name, children tend to reject the label as an additional name for the same object, assuming that the new label refers to an object part. The principle of mutual exclusivity was considered by Markman to be applicable to the distinction between object and substance. A possibility that is further investigated by Carey who devoted her chapter (Chapter 4) to this question.

Chapter 3, in this volume, not only fluently and clearly presents the scientific goals, designs, and results of many experiments, but also didactically explains how two hypothesized constraints which cannot function independently, interact and complement each other. According to Markman's view, the two principles emerge early and continue to operate beyond the single word stage as they enhance the learning of property terms as well as object terms. One issue missing in Markman's discussion is that of how far one can generalize from experimental results of well-planned training studies to the real world case of nonostensive word learning. This question, as well as a more detailed examination of how children deal with the projection of meaning for nonobject terms, are discussed by Niagles, Gleitman, and Gleitman in Chapter 5 in this volume.

Several suggestions have been recently made about the type of constraints that enhance the acquisition and generalization of early word meanings. Carey supports the view, originally proposed by Markman, that from early on the child projects noun meanings according to taxonomic categories (i.e., objects that are grouped together on the basis of similarity relations). She argues, however, that the taxonomic assumption is not sufficiently powerful to do the "work" Markman expects. This constraint does not explain why, when introducing the word "cup" in the presence of a real CUP, the child would pick out CUP as the relevant taxonomic category and not **BROWN THING, PLASTIC THING,** or **A THING I LIKE.** In order to explain the successful word mapping of very young children it is mandatory to assume that a much deeper distinction is operating within the child: the ontological distinction between object and substance. In Chapter 4 of this book, Carey focuses on the ontology underlying children's beliefs regarding the classes of referents that NOUNS label.

In a systematic and very deep discussion of what might be the origins of lexical constraints, and how they operate at the procedural level, Carey examines the ontology underlying word meaning. Unlike Dromi, who deliberately deals with the extension of early words, Carey is mainly concerned with the underlying intension of words. She explores the quantifications or logical properties of these intensions as they are related to basic ontological types, such as "object" and "nonsolid substance."

In the opening sections of the chapter, Carey deals with the inadequacy of previously proposed constraints to explain the efficiency noted in children's lexical learning, and she states her objection to the position that early meanings qualitatively differ from late meanings in the sense of being less categorical (see Chapter 2). Carey does not accept the claim that the meanings of early words might be complexive, and hence, not related to ontological commitments. She explicitly criticizes Quine's (1960) thesis that prior to the acquisition of the syntax of quantification young children do not honor distinctions between kinds of objects or portions of substance.

In order to test the hypothesis that the status of the physical object affects the similarity relations that determine its category assignment by young children, Soja, Carey, and Spelke (1990) conducted a series of word-learning studies with subjects of 2:0 to 2:6 years old. They introduced novel words in the presence of two kinds of stimuli: objects and nonsolid substances (e.g., gels, liquids, and powders), comparing children's projections of these test words' meanings. To assess Quine's conjecture about the effect of syntactic quantification on the conceptual appreciation of the mass/count distinction, these authors analyzed the subject's command of syntax in spontaneous speech. Furthermore, two learning conditions for the novel words were contrasted: (a) syntax neutral context (i.e., presenting the novel words without quantification), and (b) informative syntax context (where the novel words were introduced and embedded in quantification statements such as "a xxx" or "another xxx").

The results of the studies are summarized in the chapter, showing that 2-year-old subjects' performance on object and substance trials differed from chance. When the referent was a physical object, subjects projected the word to another object of the same kind, respecting the shape and number of the original referent. In contrast, when the word was modeled for a nonsolid referent, the subjects projected its meaning to another sample of the same substance, ignoring the shape or number of piles of the original referent. The results also clearly indicated no difference between the neutral and informative syntax conditions.

Carey discusses at length the theoretical implications of these findings. She proposes that the object/substance distinction is likely to be innate. She explains how this innate constraint might be of use to the child, and objects to Landau, Smith, and Jones's (1988) claim that shape rather than ontology dictates adult's and children's noun projection rules. Carey also enters into a somewhat philosophical discussion of whether constraints function at the linguistic or conceptual levels. She asks whether such constraints are language-specific or in fact are related to human induction capabilities in general. The distinction between extension and intension is also touched upon at the chapter's end, with a clear commitment to the view that in order to better understand the process of early word-meaning acquisition, researchers need to explore the level of the word's intension by means of comprehension tests, rather than the level of extension by means of production analyses.

Two chapters in this book are devoted to the study of young children's syntactic knowledge and its relation to the nativist position that the linguistic code is innate and, as such, strongly influences children's course of language acquisition. The manner in which children benefit from an underlying knowledge of the linguistic code and mainly of their language's syntax is of central concern to Naigles, Gleitman, and Gleitman (Chapter 5). These researchers articulately present *the syntactic bootstrapping hypothesis*, which in their opinion provides a most powerful mechanism for learning language in general and semantics of verbs in particular. In their review of a large set of experimental studies, Crain and Fodor (Chapter 6) raise and discuss the question of whether young subjects' performance in comprehension and production of syntactic structures reveals their linguistic competence. This chapter concerns the discrepancy between what are predicted to be universal and innate properties of human languages, and what children appear to know during the early years of syntactic productions. The authors argue that young subjects' linguistic performance is strongly influenced by various factors that are extraneous to language. They demonstrate how failures in experimental tasks are not necessarily related to the ignorance of grammatical principles, but rather are related to task complexity. Crain and Fodor show that when the task complexity is simplified, considerable knowledge of universal grammatical principles is revealed even in very young children. This finding leads them to the conclusion that cognitive rather than linguistic facets develop with age.

Naigles, Gleitman, and Gleitman open their discussion on the important role of syntax in determining verb semantics with a most convincing set of arguments for why verb meanings cannot be learned by mere observation of the scenes in which these verbs are modeled. They present the case of mental verbs which cannot be demonstrated or seen; they remind the readers that blind and sighted children show very similar patterns of verb usage; they are concerned with the common phenomenon whereby the same scene can usually be described linguistically in many ways; and they question the assumption that the principle of mutual exclusivity dictates verb meaning acquisition.

However, in the structural information of the language code itself, children can find resourceful evidence that will constrain their semantic conjectures, and hence, facilitate their correct semantic interpretation. Recent linguistic investigations pinpoint the fact that semantic interpretations and syntactic frames show some correlation in terms of their relative privileges of occurrence. Thus, for at least some subclasses of verbs, one can predict the syntactic environment from its semantic partitioning and vice versa. If so, the authors argue, when the language's design offers clues to potential semantic interpretation, young children will make use of this information. The syntactic bootstrapping hypothesis here mirrors Bowerman's (1973, 1977, 1983) suggestion that children use semantic bootstrapping mechanisms in making predictions about syntactic structures. Here the claim is that just as children may use semantics as a means for learning syntax, they will use structural facts about a verb as evidence for its semantic interpretation.

In order to test the syntactic bootstrapping hypothesis, the authors conducted a set of experimental studies that were designed to elicit children's and adults' interpretation of transitive and intransitive verbs in different syntactic frames. The subjects were asked to act out grammatical and ungrammatical sentences containing the same verbs, where in some cases verb semantics and syntactic structures led to contradicting interpretations. The results indicated a strong tendency by children in the three age groups tested (2, 3, and 4 years old) to show frame compliance. This was particularly true for intransitive verbs that appeared in causative constructions. The children deduced causative interpretation for intransitive verbs when these were embedded in transitive sentence frames. A slightly less significant result was observed for transitive verbs in intransitive syntactic frames, where some frames elicited more of an effect than others, and these effects diminished with age.

A replication of the experiments with adult subjects revealed quite a different pattern of responses where the overall effect of frame compliance was significantly smaller, and a clear effect of frame type was observed. More frame compliance was noted for transitive than for intransitive frames, and for elaborated transitive frames that included a prepositional phrase. The differences observed for children and adults are explained as related to the linguistic experience of the adults. Unlike children, adults are entitled to firm convictions about the meaning of the verbs used in the experiments, and hence, they responded to the odd sentences by "bringing the form into alignment with the verb meaning rather than, like the children, bringing the verb meaning into alignment with the forms" (p. 135).

The discussion sections of the chapter highlight the hypothesized origin of the syntactic bootstrapping mechanism and its co-existence with other sources of evidence about possible interpretations of new words. Naigles, Gleitman, and Gleitman very clearly state that syntactic clues to potential meaning *cannot be detected in a single hearing of a single syntactic frame.* Thus, in order to recover meaning, the child must examine a wide range of syntactic frames in which a given verb appears. Another source of evidence for verb semantics is the contingency of the verb's repeated uses in different non-linguistic environments. The child recovers the meaning of the verb lexicon by means of gathering probabilistic evidence from two imperfect databases (i.e., extralinguistic and linguistic).

A strong nativist position, which holds the view that universal properties of language are innate, is presented in Chapter 6 of this book. An original argument is developed and tested in this chapter, according to which children's violations of putatively universal phrase structure rules (or constraints on transformations) are not related to the lack of grammatical knowledge, but rather result from cognitive limitations that significantly reduce subjects' performance in complex experimental tasks. In other words, the authors argue that in many cases, the nonsyntactic demands of the task constitute the cause of children's errors. The maturation of nonlinguistic capacities, such as short-term memory, computational ability, pragmatic knowledge, and inferencing capabilities, explain why some grammatical rules seem to emerge later in language development.

In support of their nonlinguistic maturation hypothesis, Crain and Fodor examine three factors that influence performance in syntactic tasks and that are nonlinguistic by nature: *parsing*, *plans*, and *presupposition*. *Parsing* is a complex task involving decision strategies that favor one structural analysis over another when both are permitted by the input of word sequence. A *plan* is the cognitive design or mental representation of the sequence of steps for the manipulation of objects (usually enactments of toys) in response to a target sentence in a comprehension task. *Presuppositions* are the variety of pragmatic considerations that must be taken into account from extrasentential contextual and linguistic cues in order to fully comprehend a sentence. The chapter reviews a large set of experiments in which Crain and Fodor believe that nonlinguistic factors were responsible for many of the young subjects' failures. Moreover, new studies are described in which the researchers manipulated these confounding factors in order to demonstrate that when these factors are suitably controlled for, subjects' performance improves significantly.

The chapter reports on experiments on the following linguistic structures: (a) Subjucancy, (b) Backward Pronominalization, (c) Subject/Auxiliary Inversion, (d) Relative Clauses, (e) Temporal Terms, (f) Prenominal Modifiers, (g) Passives, and (h) Wanna Contractions. In all the studies that were examined, the authors succeeded to show that when performance problems were reduced in the testing situation, subjects manifested an earlier command of the constructions that were tested. On the basis of these results, Crain and Fodor conclude that the need to appeal to a maturation theory of the linguistic structures themselves (e.g., Borer & Wexler, 1987) is obviated, since non-linguistic immaturity can create the illusion of linguistic immaturity. The authors call for a much more sophisticated approach to language testing and encourage further investigation of their interesting proposal.

Chapter 7 in this collection presents an account which is pragmatic rather than semantic or syntactic. Berman's study on narrating skills in preschool and school-age children and in adults describes the major strategies that speakers apply for highlighting, focusing, and elaborating thematically relevant information. This chapter deals with relatively late-developing aspects of language acquisition which span throughout several years of school and even into adulthood. Berman suggests that linguistic, conceptual, and pragmatic factors interact in determining the quality of verbal discourse, and she refers to postulated links among these factors.

Berman's data consist of a set of cross-sectional stories of Hebrew speakers at different age levels (12 narrators at each of the following age groups: 3–4, 4–5, 5–6, 7–8, 9–10, 11–12, and adults) which were collected as part of a large-scale cross-linguistic research. In this project the same picture book was utilized as a stimuli for the elicitation of stories from speakers of German, Spanish, Hebrew, Turkish, and English. The chapter is devoted to a close analysis of a single episode in the book which depicts a searching expedition after a frog which had earlier disappeared. Various aspects are examined by the author: the contents of the episode, the inferences speakers make about the situation, the overall thematic organization of the verbal output, and the morphosyntactic and lexical devices used. The detailed analysis makes it possible to draw conclusions about perspective-taking abilities and how they develop with age.

Three major aspects of perspective taking in discourse are included in Berman's system of analysis: (a) *Local and Global Organization of Elements,* where the author tests whether the subject describes a picture as isolated or as an integrated part of the story line; (b) *Perspective on a Single Event,* where the number of components mentioned and the perspective favored by the speaker are investigated; and (c) *Perspectives on Related Events,* where the use of linguistic devices for shifting perspectives and for highlighting different events are examined.

Developmental trends were identified for each of the aforementioned aspects. Thus, with regard to the first question, Berman reports that none of the 3- and 4-year-olds related the search to the overall frame of the story; 5-year-olds described the dog and the boy as both looking and searching; 7-year-olds were the first to make the search an inclusive activity; and only 12-year-olds and adults described the scene as a generalized searching expedition triggered by preceded events. Descriptions of the events also indicated an age effect with regard to the degree of agenthood mentioned. Young subjects always took the perspective of the protagonist, who performs the search (high agency perspective), whereas older subjects (aged seven and up) seemed to downgrade agenthood by providing the perspective of the affectee. Nine-year-old subjects described the event in greater detail than younger subjects, with a growing tendency to elaborate descriptions by the inclusion of relative clauses and other phrasial components. Perspective-switching abilities were also noted only for the older school-age subjects and adults. Such perspective-switching abilities require skilled deployment of syntactic cohesiveness devices, including coordination, subordination, and anaphoric pronouns which are learned late by children.

The findings on how Hebrew-speaking subjects describe the same scene in a picture book at different age levels are discussed with reference to the following issues: the cognitive demands of the task, the developing narrative skills, the interaction of form and function in discourse, and the cross-linguistic vs. language-specific facets in expressing perspective. According to Berman, "children acquiring different languages will with age learn to perform the same range of general discourse functions on the basis of greater cognitive maturation and broadened expressive skills. . . . As they mature speakers will tend increasingly to favor the perspectives most obviously prompted by the grammar of their native tongue" (p. 198).

The concluding chapter of the book is unique in that: it deals most directly with the complicated question of the deep interrelationships between language and thought; it constitutes a theoretical chapter, summarizing the author's clear epistemological view on language's role in determining people's view of the world; it contains a vivid description of empirical studies which were designed in order to test a developmental theory and yet were conducted with adult subjects; and it presents an interesting view as to the difference between cognitive and communicative interpretations. In Chapter 8, Schlesinger presents his recent formulation of the *"Semantic Assimilation Theory,"* which is an acquisition theory, and he examines to what extent this theory is supported by evidence on the effect of structural import.

The chapter opens with a very clear formulation of the original *Whorfian* position that the structure of a language imposes its categorization on its speaker's thinking and affects the way reality is conceived. Following a confrontation of this position with the opposite view of radical conventional-ism, and a concise review of studies which failed to indicate which of the two positions is refutable, Schlesinger proposes a weak version of the linguistic relativism view which is based on his own interpretation of De Saussure (1959). In this proposal, language is perceived as an *intermediary* between thought and sounds, so that it operates at two levels. On the one hand, language helps in categorizing the sound streams into meaningful units, and on the other hand, language enhances categorization of thought. The strongest implication of this position is that a concept need not have been formed by the child prior to the acquisition of a label for it. Instead it is argued that children may develop concepts during the process of learning the correct use of words (see more in Schlesinger, 1982).

This general assumption forms the basis of Schlesinger's "Semantic Assim-ilation Theory," which explains how syntactic categories can be formed by the child as an extension of the semantic categories serving as their core. According to this claim, a process of semantic assimilation gradually expands the child's semantic categories into formal ones, and is expected to leave its mark on them. Thus, for example, the semantic core of the formal category SUBJECT (which is the notion of AGENTHOOD) is predicted to evidence itself even during adulthood, in view of the fact that "adult linguistic categories retain something of the 'flavor' of the semantic core out of which they were developed" (p. 206).

Three hypotheses are given concerning the extent to which semantic notions affect adults' processing of formal linguistic categories. The first hypothesis suggests that structural import influences the way adults conceive SUBJECT. The second hypothesis proposes that adult cognition operates with categories that conform largely to the linguistic categories of the native tongue. The third and weakest hypothesis states that structural import has an effect only at the level of language use, influencing the way a speaker *interprets a message or chooses a linguistic unit in speaking,* but not affecting the deep underlying conceptual organization of reality.

Three studies were designed to examine the effect of structural import on adults' interpretation of linguistic stimuli, including tests of the roles of the participants, the experiencer and stimulus, and the instruments. The findings substantiated the claims that structural import has communicative effects (supporting the third hypothesis), and that linguistic categories bear the imprint of the semantic assimilation process through which they were formed (supporting the first hypothesis). On the basis of these findings, Schlesinger concludes the chapter with a series of questions about whether the effect of native language on cognition is limited to the communicative situation alone, or else extends beyond it to other aspects of our mental life.

An Epilogue

My somewhat detailed presentations of the major themes expounded in the fascinating chapters that compose this volume, as well as my modest attempts to reflect on the more central issues and claims that are made here, indicate that the topic of language and cognition in development is one which will infinitely survive. As we have seen, the focus of investigation and theorizing might change from decade to decade, but the thought-provoking questions remain and continue to stimulate most interesting empirical as well as theoretical discussions. I certainly hope that by pointing to such a wide range of crucial issues and questions, and by drawing upon evidence from a very broad spectrum of research areas covering different age groups, various research methodologies, and several theoretical positions, this book will be a relevant guide to a variety of target readers, mainly those researchers and advanced students in the area of child language who wish to deepen their understanding of the mysteries of the interrelationships between language, cognition, and development.

References

Bates, E. (1979). *The emergence of symbols: Cognition and communication in infancy.* New York: Academic Press.

Bates, E., Benigni, L., Bretherton, I., Camaioni, L., & Volterra, V. (1977). From gesture to the first word: On cognitive and social prerequisites. In M. Lewis & L. Rosenblum (Eds.), *Interaction, conversation, and development of language.* New York: John Wiley and Sons.

Bowerman, M. (1973). *Early syntactic development: A cross-linguistic study with special reference to Finnish.* London: Cambridge University Press.

Bowerman, M. (1977). The acquisition of rule governing "possible lexical items": Evidence from spontaneous speech errors. *PRCLD, 13,* 148-156.

Bowerman, M. (1978). Semantic and syntactic development: A review of what, when, and how in language acquisition. In R. L. Schiefelbusch (Ed.), *Bases of language intervention.* Baltimore: University Park Press.

Bowerman, M. (1983). Evaluating competing linguistic models with language acquisition data: Implications of developmental errors with causative verbs. *Quaderni di Semantica, 3,* 5-66.

Borer, H., & Wexler, K. (1987). The maturation of syntax. In T. Roeper & E. Williams (Eds.), *Parameters and linguistic theory.* Dordrecht: Reidel.

Bloom, L. (1973). *One word at a time.* The Hague: Mouton.

Bloom, L., Lifter, K., & Broughton, J. (1981). What children say and what they know. In R. Stark (Ed.), *Language behavior in infancy and early childhood.* North-Holland: Elsevier.

Bloom, L., Lifter, K., & Broughton, J. (1985). The convergence of early cognition and language in the second year of life: Problems in conceptualization and measurement. In M. D. Barrett (Ed.), *Children's single word speech.* New York: John Wiley and Sons.

Campbell, R. N. (1988). Language acquisition and cognition. In P. Fletcher & M. Garman (Eds.), *Language acquisition: Studies in first language development* (2nd ed.). London: Cambridge University Press.

Corrigan, R. L. (1976). *Patterns of individual communication and cognitive development.* Unpublished doctoral dissertation, University of Denver.

Corrigan, R. L. (1978). Language development as related to stage 6 object permanence development. *Journal of Child Language, 5,* 173-189.

Corrigan, R. L. (1979). Cognitive correlates of language: Differential criteria yield differential results. *Child Development, 50,* 617-631.

Cromer, R. F. (1974). The development of language and cognition: The cognition hypothesis. In B. M. Foss (Ed.), *New perspectives in child development.* Baltimore: Penguin Books.

Cromer, R. F. (1976). The cognitive hypothesis of language acquisition and its implications for child language deficiency. In D. Morehead & A. Morehead (Eds.), *Normal and deficient child language.* Baltimore: University Park Press.

De Saussure, F. (1959). *Course in general linguistics.* New York: Philosophical Library.

Fischer, K. W. (1980). A theory of cognitive development: The control and construction of hierarchies of skills. *Psychological Review, 87,* 477-531.

Fischer, K. W., & Corrigan, R. A. (1981). A skill approach to language development. In R. Stark (Ed.), *Language behavior in infancy and early childhood.* North-Holland: Elsevier.

Golinkoff, R. M., Hirsh Pasek, K., Lavallee, A., & Baduini, C. (1985). *What's in a word?: The young child's predisposition to use lexical contrast.* Paper presented in the Boston University Conference on Child Language, Boston, MA.

Gopnik, A. (1982). Words and plans. *Journal of Child Language, 9,* 617-633.

Gopnik, A. (1984). The acquisition of gone and the development of the object concept. *Journal of Child Language, 11,* 273-292.

Gopnik, A., & Meltzoff, A. N. (1985). From people, to plans, to objects. *Journal of Pragmatics, 9,* 495-512.

Gopnik, A., & Meltzoff, A. N. (1986). Relations between semantic and cognitive development in the one word stage: The specificity hypothesis. *Child Development, 57,* 1040-1053.

Hutchinson, J. E. (1986). *Children's sensitivity to the contrastive use of object category terms.* Paper presented at the Stanford Child Language Research Forum, Stanford University.

Landau, B., Smith, L. B., & Jones, S. S. (1988). The importance of shape in early lexical learning. *Cognitive Development, 3,* 299-321.

Luria, A. R. (1961). *The role of speech in regulation of normal and abnormal behavior.* New York: Liveright.

Macnamara, J. (1972). Cognitive basis of language learning in infants. *Psychological review, 79,* 1–13.

Markman, E. M., & Wachtel, C. A. (1988). Children's use of mutual exclusivity to constrain the meanings of words. *Cognitive Psychology, 20,* 121–157.

McCune-Nicolich, L. (1977). Beyond sensorimotor intelligence: Assessment of symbolic maturity through analysis of pretend play. *Merrill Palmer Quarterly, 23,* 89–101.

McCune-Nicolich, L. (1981). The cognitive bases of relational words in the single word period. *Journal of Child Language, 8,* 15–34.

Quine, W. V. O. (1960). *Word and object.* Cambridge, MA: MIT Press.

Rice, M. L., & Kemper, S. (1984). *Child language and cognition.* Baltimore: University Park Press.

Schlesinger, I. M. (1982). *Steps to language.* Hillsdale, NJ: Lawrence Erlbaum Associates.

Sinclair de Zwart, H. J. (1971). Sensorimotor action patterns as a condition for the acquisition of syntax. In R. Huxley & D. Ingram (Eds.), *Language acquisition: Models and methods.* New York: Academic Press.

Sinclair de Zwart, H. J. (1973). Language acquisition and cognitive development. In T. E. Moore (Ed.), *Cognitive development and the acquisition of language.* New York: Academic Press.

Soja, N. N., Carey, S., & Spelke, E. S. (1990). *Ontological categories guide young children's induction of word meaning: Object terms and substance terms.* Manuscript submitted for publication.

Sugarman, S. (1983). Empirical versus logical issues in the transition from prelinguistic to linguistic communication. In R. M. Golinkoff (Ed.), *The transition from prelinguistic to linguistic communication.* Hillsdale, NJ: Lawrence Erlbaum Associates.

Uzgiris, I., & Hunt, J. (1975). *Assessment in infancy: Ordinal scales of psychological development.* Chicago, IL: University of Illinois Press.

Veneziano, E. (1981). Early language and nonverbal representation: A reassessment. *Journal of Child Language, 8,* 541–563.

Watson, J. B. (1924). *Behaviorism.* New York: Norton.

Whorf, B. L. (1956). *Language thought and reality.* Cambridge, MA: MIT Press.

1

Piaget on the Origins of Mind: A Problem in Accounting for the Development of Mental Capacities*

Susan Sugarman

Princeton University

The participants in this workshop were asked to address the interface between language acquisition and cognitive development. I have chosen to discuss a particular aspect of Piaget's (1936/1952, 1937/1954) theory of the origins of intelligence in children. Piaget's theory has a conceptual flaw that makes it difficult to know how the development of mental capacities is to be explained. Whether or not directly analogous problems arise in the attempt to account for the acquisition of language, the arguments presented here may have some bearing on questions relating to language acquisition.

Piaget proposes the radical thesis that all of intelligence develops out of the action of mere reflexes at birth. It is built up progressively in stages, each stage building on the one before, each leading necessarily to the next, given that the baby acts in the world. Piaget's account is the most closely detailed attempt anywhere to attribute the development of mental life to a continuous process of self-generation, or construction, whereby each form builds on the ones before it. Based on an extensive analysis (Sugarman, 1987a), summarized here, I argue that Piaget's account fails. Even if all of his claims were empirically accurate, his theory could not explain how intelligence develops. The sequence of observable stages that Piaget describes could occur without any of the mental developments that he, and common sense, would presume the stages embody.

This apparent collapse of the theory may be rooted in a deep problem concerning the explanation of mental capacities, in particular the explanation of developmental transitions. At present it is unclear what kind of alternative might succeed. I delineate Piaget's error in the hope that others may join in the effort to work out its full implications. I give a reconstruction of Piaget's theory first, then a critique, and then discuss broader implications of the critique. I comment briefly on language at the end of the chapter.

* I thank John Darley, Esther Dromi, Rachel Falmagne, Philip N. Johnson-Laird, Rachel Melkman, and Carl Olson for helpful discussion of this chapter.

Piaget's Theory: Reconstruction

All of intelligence, Piaget says, arises out of the functioning of only reflexes, at birth. Initially, at least in theory, therefore, the mental state of babies is devoid of any impulse or experience apart from what is entailed in purely reflexive action, that is, totally mindless activity. At the same time, the most basic qualities that one associates with intelligence — intentional action and the subjective experience of space, time, object, and causality — arise gradually, and necessarily, through babies' mere exercise of their initial capabilities, namely, the reflexes.

The nature of "exercise" here is all-important. Piaget grants to babies at birth certain aspects of action, called "functional invariants" (Piaget, 1936/1952), that apply to all levels of operation of the organism, including the biological level and the highest levels of intelligence. These invariants include the complementary processes of "assimilation" and "accommodation" (both aspects of "adaptation"), and "organization." Assimilation refers to the incorporation of input by an existing organization. Piaget uses it in the context of primitive action to refer to the organism's impulse to reproduce its experience, or from an external point of view, its tendency to repeat its action. Accommodation refers to the organism's adjustment of its behavior to meet the exigencies of this repetition. Organization is the organism's internal adjustment of its structures with each other, its preservation and integration of its successive attempts at assimilation and accommodation.

Hence, Piaget's thesis in full is that, given the reflexes operative at birth and the "functional invariants," babies' action will elaborate. This elaborating action, in turn, will prompt the elaboration of a mental life. This elaboration in its turn will motivate further modifications of action, and so on. Piaget and his commentators sometimes use the metaphor of a spiral to describe this relation of continuing mutual influence between thought and action in development.

Piaget outlines six stages of "sensorimotor" intelligence, extending from birth to approximately 2 years of age. He provides the most detailed account of the transition process for stages II and IV, which involve two of the most important transitions from the point of view of intelligence. The transition at stage II is the coordination of actions in different modalities (e.g., looking and reaching) and the conceptual construction of a unified "object" (an external entity that can be both seen and touched) that, according to Piaget, results from this coordination. The transition at stage IV is the development of means-ends behavior. I focus on these transitions in the following reconstruction.

I assume that Piaget's claims are empirically accurate, and I have attempted to put the sharpest and most consistent construction on his theoretical claims that his texts will allow. I follow this policy to expose what I think is the genuine underlying structure of his argument.

Stage I (0–6 weeks; for this and all subsequent stages ages are approximate) involves the use of reflexes. The reflexes of interest are those that will eventually evolve into voluntary behavior — for instance, sucking or grasping — as opposed to the eyeblink response. Although Piaget does not consider reflexive reactions to be intelligent in themselves, infants' activity extends beyond the purely automatic reaction in two ways that Piaget thinks are functionally analogous to intelligent activity and constitute its point of origin. First, babies tend to repeat their behavior (assimilation), which Piaget infers is based on an attempt on the babies' part to reproduce their immediately previous experience (Piaget, 1937/1954, p. 310). Second, the reactions elaborate. There is sensorimotor groping when the nipple happens to slip from the mouth (accommodation), for example, and a tendency over time to systematize these gropings (organization). Once a reaction has expanded in this way, it is no longer purely reflexive, the nonvoluntary result of stimulation to a specific area of the body. It is instigated by more remote and more diverse contacts and involves more active apprenticeship. Sucking, for instance, is elicited initially by stimulation of the inner membrane of the mouth. Within a day of birth, contact with the lip is sufficient. Shortly thereafter contact with the cheek will prompt a sensorimotor groping, which becomes progressively more systematic. Laurent, for example, eventually turns only to the side on which contact with the nipple is made (Piaget, 1936/1952, Observations 1–10).

The second stage (6 weeks–5 months) involves the further enlargement of these patterns. Rather than involving only the immediate adjustments necessary to allow functioning of the reflex, the core reaction itself elaborates, according to the results to which it leads. These results are accidental concomitants of the reaction that have occurred all along, but that babies now begin to incorporate as part of the (or a) repetitive cycle involving the reflex. Rather than involving only sucking itself, for instance, repetitive cycles of which sucking is a part will now include sucking, bulging the cheeks, licking the lips, protruding the tongue, and so forth (Piaget, 1936/1952, Obs. 11–14). Piaget (1936/1952) uses the term "circular reaction" (after Baldwin) to refer to these cycles that are "acquired" as opposed to hereditary. The circular reactions of stage II are "primary," as opposed to "secondary," insofar as the actions babies reproduce (e.g., bulging the cheeks) are cultivated for their intrinsic effects rather than for effects on the external "secondary," environment. The latter, "secondary" circular reactions arise in stage III.

The coordination of actions in different modalities (which Piaget calls the coordination of "heterogeneous schemata"), also seen at this stage, has a similar structure, according to Piaget. It involves the attempt to reproduce an effect that previously occurred intermittently with babies' behavior but that babies did not specifically attend to. Classic examples are hearing and looking (turning in the direction of a sound), and looking and grasping (grasping objects that are seen; bringing objects contacted into the visual field). The account in outline is that babies look by chance, for example, at the hand that grasps. They then attempt to reproduce this result. The reproduction is accomplished through the reciprocal enlargement ("reciprocal assimilation") of the two actions in question. Out of this reciprocal enlargement grows the recognition of the entity grasped and the entity seen as the same object, external to either action.

Thus, according to Piaget, the initial conjoining of the two actions in question is not motivated by, and does not involve, the perception of a distinct object on which some other action could be brought to bear. Before the end of stage II, according to the theory, babies have no concept of "object" as external to themselves. Theirs is a complex experience that we adults would divide into the perception of an external object (e.g., the nipple, in the case of sucking), and babies' response (e.g., sucking), but which for the babies is not yet distinguished. What is seen is experienced as an extension of seeing and of the effort involved in seeing. Hence, when babies first turn toward a sound, they are not turning to see the source from which the sound emanates. They are trying to see at the same time as they hear. One system has been stimulated, and there is a tendency for the other systems to seek stimulation too.

The data on which Piaget bases this interpretation are contained in his study of babies' concept of "object" (Piaget, 1937/1954), which involves babies' reactions to the displacement and disappearance of objects. Initially babies do not seem to pursue (with their eyes or hands) objects that vanish from sight or touch, whereas at a slightly later age various kinds of search are seen. When stimulation ceases, babies simply direct their attention elsewhere, hold the position they were in when the stimulation occurred, or repeat the behavior (e.g., sucking) that was in progress then. According to Piaget, this group of reactions, unlike later-appearing reactions, is compatible with the hypothesis that stimulation that we would distinguish as "object" is experienced by babies as continuous with (what we would distinguish as) the acts through which that stimulation is received.

Insofar as actions in separate modalities are initially conjoined in the absence of a perception of an external, unified object, how does this conjoining come about? In the case of hearing and looking, turning to look *when* something is heard usually produces novel visual stimulation. Something is seen that the baby did not see before. As specified by the principle of assimilation, babies will try to reproduce this experience. Hence, hearing will come to provoke looking, just as starting to suck comes to provoke bulging the cheeks (the "primary circular reaction" described earlier). This expansion is an instance of the "reciprocal assimilation" of actions.

The mental transition, that of turning to look at *what* is heard, follows naturally from here, as a matter of logical necessity, according to Piaget. Insofar as the same "sensorial image" is at the point of "intersection" of several currents of assimilation, that image will tend to become solidified and projected into an external universe (Piaget, 1936/1952, p. 143). The "image" perceived can no longer be experienced as an extension of hearing, for example, because it is also seen. The account of the coordination of looking and reaching (ultimately reaching for "what" is seen) is parallel.

The principal acquisition of the third stage (5–9 months) is the secondary circular reaction, in which children cultivate and repeat actions for the purpose of producing effects on the external environment. Classic examples include shaking noise-making objects to make them sound, striking an object on another surface to produce a noise. Two "primary" schemas come together to form these reactions in much the manner in which visually guided reaching is acquired in stage II. Piaget describes how, in theory, Lucienne came to beat her legs in her bassinet so that the dolls hanging overhead would swing (Obs. 94, Piaget, 1936/1952). Before connecting the movements of her legs with the swinging of the dolls, Lucienne would already have been looking at and listening to the dolls as they swung. At this early point, she would have tended, separately, to "conserve" the activity of her legs and the spectacle before her eyes. She would have continued to try to see by continuing to look and would have continued to try to feel the kinesthetic sensations produced by her actions by continuing to beat her legs. The cycle would have become self-perpetuating, because continuing to beat her legs would have continued to produce a lively spectacle to look at. Paralleling his argument for the coordinations at stage II, Piaget thinks that once this cycle were formed, it would follow as a matter of course that Lucienne would come to understand that the results she was observing depended on her beating of her legs (Piaget, 1936/1952, p. 175).

The unifying feature of all the developments of the fourth stage (9–12 months) is the intercoordination of secondary "schemata" (acquired patterns that arose through secondary circular reactions). The most important advance associated with this feature is the development of means-ends behavior, in which means are unambiguously distinguished from ends and in which the end to be achieved is known by children before the action takes place. In the fully developed reaction, the end to be attained is novel, by contrast with the "end" involved in a secondary circular reaction, in which children are attempting only to reproduce a previously observed result. Examples would include removing an obstacle to grasp an object beyond it, using intermediate means to obtain a desired object or effect: pushing mother's hand toward a piece of material to get her to swing it; pulling the bassinet strings to occasion the fall of an object lodged overhead. The important conceptual advance associated with these behavior patterns is coming to do one thing *in order to* do another, as contrasted with doing one thing *instead of* another.

The "reciprocal assimilation" of two action patterns is again the mechanism of change. Piaget builds the case from a transitional example (Piaget, 1936/1952, Obs. 120). Piaget has placed a piece of paper on Laurent's bassinet hood, just where the hood is joined by a string connecting the hood to the bassinet handle. First Laurent tries to reach for the paper directly. Eventually he stops reaching and grasps the string and pulls it harder and harder. The paper starts to fall. He extends his hands and catches it. Piaget considers the example transitional, because it is unclear, he thinks, whether Laurent pulled the string *in order to* get the paper or *instead of* getting the paper, because he could not get it.

Piaget uses this ambiguity in deriving a theoretical account of how behavior "in order to" carry out another behavior might come about. After having failed to grasp the paper directly, according to this account, Laurent began instead to "assimilate" the object to the schema of pulling the string. He pulled the string at first not through any intention of making the paper fall (so as to catch it), but to provoke the usual effect that pulling the string creates, namely the movement of the bassinet hood or of things hanging from it. Thwarted in his attempt to get what he wanted, Laurent did something else instead, this latter activity having been provoked by his attention to an area — the top of the bassinet — normally associated with that activity. But, theorizes Piaget, Laurent continues all the while to "apply" the schema of grasping the paper, insofar as he continues to desire to grasp it (Piaget, 1936/1952, p. 231). As a result of this simultaneous "assimilation" of the object by two schemas and the fact that the paper eventually does fall, pulling the string thereafter becomes a means of grasping the paper.

The standard cases of means-ends behavior associated with stage IV, obstacle removal and the use of an intermediary, are more complicated, according to Piaget, because the different objects involved are not already in a relationship. Mother's hand is not already attached to the material that is to be swung. Children achieve the necessary relationship in two steps, Piaget theorizes. First they try to "assimilate" one object to the other. They transfer to the object they can reach (mother's hand, or the obstacle to be removed) the actions they wish to perform, or to have performed, on the more distant object. They beat on mother's hand. As with the strings-and-paper example, the transferred activity in these cases is initially a substitute activity, not an intermediate step toward a more distant end. Simple substitution (simple "assimilation") does not work in these standard cases, however, because the objects are not connected. The mere movement of one of them will not necessitate the movement of the other. Mother's hand has to be maneuvered in a particular way to get the material swung. The solution, according to Piaget, is that children subordinate one schema to the other, rather than simply fusing them as at previous stages (Piaget, 1936/1952, p. 234).

In Piaget's theory, the central developments of stages V (12–18 months) and VI (18–24 months) can be seen as elaborating the basic means-ends framework established in stage IV. In stage V, when confronted by an initially insoluble problem, children devise completely novel means to solve the problem; stage IV involves only the application of "known schemata." The children arrive at these novel means through a process of cumulative groping, whereby they capitalize on chance effects of failed attempts to accomplish some end. For instance, after Jacqueline has tried unsuccessfully to pull a large cardboard rooster through the playpen bars, the rooster falls on the outside. In picking it up, Jacqueline happens to tilt it at an angle that is sufficient to allow it to pass through the bars. On subsequent trials of the experiment, Jacqueline deliberately lets go of the rooster before trying to pull it through the bars. Later, letting go is replaced by simply lowering the toy (Piaget, 1936/1952, Obs. 165). In stage VI, the beginning of "representational" intelligence, this cumulative groping is speeded and internalized. Confronted with the rooster problem for the first time in stage VI, children would anticipate that the angle of the rooster needed to be adjusted and would lower it spontaneously without needing to have this procedure suggested to them by external events. There would be "invention by mental combination" (Piaget, 1936/1952).

Piaget gives no systematic account of the transition process into either of these stages, except insofar as to trace the historical roots of the particular "schemas" the children bring into play in their new procedures. Given that the account of the earlier stages is sufficient for my demonstration, I omit any further consideration of stages V and VI.

Piaget's Theory: Critique

The main problem with Piaget's theory is that it is circular. Piaget gives what seems to be a coherent account of how, given his theory of the starting point (that it consists of reflexes, the "functional invariants," and an inchoate view of reality), babies could develop the behavioral coordinations he describes: visually guided reaching (hearing and looking, etc.), means-ends behavior. The mental states that are allegedly realized in these behaviors must be presupposed for the theory to "explain" them. These mental states include the perception of a unified, external object (stage II) and the motivation for acting that involves doing something "in order to" do something else (stage IV).

Consider the theory of stage II. Initially, according to the theory, children look only *while* they hear, or grasp only *while* they look. They do not look at *what* they hear, or grasp *what* they see. At that point a visual impression would be experienced only as part of the act of looking, not as something external to looking. Through "reciprocal assimilation," the simultaneous engagement in the two patterns would intensify, because they would provide stimulation for one another. The child, however, would not identify the one (e.g., heard) image with the other (the seen image). This identification would follow as a matter of course, according to Piaget, as the "geometric point of crossing lines" (Piaget, 1936/1952, p. 108). By virtue of being at the "intersection" (p. 143) of several action patterns simultaneously, the object would tend to become external to any one of those patterns. The thing that is grasped while seen can no longer be viewed by children as an extension merely of seeing, because it is also grasped.

To come to the resolution that the thing that is seen is not just an extension of seeing, however, babies would have to know that the very same thing is also being grasped. According to the theory, they have no way to know this. Moreover, to know either that the thing that is seen is not an extension of seeing, or that it is the same thing that is being grasped, requires distinguishing a "thing" from the act of seeing. This is what the theory explicitly denies babies understand and is what Piaget is attempting to explain.

Intermediate arguments that Piaget proposes, or that could be constructed from the theory, do not break this apparent circle. Piaget describes how in due course the individual actions (e.g., looking *or* grasping) that come to be conjoined tend to diversify as a result of contact with increasingly varied circumstances. For instance, babies grasp things increasingly from different positions and through the use of different arm movements, to the point where they adjust their arm differently in anticipation of grasping, say, a handkerchief versus a pencil. This diversification, says Piaget, results in the externalization of the things grasped (Piaget, 1936/1952, p. 121). If babies now come to grasp something while seeing (what we know to be) the same thing, the argument would presumably continue, what has been combined with looking is the grasping of a thing that is already partly detached from the act of grasping. Under these circumstances, according to the argument, when encountering the seen image, babies would be better situated to "falsify" the theory that they are only grasping and to recognize that they are grasping a thing that they also see.

This argument still does not explain how that which is differentiated from the grasp would become identified with what is seen. It is not clear, in any case, how the differentiations Piaget describes would lead to a perception of the externality of the thing grasped. If one interprets the "functional invariants" (assimilation, accommodation, and organization) as they are defined for stage I, babies could just be adjusting their grasp to deal with the exigencies of the moment. Each resulting variant of the action could still be viewed by babies as continuous with the thing grasped. To argue otherwise would be to attribute babies with an appreciation of a class of differentiated grasping acts. Piaget would not want to make this attribution at this stage.

Piaget might appeal, alternatively, to the functional invariant specifically of organization. From the beginning even of the reflex stage, according to the theory, infants tend over time to systematize the accommodatory movements they make in connection with their actions and that allow these actions to continue when they have been impeded. Piaget might have argued that babies' transition from grasping *when* they see to grasping *what* they see reflects the same tendency toward internal organization, this time involving babies' mental schemes. To argue this point, however, would be circular. Piaget would be shifting the meaning of the purported functional invariants depending on the stage in question. Whereas organization referred to a systematization of behaviors at stage I, it would refer to a systematization of mental schemes in stage II. If (again) one interprets the functional invariants as they are defined for stage I, organization at stage II would add only the likelihood that grasping-while-seeing would become systematic or habitual. It would not become the psychologically new experience of grasping what is seen.

Piaget's argument regarding stage III, which introduces the notion that infants are bringing about the (external) effects they observe, parallels the account of the coordination of actions at stage II and has the same flaws. I therefore proceed to the account of stage IV.

Assume for the sake of the argument that babies now experience grasping what they see as grasping what they see. The account has other gaps. The central acquisition of stage IV is that children come to do one thing (move an object, pull a string) *in order to* do another (retrieve a different object, occasion some action on another object). Children develop these coordinations, according to the theory, by first engaging in one action *instead of* the desired one, using one object (that will eventually become the "means") instead of the other (the original goal object). In the standard kind of case, when the goal and intermediate objects are not in fact in contact, this replacement activity will be insufficient to get children to their goal. The children must instead subordinate one action, or one object, to the other, Piaget says. The problem here is that Piaget is just asserting, rather than explaining, what has to happen.

One might envision a transition process here whereby children hit upon the properly oriented intermediate action — for instance, displacing the obstacle or directing mother's hand effectively, by chance. They then attain their goal. Subsequently they attempt only to "reproduce" the effective action. This process would be analogous to the process of forming the secondary circular reactions of stage III. This hypothetical account has the problem that it cannot explain how children could come to understand patterns of this kind as consisting of distinct goal-actions and means-actions. An understanding of the pattern at the level of stage III would involve conceiving of the purported goal action only as an inherent consequence of the action that we would distinguish as serving as means.

In stage III a baby bangs an object and a sound is produced. In theory, although the banging might be prompted by the sight of the object, the baby could in principle strike the object and forget why he or she did so. Once the sound is produced, this would prompt the search for the antecedent action, and the cycle would begin again. Means-ends behavior in the strict sense of stage IV involves keeping in mind the separate goal-action while undertaking the means-action, and undertaking the means-action *because* it should make the goal-action feasible. The goal-action would then be undertaken when the means action is complete, not because it would follow as a necessary byproduct of the means-action or because of an on-the-spot association with the outcome of the means-action, but because it was the plan all along. A transition process involving only the reproduction of a chance effect (from the baby's point of view) would not account for this advance.

Piaget inserts an extra transitional step that might appear to address this problem. The account is based on the "transitional" example in which Laurent pulled his bassinet strings and eventually caused the fall of the paper. Piaget introduces the idea that Laurent, who did not yet coordinate discrete actions, continued to *desire* to grasp the paper, and hence to "apply" the schema of grasping it, while he engaged in the alternative, unrelated action of pulling the string. When the paper eventually fell, he had only to grasp what he wanted all along and subsequently to repeat the effective action when confronted with the same problem.

This account displaces the original question. It addresses how, *given* that children have some long-term goal, they come to discover a way of reaching it. The central advance of stage IV was supposed to be, however, precisely that of having long-term goals, or acting with "intention" (Piaget, 1936/1952).

The problems I have discussed here, which arise in Piaget's original (1936/1952, 1937/1954) account of infancy, are not solved in his later work that purportedly elaborates his model of developmental change (e.g., Piaget, 1974/1980, 1975/1985). Although it uses different terminology, the later theory is essentially the same as that presented in *Origins* (Piaget, 1936/1952) and depends on the account in *Origins* (see Sugarman, 1987a, for elaboration).

Implications

Piaget described a sequence of stages in the development of the organization of behavior in babies. With that sequence common sense would associate a certain number of mental states: that when babies grasp an object that is in front of them, they are grasping the thing they see; when they draw a book forward and retrieve an object resting on its far end they are drawing the book forward in order to retrieve the object. Piaget was brilliant in showing how, in fact, these behaviors need not be accompanied by the mental states we normally associate with them.

He seemed to think, however, that a cogent account of these states would emerge from an account of the transitional stages leading to their purportedly associated behaviors. They would follow as a matter of course, given the state of the baby, including his or her mental state at the previous stage, and given the results of behavior. The account does not work, no matter how minute a step one attempts to account for (in addition to the preceding critique, see, for example, the closing discussion of Piaget's account of children's development of the concept of number, and the analyses of visually guided reaching and "equilibration" theory, in Sugarman, 1987a). One always ends up having to presuppose the development in question, or else having to give it up. The result is that one can envision the whole (behavioral) development occurring with no integrated perception of objects, no strictly goal-directed behavior, from the subject's point of view.

To show that it is possible to generate the right behavior, or the right developmental sequence, without positing these psychological correlates does not prove that human intelligence can develop without them. Human intelligence *is* the subjective experience of grasping what we see, and of doing one thing in order to do another. A theory that does not account for these experiences is not a theory of human intelligence.

The gap in Piaget's theory is not closed by recent demonstrations that intermodal behaviors may be coordinated by babies earlier than Piaget supposed. That babies may innately turn toward a sound they hear, for example, rather than developing this coordination, does not imply that babies perceive a unified object that can be both seen and heard (and that is external to either seeing or hearing) (see, e.g., Harris, 1983, and Spelke, 1987, for relevant discussion and reviews). Some authors have suggested that this early coordination may nonetheless provide babies with a tool for forming a concept of object, or space (e.g., Gibson, 1983; Harris, 1983). Although this position is plausible, it, too, would appear to be incomplete, for the same reason that Piaget's account is. Given the starting point (in which "object" is unformed), there does not seem to be anything in the experience of a joint orienting of different receptors toward [what the observer knows to be] a common object that would lead babies to induce "object."

Yet we adults experience objects. One solution is that we are simply wired to code "object" by some age (see also Spelke, 1983), although, as Piaget's demonstration suggests—despite Piaget—*which* age is unclear. One potential difficulty with this solution is that the same problem appears to arise for all of the developments that Piaget described. Every advance needs to be postulated ahead of time (Sugarman, 1987a; see also Melkman, 1988). The implication of this outcome is not presently clear. The tautologies may mean either that Piaget's account is in error substantively or that there is some deeper and more generic problem with the nature of explanation of mental capacities. Although the necessary analyses remain to be done, it could turn out that most alternative accounts to Piaget's would ultimately also reduce to tautologies.[1] That outcome might mean either that the accounts have a substantive gap or that we simply do not yet have an appropriate language within which to talk about emergence.

Insofar as Piaget's account is in error substantively, the tautologies may indicate either that there is a vast class of mental properties that is innate or that some of these properties develop, but it is presently unclear through what process they do. Insofar as a class of innate properties exists, it remains to delimit that class. Are humans innately programmed to code "object" fully blown, for instance, or do they begin with a more general synaesthesia (see, e.g., Marks, 1975; Marks & Bornstein, 1987; also Nabokov, 1947), which is gradually honed to produce "object"? Regarding the goal-directed orienta-

---

[1] Many alternatives can be questioned on other grounds, that also apply to Piaget's theory (Sugarman, 1987b).

tion that Piaget ascribes to sensorimotor stage IV, humans might have some form of primitive intentionality from birth, of which the mental state Piaget describes for stage IV is an eventual outgrowth. That some form of intentionality must be built into the system has been suggested independently of this investigation (Melkman, 1988).

Regardless of what the proper set of developmental primitives may be, it seems possible that the stages of development that Piaget delineated may not be connected to one another, as he envisioned, as links in a chain. As just illustrated in the preceding paragraph, although they may always follow one another in development, stages III and IV of sensorimotor intelligence may be rooted in different primitive capacities and may come about through different developmental pathways.

Whichever account is correct, there is a profound mistake in Piaget's explanatory strategy. At least in his infancy works, it appears that Piaget was attempting to derive a causal explanation of how the internal aspects of intelligence come about, from a description of changes in external behavior. An account of mind will not drop out of an account of behavior. It must begin from mental primitives. Assimilation, accommodation, and organization, the "functional invariants" that Piaget claimed drive behavior, are not feasible candidates. They apply, by Piaget's own definition, to all aspects of operation of the organism: mental, behavioral, biological. Mental assimilation, therefore, must already presuppose a description of mental life with respect to which assimilation is to be specified. That description remains to be provided.

Some aspects of mental life must develop, and it must also be the case that experience is the basis for some of these developments. Piaget perhaps went further than any other theorist in attempting to explain how this interaction could occur. The explanation ends up being vacuous, because it must presuppose its endpoint. It remains to determine what sort of mechanism would do better.

Language and Thought

The arguments raised in this chapter have at least superficial relevance for child language insofar as language use, like human spatial-adaptive behavior, is considered to involve an internal organization, and the development of that organization eludes any simple explanation. Language also has been observed to develop in stages, and the stages have sometimes been incorporated in models of the language acquisition process. One might question, therefore, whether the internal organization ascribed to language use will also elude explanation, in the way that "object" eludes Piaget's theory. Further, the stages observed in language development might turn out to be epiphenomenal, in the way that Piaget's stages may lie outside the central sources of the developments he tried to explain.

There are disanalogies between language as it is normally studied and the aspects of thought considered here, that might affect the answers to these questions. In attempting to account for the development of human thought, Piaget was trying to explain the subjective experience of, for example, grasping what is seen. Grammar, which is the usual target of explanation in linguistic study, is an internal organization that, while mental, is not clearly part of the experience of learning or using language in the same way that "object" is part of our experience of the world. It refers, rather, to an integration of information that must exist somewhere in the system in order for linguistic behavior to be produced.

The proper analogy to grammar in the experience of "object" would seem to be something more like the geometry involved in spatially adaptive behavior. We know that somewhere in the system the information from different modalities must be put together. In principle there is a geometry that will specify that integration, a set of rules that will specify the coordination of angle of gaze with joint angles of the arm, for example.

Grammar and the geometry of spatial-adaptive behavior could be conceived as computational aspects of language and spatial adaptive behavior, respectively. Both refer to an organization that must exist somewhere in the system in order for the resulting behavior to take place. The subjective experience that underlies the behavior is something else, and bears a complex relationship to both the behavior and its computational aspect. Regardless of what the "system" may be computing to produce eye-hand coordination, the *agent* may or may not be experiencing a unified object that can be both seen and felt (e.g., Stein, Magalhães-Castro, & Kruger, 1975; Weiskrantz, 1986).

The issues raised in this chapter might apply differently to the computational and experiential aspects of behavior, or at least to grammar and the experiential aspects of thought discussed here. In the case of grammar, the argument has been made that although the stage-wise development that occurs may aid the learner, the data of experience are still insufficient to account for children's eventual production of grammatically correct sentences (Chomsky, 1972). The problem with "object" and the other mental states discussed by Piaget is not that the correct behavior cannot be generated on the basis of the input. The mental states purportedly embodied by that behavior fall outside the theory.

It might be the case that stage models, with or without innate constraints on the learner, would account for linguistic behavior, and for spatial-adaptive behavior. Insofar as they do that, they might also account for knowledge of a grammar and the acquisition of a geometry of spatial behavior. These models might, at the same time, fail to account for the experiential properties of thought discussed here. Cleavages of this kind might help to clarify where the gaps in our understanding of mental capacities lie, as well as to clarify similarities and differences between "language" and "thought."

References

Chomsky, N. (1972). *Language and mind* (enlarged ed.). New York: Harcourt, Brace, and World.

Gibson, E. J. (1983). Development of knowledge about intermodal unity: Two views. In L. Liben (Ed.), *Piaget and the foundations of knowledge* (pp. 19–41). Hillsdale, NJ: Erlbaum.

Harris, P. (1983). Infant cognition. In P. Mussen (Series Ed.), *Handbook of child psychology* (4th ed., Vol. 2), *Infancy and developmental psychobiology* (M. Haith & J. Campos, Vol. Eds.) (pp. 689–782). New York: Wiley.

Marks, L. E. (1975). On colored-hearing synesthesia: Cross-modal translations of sensory dimensions. *Psychological Bulletin, 82,* 303–331.

Marks, L. E., & Bornstein, M. (1987). Sensory similarities: Classes, characteristics, and cognitive consequences. In R. E. Haskell (Ed.), *cognition and symbolic structures: The psychology of metaphoric transformation* (pp. 49–65). Norwood, NJ: Ablex.

Melkman, R. (1988). *The construction of objectivity: A new look at the first months of life.* Basel: Karger.

Nabokov, V. (1947). *Speak, memory.* New York: Grosset & Dunlap.

Piaget, J. (1952). *The origins of intelligence in children.* New York: International Universities Press. (Original work published 1936 [in French]).

Piaget, J. (1954). *The construction of reality in the child.* New York: Basic Books. (Original work published 1937 [in French])

Piaget, J. (1980). *Experiments in contradiction.* Chicago: University of Chicago Press. (Original work published 1974 [in French])

Piaget, J. (1985). *The equilibration of cognitive structures: The central problem of intellectual development.* Chicago: University of Chicago Press. (Original work published 1975 [in French])

Spelke, E. S. (1983). Constraints on the development of intermodal perception. In L. Liben (Ed.), *Piaget and the foundations of knowledge* (pp. 43–48). Hillsdale, NJ: Erlbaum.

Spelke, E. S. (1987). The development of intermodal perception. In P. Salapatek & L. Cohen (Eds.), *Handbook of infant perception* (Vol. 2, pp. 233–273). New York: Academic Press.

Stein, B. E., Magalhães-Castro, B., & Kruger, L. (1975). Superior colliculus: Visuotopic-somatopic overlap. *Science, 189,* 224–226.

Sugarman, S. (1987a). *Piaget's construction of the child's reality.* New York: Cambridge University Press.

Sugarman, S. (1987b). The priority of description in developmental psychology. *International Journal of Behavioral Development, 10,* 391–414.

Weiskrantz, L. (1986). *Blindsight: A case study and its implications.* Oxford: Oxford University Press.

2

The Mysteries of Early Lexical Development: Underlying Cognitive and Linguistic Processes in Meaning Acquisition*

Esther Dromi

Tel Aviv University

Introduction

How do children acquire the conventional meanings of words? This comprises one of the most intriguing questions for philosophers, linguists, and psychologists who wish to gain a better understanding of the complex relationships among the conceptual, linguistic, and social factors underlying language development. Word learning has been conceptualized in several, quite different, ways. According to one view, meaning is acquired gradually through a long process involving repeated hearings of the same words in different nonlinguistic contexts. The proponents of this view have emphasized the mechanism of pairing words with real-world contingencies for their use (e.g., the Augustian view, as elaborated by Schlesinger, 1982; or Locke as discussed in Gleitman, 1989; see also Nelson, 1988). A second approach has highlighted the claim that children are very efficient word learners who, with almost no evidence for confusion, correctly induce meanings even from a single hearing of a novel word in a new context (e.g., Carey, Chapter 4; Carey & Bartlett, 1978; Markman, Chapter 3).

Researchers who proposed that word meaning acquisition constitutes a long-term process that reflects complex interactions between cognitive and

* This chapter is based on a paper presented at the Fifth Annual Workshop in Human Development and Education held at Tel Aviv University in December 1987. The data presented here were collected during 1980–1981 and were analyzed for the first time in my doctoral dissertation under the direction of Melissa Bowerman. My perspectives on the issues explored here have been greatly broadened by invaluable opportunities to discuss my work with workshop participants, with my graduate students at Tel Aviv University, and with colleagues who expressed interest in my project. I appreciate their input and would mainly like to thank Martyn Barrett, Melissa Bowerman, Steven Gillis, Lila Gleitman, Carolyn Mervis, Dan Slobin, and Susan Sugarman for their informative and thoughtful commentary on earlier drafts and exciting long discussions. I am also grateful to my research assistants Smadar Eilata, Dalia Ringwald, Hana Tur-Kaspa, and Sara Zadunaiski for providing considerable help in various phases of the research and during preparation of this manuscript. Thanks are extended to Dee Ankonina for her editorial contribution. This is working paper #103 of the Tel Aviv University Unit of Human Development and Education.

linguistic developments in the child have described the differences between adults' and children's categorization abilities (e.g., Barrett, 1986; Bowerman, 1980; Mervis, 1987). On the other hand, researchers who suggested that meaning acquisition is strongly determined by innate grammatical and/or conceptual knowledge have argued that, despite the fact that meaning acquisition requires hypothesis testing and induction (Quine, 1960), children's initial lexical notions are adultlike and correct (e.g., Huttenlocher & Smiley, 1987).

Our present-day understanding of how young children build up productive vocabularies of conventional words is still tentative. During the last decade, considerable experimental efforts have been devoted to empirical testing of proposed hypotheses. Innovative research paradigms have produced an impressive body of results on strategies children apply in learning new words (see Chapters 3, 4, and 5, respectively). However, experimental studies, as telling as they are, suffer from a number of limitations: (a) the difficulty and often impossibility of running experiments with subjects under the age of 3:0 years (see Gelman & Markman, 1986); (b) the strong constraints placed on experimental, controlled conditions by the stimuli and manner of testing (i.e., the set of pictures or objects used, the list of words, and the method of instruction); and (c) the tendency for experimental results to provide answers to very specific questions and the ensuing difficulty in generalizing from them about the complex interactions among variables in real-world learning situations.

Comprehensive case-study investigations (or intensive longitudinal naturalistic observations) may serve as an alternative research method for studying how meanings are constructed by children. Diary investigations provide detailed descriptions of how the child uses the same words over time in naturalistic contexts. It has been justifiably argued that it is hard or even impossible to single out the notion of word use from the notion of word meaning on the basis of any one particular speech event (Dromi, 1987; Huttenlocher & Smiley, 1987).[1] The problem of interpretation is greatly reduced, however, in comprehensive studies that allow the analysis of repeated data points for each lexical item. In the majority of cases, a close look at how the child uses the same word in various situational contexts reveals the intended meaning of a single word. Such analysis, if done systematically, can provide firsthand information about the scope of extension for a given word at any given point in the developmental case history of that word.

In recent years, a number of research reports on the course of early lexical development have been published (e.g., Barrett, 1986; Bowerman, 1978;

---

[1] The problem of determining meaning from context of use is complex. The claim made here is that it is hard to distinguish between associations and overextensions of terms when they are uttered in the absence of the intended referent in the immediate here-and-now context. See Dromi (1987, Chapter 8 and pp. 55, 99) for several examples and for proposed operative definitions that were utilized in order to minimize this problem. I will return to the issue of how one determines meaning from use in the section on words' extension and intension.

Dromi, 1987; Gillis, 1986; Mervis, 1987; Huttenlocher & Smiley, 1987). My goal in this chapter is to review my own results on the early lexical behaviors of my daughter, to test their generalizability against reports of other diarists, and to draw inferences from the case-study findings regarding the course of meaning acquisition throughout the one-word stage. Despite my recognition of the clear limitations characterizing case-study results (e.g., the small number of subjects, the restriction to production data only, the limitations of recording, etc.), some interesting hypotheses concerning the covert process of learning meaning emerge from present-day case descriptions. In the discussion sections of this chapter, I make an attempt to spell out some hypotheses and questions that require further investigation.

The present chapter describes the course of the early lexical development of my own daughter, Keren, who acquired Hebrew as her first and only language (see Dromi, 1987, for a more detailed report of this large-scale investigation). Four aspects of the subject's linguistic development throughout the one-word stage will be reviewed and discussed: the rate of word acquisition; the contents encoded by the one-word lexicon; the development of word reference; and the changes over time in the extension behaviors of words.

From the rich body of data on the course of development of the complete one-word lexicon of the child, I concluded that the behaviors observed during the beginning of the stage were qualitatively different from those observed toward its end. Observed changes in the child's lexical behaviors reflected underlying conceptual and linguistic developments. In the discussion sections of this chapter I will elaborate on this proposal and specifically address the following topics: (a) irregular uses of early words, (b) the role of input conditions, (c) linguistic and conceptual correlates, and (d) constraints on word-meaning acquisition.

The Nature of the Hebrew Corpus

The database for my investigation was the complete record of all the words that were acquired and used by my subject from the emergence of the first comprehensible word and until the subject started to productively combine words. During the developmental stage between the ages of $10(12)^2$ and 17(23), the child accumulated a productive lexicon of 337 different comprehensible words. A carefully controlled case-study design was employed to collect as much information as possible on the use of each of these words in different contexts over time.

---

[2] Throughout this chapter child's ages are given in months and days; hence 10(12) is to be read as 10 months and 12 days. Hebrew examples are underlined and are followed by English gloss; a Hebrew word enclosed in parentheses following another word indicates the adult equivalent of the child's phonological approximation. / represents end of utterance. K = Keren, F = Father, and M = Mother.

Three independent means were employed for the collection of data: (a) a handwritten diary that included descriptions of the phonological forms, together with the linguistic and nonlinguistic contexts for their use; (b) nine periodic audiorecordings ranging in length from 55 to 180 minutes each, which provided a representative picture of the child's regular use of words in the course of natural interactions and typical discourse; and (c) four 30-minute video-recorded sessions which presented visual aspects of early interactions in semistructured situations. The combination of these data collection procedures was designed to compensate for the drawbacks inherent in each individual procedure. It also provided the means for conducting various measures of reliability and validity on the data, which were found to be reasonably high.[3] The reliability and validity measures indicated that although the mother-researcher collected data constantly and for a relatively long period of time, the record was quite accurate and representative of the actual course of the lexical development of the child, reflecting both the emergence of new words and the changes in the use of old words over time.

In the course of data analysis, each of the child's productive words was scored repeatedly in every successive week of the study. Scores were given to each word on various dimensions on the basis of preplanned analysis codes that were operatively defined and tested for reliability (see description and illustration of the coding system in Dromi, 1987, Chapter 8). As will be shown below, the procedure of repeated scoring for each word provided crucial information for the identification of underlying conceptual and linguistic processes.

The Rate of Word Acquisition

The one-word stage, in the case of my subject, spanned 8 months and 12 days (i.e., 32 weeks), during which words were accumulated at a nonlinear pace. The acquisition curve of new words was curvilinear, starting with a very slow rate of vocabulary growth which increased gradually until it reached an average of 18 new words per week between the 21st and 24th week of research. An abrupt change in the rate of word acquisition was noted during Weeks 25, 26, and 27. During this lexical spurt, between the ages of 15(27) and 16(10), the subject acquired a total of 111 new words, constituting one-third of her productive lexicon. After three weeks of intensive learning, the rate of addition of new words began to decline. During the last two weeks of the stage,

---

[3] Interjudge agreement on what constituted a comprehensive word was 95%. Mother's description of the contexts of each utterance and independent judges' descriptions of the same contexts were also found to be very close (interscorer agreement ranged from .80 to 1.00). Intertranscriber agreement on phonetic transcriptions was 98% and 99% for two different recordings. Comparisons conducted between the diary record and the audio recordings revealed that 66% of the words recorded in the diary also appeared in the audio recordings, and that the agreement on the date of acquisition for these words reached a level of 91%.

the subject learned only 14 and 6 new words, respectively. It was noticed during the last eight weeks of study that the child was improving existing lexical items in terms of both form and meaning, rather than simply enlarging her productive lexicon.

The quantitative characteristics[4] of Keren's lexical growth throughout the stage were strikingly similar to available reports on other children. Keren's ages at the outset and at the end of the stage corresponded to the ages of the subjects studied by Braunwald (1978) and by Greenfield and Smith (1976). The size of Keren's productive lexicon substantiated Anisfeld's (1984) estimate that single-word lexicons exceed 250 different words, whereas it disproved earlier estimates of lexicons consisting of about 50 to 100 different words (e.g., Nelson, 1973). The exact count of 337 words for Keren approximated Brawnwald's (1978) count of 391 different words in the productive lexicon of her English-speaking daughter, although Keren's count was smaller than Gillis's count of 451 different Dutch words for his subject (Verlinden & Gillis, 1987) and lower than the count of 600 different English roots in the productive vocabulary of Mervis's (1987) 21-month-old subject. A number of intensive studies of one-word stage subjects, then, have indicated that in Western cultures children of educated, middle- to upper-class parents establish a large-sized vocabulary of 300 or more different words prior to the emergence of productive word combinations.

The rate at which children accumulate new words has been shown to be unsteady throughout the stage. The lexical spurt phenomenon was anecdotally described by Bloom (1973), Corrigan (1976), and more recently by McShane (1980) for several English-speaking children. Although during the first few months, words were found to be added slowly, in the second half of the stage a change in the rate of learning was observed. Keren's continuous record provided strong evidence for a spurt in lexical learning several weeks prior to initial evidence for productive multiword strings. My observation of a slowed rate of word acquisition following the spurt corroborated McCune-Nicolich's (1981) finding that the rate at which her subjects learned new words decreased sharply as morpheme per utterance (MLU) values exceeded the level of 1.0.

Several factors considered together suggested that lexical acquisition does

---

[4] Carey (1978) estimated the rate of acquiring new words during the first years of life at about 8 to 10 new words a day. This figure is extensively cited in the word meaning literature, yet most writers today fail to mention that this figure was only a general estimate based on Templin's (1957; cf. Carey, 1978) proposal that by age six the average child learned 14,000 words including inflected and derived words as measured in comprehension. The exact count of the rate of learning new words in production throughout the one-word stage was lower for my subject than was predicted by Carey. Even during the most hectic week of accumulating new words, Keren only added 44 new words. In addition to the discrepancy in quantities, it should also be emphasized that the rate of Keren's lexical learning during the stage was not constant. This finding, in my opinion, implies that the notion of average lexical learning per day is not authentic; therefore, I believe researchers should introduce this concept more cautiously.

not constitute a simple additive procedure: (a) the considerable size of single-word lexicons, (b) the relatively lengthy period of time throughout which the child accumulates words at a slow rate before the lexical spurt is observed, (c) the clearly identified spurt, and (d) the decrease in word learning following the intensive spurt period. As is shown below, several changes in the way Keren used her words clearly indicated that her word learning pattern was related to qualitative underlying changes in the way words were learned during the beginning phase and toward the end of the one-word stage.

The Contents of Early Words

The contents that one-word stage speakers choose to lexicalize are remarkably similar. This appears to be true for children acquiring the same language, and also for those acquiring different languages (e.g., Braunwald, 1978; Dromi & Fishelzon, 1986; Nelson, 1973). My analysis of the contents of Keren's vocabulary and the timing of learning-specific terms indicated that her early words comprised labels of objects and actions that were commonly encountered in her immediate and familiar environment, whereas words acquired later were more generic in the sense that they encoded classes of equivalent instances (i.e., compare the more personal terms *aba* 'father' or *xitul* '(a) diaper' with the terms *kapit* '(a) teaspoon' or *ec* '(a) tree').

An analysis of the various semantic classes and their differentiation by Keren and by three other one-word stage Hebrew speakers revealed similar patterns of lexical accumulation (Dromi & Fishelzon, 1986). During the first three months of the stage, a trend was observed for all subjects to learn unrelated words belonging to different semantic classes in adult language. This trend was termed a "horizontal" pattern of lexical accumulation. During the second half of the stage, a "vertical" pattern of word accumulation was observed. This pattern was manifested by the learning, in great proximity of time, of related terms in adult speech.

Keren's lexicon and the lexicons of the three other Hebrew-speaking subjects included words for animals, food, toys, clothes, furniture, household accessories, jewelry and small personal accessories, social words, words for motion, and words for locations — even before they reached the count of 50 different words. The initial lexicon (up to Week 18) covered several contents which were semantically unrelated. In almost all cases, only one or two words belonging to the same semantic field in adult language were learned by the child at this time. The words that were chosen to encode each of these contents were those that were frequently modeled to the child within repeated routinized experiences. During the following month of recording (Weeks 18–25) and before the lexical spurt was noted, new entries were added to existing classes of words, and new classes emerged. The child started to name body parts, to talk about qualities of objects, to encode transactions and changes of location, and to talk about states.

As reported above, Weeks 25–27 were characterized by a lexical spurt. During this period of time, new members of all the already known semantic classes entered the child's productive lexicon. The category of object words was greatly enlarged and several generic terms emerged (e.g., *even* '(a) stone'; *perax* '(a) flower'; *apit (kapit)* '(a) teaspoon'). An interesting finding was that during these and subsequent weeks I noted a proximity in the time of emergence of semantically related words. Thus, additional names of body parts (e.g., *ozen* '(an) ear'; *pupik* '(a) bellybutton'; and *cici* '(a) breast'), new words for items of clothing and the action word for putting on clothes (e.g., *abis (lehalbish)* 'to put on'; *gufia* '(an) undershirt'; *taic* 'tights'; and *bayi (garbayim)* 'socks') were recorded for the first time within the same week and often even on the same day.

The change in the pattern of word acquisition, from a more horizontal course of picking up terms for unrelated contents to a more vertical course of learning terms for semantically related contents, revealed that with time the child's lexical system became increasingly differentiated, as closely related contents were named. The growing lexical diversity reflected by the use of semantically related words may be attributed to the child's general ability to form classes of objects or actions on the basis of the identification of similarity relations. The rapid, accurate learning of two semantically related words requires that the child succeed in differentiating between members of the same and different classes, and also in entertaining the idea that each class possesses only one name. As proposed by Markman (Chapter 3), the mutual exclusivity constraint may considerably enhance word learning during the lexical spurt period.

During the last five weeks of the study, Keren learned relatively fewer new words. She added attributes to her active vocabulary, acquired her first pronoun, and started to differentiate between kinship terms which she had previously confused (i.e., started to use *saba* 'grandfather' and *savta* 'grandmother' correctly). The last three words in Keren's lexicon were *para* '(a) cow'; *kelev* '(a) dog'; and *tiyul* '(a) walk.' Importantly, these last words were conventional Hebrew words for contents that Keren earlier lexicalized by means of nonconventional forms or nursery words. The substitution of nonconventional or idiosyncratic forms by conventional adult forms for the same or closely related meanings showed that, at the end of the stage, Keren was very attentive to the ways by which meanings were encoded in adult speech. In my opinion, the replacement of old by new forms reflected the child's linguistic awareness that words are a conventional means for encoding consistent meanings by arbitrary, agreed-upon forms.

The Distribution of Children's Words in the Various Categories of Reference

It has often been reported that children's early vocabularies consist primarily of object reference words or nouns in adult speech (e.g., Dromi, 1987; Farwell,

1976, 1977; Gentner, 1978, 1982; Huttenlocher & Smiley, 1987; Verlinden & Gillis, 1987). Keren's complete one-word stage lexicon of 337 different Hebrew words contained five classes of words. A pronounced similarity was found between the distribution of these different classes in the Hebrew corpus and the distribution reported by Gentner (1982) for English, Japanese, German, Kaluli, and Turkish, and by Verlinden and Gillis (1987) for Dutch. In all of the languages studied, the largest category of words learned was of object words, whereas modifiers, words for actions, and social words were less well represented. Object words constituted 59 percent of the words that were learned and used by Keren throughout the stage; indeterminant words accounted for 16 percent of the total lexicon; action words 14 percent; social words 7 percent; and modifiers, the smallest category, only 4 percent.

My results indicated that by examining detailed descriptions of contexts, it was possible to decide whether or not a single word referred to a specific aspect of a given situation. In Keren's record, as in the records of other subjects (e.g., Gopnik, 1984; Huttenlocher & Smiley, 1987; Verlinden & Gillis, 1987), some words were used as names of classes of objects from the very start. Consider the following entries for the word *oto* '(a) car,' that were recorded during the first week of emergence:

1. Age 12(16): Outside, in front of the house; K and M stand and watch a group of children playing. When a car comes into sight K says *oto* '(a) car.'
2. Age 12(17): On the stairs; K is playing with one of her toy cars. F comes home. K shows him her toy and says *oto* '(a) car.'
3. Age 12(19): In the parents' room; K is walking around swinging a large shopping bag. F asks K: *ma yesh lax sham?* / 'What do you have there?' K comes closer to F, shows him the bag, looks inside it and says: *oto* '(a) car.' F and M are puzzled; they look into the bag and realize that K was right. There is a toy car in the bag.

The above examples clearly demonstrated that the term was used by the child for several object referents belonging to the adult category of "car." Similarly, other words were used correctly for actions only, or as modifiers or social words from their very first recordings. For example:

4. Age 16(18): In the living room; M who has just returned from work, takes off her shoes; K puts M's shoes on and walks around in them saying *alax* 'walked.'
5. Age 16(18): In K's room; M is sitting on the floor with K who is eating potato chips. K hands a chip to M and says: *ki (kxi)* 'take.'
6. Age 16(18): In the living room; M and K are drawing on a piece of paper. K says *myau* (her sound for a cat) and M draws a little cat. K says: *an*

(katan) 'small.' M draws a smaller cat. K seems delighted and points excitedly to the two drawings.

7. Age 17(2): In the living room; F and K are sitting and watching television. M is in the kitchen. F asks: *eifo ima?* / 'Where is mommy?' K says: *ulayim (yerushalayim)* 'Jerusalem.' (Several days before this recording M had gone to Jerusalem and had told K about it. K herself had never been to Jerusalem and therefore it was very unlikely that she knew what the term meant. I assume that the word was used here as a social routine.)

A number of early acquired words (45 of the 337 words) were used for some time ambiguously, for both actions and objects or for objects and attributes. These words were classified as indeterminant. Most of them were nouns in adult speech, or nonconventional forms (i.e., sounds that animals make or other nursery words that were modeled mainly by her nanny, who was a nonnative Hebrew speaker). The word *tita* 'tick-tock,' for example, was used simultaneously by Keren for the action of bringing small objects towards the ear, and also as a name for several jewelry items. Consider the following example:

8. Age 13(9): In the dining room; K is playing with M's pen. She is putting it close to her ear as if she is listening. While performing the action K says: *tita* 'tick-tock.' (I recorded the word in a similar context before, but on earlier occasions K brought jewelry items close to her ear. K utters the word *tita* when pointing to my ring, necklace, and F's watch.)

Other words which encoded more than one aspect of a situation included: the word *xam* 'hot,' which was concurrently a word for heaters and ovens, and a modifier denoting the property of being either cold or hot; the word *iga (rega)* 'a moment,' which was used for the action of diapering and for a diaper; and the word *hopa* for round objects and also for sharp contact between the body and the floor (i.e., jumping, climbing the steps, falling down).

Simultaneous use of the same word for more than one aspect of a given situation is not typical of adult language or the linguistic input to the child. This behavior, however, has been previously documented (e.g., Bowerman, 1978, 1980; Gillis, 1986; Nelson & Lucarriello, 1985), and was attributed to the complexive nature of young children's thinking (e.g., Vygotsky, 1962). It has been argued that early words, rather than standing for particular instances of a category or a class of objects, might initially be produced to indicate loose association between the sound pattern and several features of the contexts in which they occur.

Indeterminant uses of words in Keren's data were considerably more frequent during the first two months of the one-word stage than later. Moreover, early acquired words persisted in this pattern longer than did later acquired words. The finding that some words in Keren's record indeed showed indeterminant behaviors (i.e., were used by the child across grammatical classes) indicated that during the first few months of production she did not strictly observe the constraint of grammatical class membership which is assumed to be universal in adult language (see Nelson, 1988, for similar claims). As I argue below, irregular uses of words were recorded especially when Keren failed in the initial pairing of the word with its intended referent. I further discuss this finding following the summary of the results on extension.

The Extension Behaviors of Early Words

In addition to the question of whether a word referred to either objects or actions or both, I was interested in defining the scope of extension behaviors for each word in Keren's vocabulary and the manner in which these changed over time. My analysis addressed only the level of word extension, as a result of the fact that this level was traceable in the kind of naturalistic production records maintained for my subject.[5] Even a very detailed database of the contexts in which words were produced over time did not enable appropriate investigation of the development of words' intensions. This is not to say that meaning in the one-word stage was confined to the level of extension only. As was recently shown by Gelman and Markman (1986) and by Carey (Chapter 4), intension in a rudimentary form can be demonstrated as existing in very young children (i.e., 3 years of age and younger). However, under this age, it is extremely difficult (or even completely impossible) to evaluate sense relationships among different lexical items, primarily because such relationships can be identified only through well-planned experimental manipulations, especially during this stage, when syntactic evidence is still unavailable (e.g., Anglin, 1977).

The distinction between *extension* and *intension* is particularly helpful in analyzing spontaneous productions of early words, thereby allowing one to describe words' denotation properties while ignoring other aspects which cannot be directly tested without very young subjects' cooperation. In my study, the distinction served to separate (a) the class of items to which a term was applied, from (b) the properties which determined the applicability of that term by the child.[6]

The analysis of word extension was selected as a heuristic for comparing the

---

[5] My investigation of Keren's early lexical development was a naturalistic study, and therefore I intentionally did not perform any formal testing throughout the period of data collection (see Dromi 1987, Chapter 6, for the rationale of the methodology selection).

[6] The distinction between extension and intension is derived from Frege's (1892) work on reference and sense. Throughout the years, this notion has been modified in a number of directions by logicians and philosophers. Anglin (1977) integrated this distinction into child language research. I wish to thank Lila Gleitman for introducing me to the applicability of Frege's work.

child's extensions with those of adults' for the same lexical items. This analysis showed the extent to which Keren's uses of words resembled conventional uses; it also served as a means of documenting changes in the ways a particular word was used by the child over time. The extension patterns of 276 of Keren's words were identified; 61 words were excluded from this analysis because of insufficient information about their repeated use. The classification system for extension included four distinct categories: underextension, regular extension, overextension, and unclassified.

Underextension

Words which were used restrictively for a single or very limited subset of instances of the corresponding adult category were assigned to this category. Consider the following two examples:

9. Age 12(7)–15(7): K produces the word *pil* '(an) elephant' only in those contexts in which her white elephant toy is present. However, she fails to supply the word when she sees or plays on a slide in the shape of an elephant or when I show her pictures of elephants or plastic toys.
10. Age 16(15)–16(30): K produces the word *alax* 'go' (past singular masculine) only when she is walking around the house and wearing her parents' shoes. She never utters the word as a response to my questions about other people walking or herself walking without shoes.

Regular Extension

Words demonstrating flexible use for a number of different referents which all belonged to the corresponding adult category were assigned to this category. Note that regular use of a word may sometimes be identified in a single speech event in which the child names a nonprototypical instance of a class. Compare examples 11 and 12.

11. Age 12(16)–12(19): During these three days the word *oto* '(a) car' was recorded in a number of different places and while the child pointed to different instances of cars: real cars, toy cars, pictures of cars in different colors and shapes, etc.
12. Age 16(6): In K's room; M is standing on a chair. She is looking for something in the closet. One of the items she takes out is a hot water bottle which K has never seen before. M gives the bottle to K who shows it to F. When F takes the bottle K says: *babuk (bakbuk)* '(a) bottle.' Parents are surprised because this is not a typical bottle and before K used the term only for her own bottle.

Overextension

An overly broad use of a word for a class of referents, some of which fall outside of the corresponding adult category for the same word, was classified as overextension. The identification of overextensions in the speech of young children appears *far more complicated* than the identification of either underextension or regular extension. The main difficulty lies in the need to distinguish between irregular uses which arise from overly broad semantic definitions, and other types of irregular uses which are related to other factors (e.g., the growing communicative needs in the absence of large enough vocabulary, and/or the extent to which existing lexical items are differentiated).

In the present study, words included in this category were only those which persisted over time (i.e., were recorded in the same unexpected context at least three times and over at least several days), and for which a possible basis for overextension was identified (i.e., extension on the basis of similarity in function, form, location, or possession). Transient misuses of words and unclear extensions were assigned to the category of unclassified. Consider the two examples of irregular uses of the word "broom" which was overextended for several weeks to all the items that were kept in one closet in the kitchen.

13.   Age 16(17): In the kitchen; M is washing dishes. K is playing with one of the doors of the closet. M hears K saying *matate* '(a) broom.' She thinks that K sees a broom inside the closet. When M turns around she realizes that K is playing with a green funnel used for watering the plants.
14.   Age 16(19): In the kitchen; K is walking around holding a dustpan and swinging it back and forth. M asks: *ma ze?* / 'What is this?' K answers confidently: *matate* '(a) broom' /.

Other typical examples of overextensions were the use of: the word *tik* '(a) purse' for several containers: plastic and paper bags, a hat which was carried around upside down, pockets etc.; the word *na'al* '(a) shoe' for shoes and socks; the word *pe* '(a) mouth' for mouth and lipstick; the word *ikanes (lehikanes)* 'to go in' for the action of going in between two objects (e.g., when Keren asked to walk through in between two chairs, or between her bed and the wall, etc.); and the word *oax (liftoax)* 'to open' for the action of folding back shirt sleeves.

Unclassified
A number of words were used by the child repeatedly in different contexts. Although these words were uttered consistently, and recorded in high frequency, it was never clear which aspect of the situation they encoded. Some words were used ambiguously for actions and related objects (e.g., the word *dio* 'giddi up' for bouncing movements, riding, and for horses); others sounded as if they were used associatively rather than in a referential manner (e.g., the word *dod* '(an) uncle' used for strangers and for whenever the child heard noises coming from outside); still other words exhibited a pattern of shifting referential behavior so that it remained unclear as to whether they were terms for specific objects, actions, or relations or were employed as cover terms for

whole unanalyzed situations (Dromi, 1984). This category was exemplified by Keren's uses of the word *niyar* '(a) piece of paper.' This word, which was recorded many times throughout the stage, may have referred to pencils, pieces of paper, typed pages, the action of writing/drawing, or the drawing itself. Consider the following descriptions of the contexts in which Keren used this word:

15. Age 14(5): M is writing notes in K's diary; K observes M. Suddenly K starts to yell repeatedly: *niyar / niyar / niyar /* 'paper.' M gives K a piece of paper. K continues to whine. She says again and again: *niyar / niyar / niyar /* and tries to catch M's hand. M gives K a pencil. K takes it and sits down. K draws on her piece of paper.

16. Age 15(7): In K's room; K is lying down on her back and sucking her thumb. M enters the room. K gets up, picks up her little pillow, and shows it to M. She points to the applique of two birds on the cover of the pillow and says: *niyar /* 'paper.'

17. Age 15(17): Outside; M and K are walking on the sidewalk. K stops, points to an arrow on the sidewalk (a chalk drawing from a children's game), and says: *niyar /* 'paper.' M is surprised. She says *ze ciur /* 'it is a drawing.' Later on when we pass another arrow M stops, points at the arrow and asks: *Kereni ma ze? /* 'Keren what (is) this?' K answers confidently: *niyar /* 'paper.'

18. Age 16(4): In M's study; K takes out a pen from M's bag, hands it to M, and says: *niyar /* 'paper.'

19. Age 16(4): In the living room; K is playing with an empty plastic container of food. She points to a sticker on it with the name of the product. K gives M the container and with a rising intonation she asks: *niyar? /* 'paper?'

Summary of the Results on Extension

The four extension categories were unequally represented in the corpus. Of all the words that were learned throughout the stage, 66 percent exhibited the behavior of regular extension at one time or another, and the other 33 percent of the sample showed underextended, overextended, or unclassified behaviors. It was interesting to note that overextensions, which have so often been discussed in the word meaning literature (e.g., Clark, 1973, 1975; Rescorla, 1980), were recorded for only 77 of the 276 analyzed words. This behavior appeared as rarely as underextension or unclassified extension; it emerged relatively late and was recorded much more often toward the end of the stage.

The question, of when in its history a word shows certain extension behavior, is relevant to the present discussion. I found, as expected, that almost all underextensions were recorded during the initial uses of a word and that this behavior persisted for short periods of time (mean = 2 weeks, range = 1–10 weeks). In contrast, overextensions were almost always re-corded **after** a few weeks of correct or restricted use. This behavior was transient for some words and longer lasting for others. Half of the words that showed regular extension were recorded as such from the first week of their use, whereas the other half showed underextension or unclassified behaviors prior to the recording of regular uses. Unclassified behaviors were mainly recorded during initial weeks of production. Words that showed this behavior exhibited it over a long period of time (mean = 7 weeks, range = 1–24 weeks), despite regular attempts on the part of the mother to provide conventional words in cases of the child's irregular or unclear productions. Consider the following conversation which was audio-recorded when Keren's age was 15(20):

20.   In the living room.

> K: *?am /*
>   ?
> M: *nelex sof sof lamitbax? /*
>   '(shall) we finally go to the kitchen?'
>   *ma at roca le'exol? /*
>   'What do you want to eat?'
> K: *?am/*
>   ?
> M: *ma le'exol? /*
>   'What to eat?'

Timing of Acquisition and Extension Behaviors

A strong relationship was found between the timing of acquisition (i.e., child's age and linguistic maturation) and the pattern of extension. During the first four months of data collection, an unpredictable pattern of extension was noted for newly acquired words. The distribution of extension types was uneven, and it was difficult to identify a single factor that would explain why some words were initially underextended, while others were used regularly from the outset, and yet others demonstrated unclassified behaviors. In some weeks during this period, all of the new words acquired showed unclassified extension, and in other weeks some words were extended regularly from the outset. A striking finding for this first phase was the total lack of initial overextensions. No word in the record was overextended by the child during its first week of use. Initial unclassified behaviors, on the other hand, were recorded frequently, and during some weeks predominated.

The unpredictable pattern of extension was altered toward the fifth month of study, shortly before the lexical spurt was observed. Starting at this time, 30–40% of the new words showed underextension during the first week of use, and over 50% of the new words were recorded showing regular extension from the very first recordings. Starting at this point in time and onward, with an ever-growing tendency toward the last few weeks of the stage, most of the new words learned (70–100%) exhibited adultlike meanings from their outset.

Overextensions of new words during their first week of production were recorded only during the last three months of research. Unclassified behavior in new words declined considerably until completely disappearing five weeks before the end of the stage. This change revealed that only toward the end of the stage did Keren become aware that words are conventional tools, and therefore that strict rules for word application must be followed. This finding might also indicate that only toward the end of the stage the child more fully entertained the idea that words name classes of similar instances rather than label single examplars.

As words change their extension behaviors over time, it becomes obligatory to examine extension patterns not only for new words but also for old ones. Figure 2.1 depicts the relative distribution of all words used by the child during each week of study.

The interrelationship between the four extension types represented by the four curves in the figure reveals that overextension and underextension behaviors were relatively low and stable throughout the stage, whereas unclassified extension and regular extension were negatively correlated. It is obvious that with time more and more words entered the category of regular extension, as fewer and fewer words showed unclassified behaviors. The gradual, systematic increase in the number of regularly extended words suggested that with time the lexical system of the child became more and more conventional, with very few words showing too restricted or too broad extensions.

The analysis of extension behaviors supported the claim that the subject's lexical abilities at the beginning and the end of the one-word stage were qualitatively different. I believe that underlying cognitive and linguistic developments taking place throughout the stage were linked to the variance in: the rate of word acquisition; the contents that early and late acquired words encode; the clarity of referential behaviors; and the prevalence of the different extension behaviors. In the remaining sections of this chapter, I elaborate and discuss this proposal with reference to current theoretical issues related to this claim.

Irregular Uses of Early Words

The question of whether early uses of words reflect adultlike meanings or rather are loosely associated with idiosyncratic, unstable meanings has important theoretical implications. Examples of children's irregular uses of words have proliferated in the child language literature; for instance, extensive work

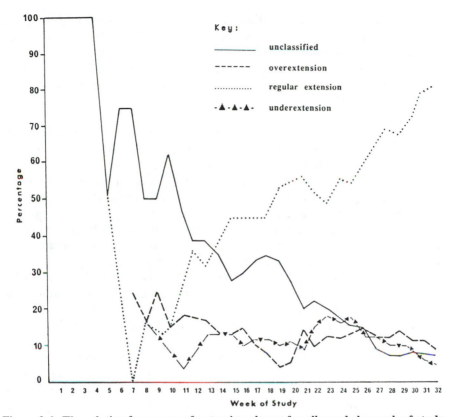

Figure 2.1. The relative frequency of extension classes for all words by week of study.

has been conducted on overextensions of meaning (e.g., Bowerman, 1978; Clark, 1973, 1975; Rescorla, 1980). In a previous section (see also Dromi, 1982, 1987), I argued that a clear distinction must be drawn between semantic overextensions and other types of irregular word uses. Judgments about correct or incorrect applications of a child's words are usually based on the adult's expectations as a listener. Such expectations arise from knowledge of the conventional meaning of the word. Irregular uses of words (i.e., their productions in unexpected contexts) may not always reflect an underlying, overly broad category associated with the misused word.

My analysis of Keren's data clearly indicated that categorical and comple-xive overextensions (i.e., misuses which are based on the identification of similar features) did not emerge early in the one-word stage. Such uses were recorded late in the case history of single words, and were far more prevalent (especially for new words) during the second phase of the stage. This is not to say that all the words that were learned early by Keren were recorded in expected contexts. As reported above, several early words exhibited irregular uses. Some were used for both actions and objects, some showed shifted referential properties, and in some cases it was difficult to identify the reference or extension of a word despite frequent recordings in similar contexts.

The following common characteristics were noted for the irregularly used words which were thereby assigned to the category of indeterminant or unclassified extension:

- All of these words were acquired during the first five months of research and before the change in the rate of acquiring new words was noted (i.e., at the age of 15(21) in the 21st week of investigation).
- A recognizable number of these words were nonconventional words in adult Hebrew (see Dromi, 1984, for a list of the unclassified words).
- The nonlinguistic contexts for learning these words were best characterized as everyday repeated experiences, and their introduction by the adults did not involve a clearly ostensive definition (e.g., pointing to a picture book, giving or showing an object, or demonstrating an action).
- Many of the words were modeled when embedded in speech routines (i.e., appeared in frozen linguistic strings); several appeared in the input records as single-word expressions (e.g., "don't paint on the floor — paint only on paper"; "just a minute"; and "hopa" when climbing the steps).

Early irregular uses of words may have initially been associated with the child's overall unanalyzed representations of early everyday experiences. I suggested that words exhibiting irregular, noncategorical uses should be termed **situational words** (Dromi, 1982, 1984, 1987). I argued that situational words comprised words that the subject started to utter long before she carried out a detailed analysis of their underlying categorical meanings. My hypothesis was that these words were elicited on specific occasions only, on the basis of the subject's knowledge of the appropriate contexts for their application. A simple and linguistically immature *word-context production strategy* that was related to the recognition of a familiar object, or that accompanied the performance of a familiar action, may explain the consistency and yet the nonanalytic meaning of a situational term (Dromi, 1984).

My records showed that during the first phase of the one-word stage Keren uttered words even when she just heard a familiar sound pattern that she recognized. The two examples below illustrate this point:

21. Age 13(8): In K's room; F and M are talking about going out tonight. K seems not to be paying attention. She is running around with her ball. M draws a schematic map of town on a piece of paper and says to F: *ani efgosh otxa po al yad hasha'on shel yaffo / 'I shall meet you right here near the Jaffa clock.'* K comes closer to parents. She points on the piece of paper and says: *tita* 'tick tock' (her word for watches, clocks and other jewelry and also a word for bringing little objects to the ear). It seems to

me that the word was elicited in this particular context because K recognized the word *sha'on* '(a) clock' which is the name of the central square in Jaffa.

22.   Age 15(21): At the playground; K and M are playing on a slide. Another girl approaches the slide. K points to her and says *ada (yalda)* '(a) girl.' Suddenly the girl falls down and starts to cry. K looks at M and says, while pointing at the crying girl, *nok (tinok)* '(a) baby.'

The last example illustrated that even when the child uttered a conventional word in expected contexts, the word may not have encoded socially agreed-upon meanings. At specific times during the early phases of production, many words conveyed subjective or local meanings.

Is it possible that Keren's production of situational words was idiosyncratic? To what extent was this behavior generalizable across subjects? My examination of other diary reports revealed remarkable similarities between the descriptions of Keren's early uses of situational words and the descriptions of irregular usage by other one-word stage speakers. Braunwald (1978) described her English-speaking daughter's uses of the word "bow-wow" as "a multi-purpose word referring to the sounds of barking, birds chirping, car and airplane engines or noises audible in the house from outside as well as the sight of dogs and cars" (p. 520). Braunwald's transcript read like a translation of the Hebrew term *dod* '(an) uncle' as used by Keren for unfamiliar faces and loud voices coming from outside.

Ferrier's (1978) descriptions of her child's uses of the term "phew!" were strikingly similar to my descriptions of Keren's word *pipi* 'urine.' *Phew* was an exclamation word used by the mother to express her feelings toward the unpleasant smells of wet diapers. The subject learned this word and extended it to several referents that were somehow related to the routine of "nappy changing." She subsequently used the word even outside of this situation for clean and dirty objects and for the nappy bucket and full or empty buckets in general. Some of Bowerman's (1978, 1980) examples of Eva's complexive word applications also resembled Keren's uses of some situational words. Bowerman's examples for the word "giddi-up" for horses and riding was identical to Keren's *dio*. I assigned *dio* to the categories of indeterminant reference/unclassified extension since Keren used it for horses, gallop sounds, and repeated movements of riding or bouncing (e.g., as a request for an adult to pick her up and let her "jump/ride" on his/her lap).

Descriptions of highly context-dependent word uses which did not show any evidence for initial categorical extension appeared in publications of two other diarists (Barrett, 1986; Gillis, 1986). These researchers documented in detail the contexts in which first productions were used, and they concluded that at least some early words are uttered by children prior to the establishment of categorical representations (see also Lucariello, 1987; Nelson & Lucariello, 1985).

Barrett (1986) reported that a few of his son Adam's first words were event-bound productions. For some time prior to their extension to various novel referents, these words were uttered only in particular contexts of routinized events. The word "duck," for example, was for a few weeks uttered only when the child was engaged in banging one of his toys, a yellow duck, on the edge of the bathtub. This word was never recorded when the child was playing with two other ducks in the same manner and setting, with the yellow duck in other ways, or while he was looking at or feeding real ducks.

Barrett hypothesized that the word was initially associated with the representation of an event which consisted of a single action (the banging during bath-taking time), a single person (Adam), and a single object (the yellow duck). Barrett reported that the subject gradually separated out the major constituents of this representation. First, the word was used for the other duck toys in the same situation, and only later was it generalized beyond this to other instances of ducks that were encountered in different contexts (e.g., when looking at picture books, pointing to toy and real ducks in other locations, etc.). According to Barrett, such evidence on early extension of words by children provided a basis for the claim that two main routes exist in early lexical development: one for context-bound words and the other for nominal and nonnominal words which exhibit early referential behaviors. Barrett suggested that words are attached to taxonomic categories only when children start to appreciate semantic relationships among them, and this achievement has been documented only during the early preschool years.

A contextualized description of early productions was also provided by Gillis (1986, 1987). Gillis reported that during the first six months of word learning (from the emergence of first words and until the lexical spurt was noted), some of his subject Maarten's words demonstrated unstable extension. These words were sometimes used for objects and at other times for related actions or for the relationship between objects and/or actions. Gillis postulated that these productions were highly contextual and were triggered either by the identification of single components of an event, or by the identification of the overall scripted event. Gillis's proposal, that early productions are in fact expressions lacking denotation properties, is very similar to my claim that situational behaviors of words are noncategorical word applications, which are associated with holistic, unanalyzed representations of situations or scenes (Schank & Abelson, 1977).

Throughout the one-word stage, fewer and fewer of Keren's words showed situational behaviors. I observed a gradual, continuous increase in the number of categorical uses of words as the frequency of situational uses of words decreased. During the last eight weeks of the study (and following the lexical spurt), object words were often recorded when their intended referents were not present in the immediate contexts. On several occasions Keren used an action word when pointing to object referents, and it was obvious that she was talking about the action or state of the object rather than naming it. Sequences of single word utterances were often recorded toward the end of stage, reflecting the successive encoding of differentiated aspects of the same situation (Bloom, 1973). For example:

23.   Age 16(26): At the doorway; K and M are about to go out for a walk. M says: *boi albish lax cova* / 'Let me put your hat on.' K says: *kova* / *os* / '(a) hat,' '(a) head.'
24.   Age 16(30): In parents' room; K is pointing to a picture of a bird which is hanging on the wall. She says to F who is holding her in his arms *ipor (cipor)* / *afa* / '(a) bird,' 'fly.'

During the last few weeks of the study Keren started to replace old nursery forms with conventional Hebrew words. It was interesting to note that at first Keren often juxtaposed new (conventional) and old (situational) words. Consider the following two examples:

25.   Age 17(5): In the living room; K brings a red balloon to M. She hands it to M and says: *alon (ballon)* / *hupa* / '(a) balloon' '?'. *hupa* was K's earlier word for round objects and any abrupt contact of body parts, mainly legs, with the floor; it was also used for jumping.
26.   Age 15(16): In K's room; K is sitting on the floor and playing with plastic toy animals. She takes a horse out of the box and says: *dio* / 'giddi-up.' M asks K: *ma ze?* / 'What is this?' K answers: *sus* / *dio* / '(a) horse,' 'giddi up.'

I propose that the subject's strategy of leaning on her old words, when she first started to utter conventional words, indicated that the appreciation of the underlying principles for conventional word uses was not instantaneous, and that schematic and categorical uses of words co-existed during the first few months of verbal production.

Cognitive and Linguistic Correlates

In recent years a number of researchers have suggested that the earliest forms of gestural and verbal communication occur within repeated contexts of routinized everyday experiences (e.g., Barrett, 1986; Bates, 1979; Dromi, 1984, 1987; Gillis, 1986, 1987; Nelson & Lucariello, 1985). This suggestion implies that early vocalizations are not referential, but rather are procedures that constitute parts of the contexts in which they are uttered. By a continuous process of decontextualization, early vocalizations become increasingly symbolic. They are detached from the restricted action schemes in which they are initially embedded, and begin to represent sets of referents or relations. As symbolic tools, words are separated from their intended referents not only in time and space, but also by the very fact that they become arbitrary and that they start to convey socially agreed upon meanings (Bates, 1979; Piaget, 1962).

The question of how and exactly when first words become symbolic has been studied by a number of researchers. Bates and her colleagues (1979) reported that in both the nonlinguistic and the linguistic arenas symbolic capacities emerge at the age of 13 months. Huttenlocher and Smiley (1987), Gopnik and Meltzoff (1985, 1986), and Mervis (1987) have also claimed that symbolic, referential, and categorical uses of words are evident at the outset of speech. Other researchers have indicated that evidence for symbolic uses of words is not obtainable prior to the lexical spurt (Bloom, 1973; Corrigan, 1976; Gillis, 1986).

Nelson, for example, has discussed the possibility that early productions are not true words (e.g., Nelson, 1988, 1990; Nelson & Lucariello, 1985; also see Lucariello, 1987). She estimated that the first 30 vocabulary items acquired by the child are prelexical terms that lack denotation properties and that are not conceptual, in that they do not name classes of things, people, actions, and events. Nelson (1988) speculated that only after the child becomes proficient in forming concepts does s/he master the realization of the one-to-one correspondence existing between words and concepts. Starting at this phase, "the child looks for words for established concepts and also tries to form concepts for new words" (p. 225).

Sugarman (1982a,b; 1983), who studied the development of the non-linguistic categorization abilities of very young children, gathered empirical support for the hypothesis that *a qualitative change* in the classification abilities of children occurs between the ages of 18 to 24 months. She found that at this age her subjects started to successively compare individual instances before making a decision as to their class membership (i.e., a classification strategy reminiscent of Gillis' observation that at a certain point during the one-word stage, when children produce a word, they search around for other referents that are named by the same term). According to Sugarman, while the classification of discrete objects by 12-month-old subjects is motivated by the recognition of some familiarity with that object, 18–24-month-old children categorize objects on the basis of the identification of similarity among them. Only when subjects start to realize that A and B are distinct objects, but that they can be equated because they look alike or serve the same function, can it be concluded, Sugarman argued, that the subjects show genuine categorization abilities. Initial evidence for this important cognitive ability was recorded by Sugarman only toward the end of the sensorimotor period.

My analyses showed qualitative differences between Keren's early and late lexical behaviors, which can be linked to the development of general symbolic capacities and more specifically to the formation of class relationships at the nonlinguistic level. However, can conceptual attainments alone account for the differences in the overt behaviors of words?

Mandler (1979, 1983) distinguished between categorical and schematic cognitive structures of representation. She claimed that a scheme is a structure which is organized around contiguities of space and time, unlike categories which are based on similarity relationships among the members of a class. According to Mandler, schematic and categorical structures co-exist in humans and serve different cognitive functions, enabling subjects to shift from one mode of representation to another.

Words which showed situational behaviors appeared to be initially attached to schematic representations of early everyday experiences. I suspected that when the child failed to pair a word with a single component of a situation (e.g., an object or an action), she associated the word with a schematic representation of the context in which it was learned. As we have seen, not all the words that Keren learned during the first phase of the stage showed situational application. Some words were used regularly from their outset.

The detailed record of Keren's lexical development showed that, as predicted by Carey (1982), words followed different routes to conventional meanings, and a simple model postulating a linear progression from holistic to highly differentiated meaning representation, or from contextual to categorical word usage, is not sufficiently comprehensive to account for the diversity of findings. Several additional factors, other than the observed progress in categorization abilities, must be invoked in order to explain the diversity of patterns observed. Candidate factors that determine initial and subsequent word extension will be examined below.

The Role of Input Conditions

As we have seen, the question of why some words are mapped correctly while others are not is multidimensional and complex. It does not yield a simple answer. My detailed longitudinal records of Keren's lexical development indicated that a complex interaction between several major factors determined the initial mapping of a word and the path it took toward conventional meaning. The course of both initial and subsequent extension were affected by the timing of acquisition within the one-word stage; the linguistic and the nonlinguistic contexts for learning a new word; and the grammatical status of the word in adult speech.

Detailed descriptions of the natural linguistic and nonlinguistic contexts for learning words are very limited to date. Harris, Barrett, Jones, and Brookes (1988), identified a strong relationship between four children's initial uses of their first 10 words and the characteristics of their mothers' modeling practices. Harris et al. found that words that initially revealed event-bound behaviors were most frequently modeled by the mothers in very similar nonlinguistic contexts. Mothers' modeling behaviors were consistent across time and could be successfully predicted from the child's records. The relationship between mothers' input practices and the subsequent contexts of production of the same 10 words was dramatically weaker. The contexts of the child's initial productions revealed a pronounced resemblance to the most frequent contexts in which the words were modeled to the child, whereas later productions seemed not to be so closely tied to the nonlinguistic characteristics of input. On the basis of a set of correlational results, Barrett et al. (1991) concluded that the effect of maternal speech characteristics seemed to decline once the child had established an initial productive lexicon.

If the hypothesis is correct that the meaning of early words is strongly affected by input conditions, then great variability in initial extension is to be expected. Variability in the modeling conditions for different words within a single mother–child dyad might explain why some early words show situational behaviors while others seem to manifest regular extension patterns from their outset. During the early phases of production, words that are learned within clear, ostensibly defined contexts are used regularly by the child from the outset. Words that are frequently modeled in opaque contexts are initially embedded within undifferentiated schematic representations of the contexts in which they were learned. The assumption, that the effect of modeling conditions on extension behaviors is not constant across the one-word stage, must be carefully tested.

The characteristics of different mother–child dyadic interactions may explain why some researchers identified more regularly-extended words among early vocabularies, whereas others documented more frequent use of situational or context-bound behaviors (Mervis, personal communication, October 1988).[7] Caretakers' linguistic and nonlinguistic modeling behaviors, and the extent to which mothers' interaction styles tend to be instructive or not, cry out for careful future examination.

To what extent do children rely on their observation of real-world contingencies for using words in constructing hypotheses about lexical meaning? This fascinating question has been recently investigated by Gleitman (1989); Landau and Gleitman (1985); and Chapter 5. These researchers cited convincing empirical evidence for the syntactic bootstrapping hypothesis. The role of syntactic cues in directing the young child to correct projections of word meaning seems fundamentally important. Similarities between blind and sighted children's production and comprehension of vision-related terms, and experimental studies in which subjects aged 3:0 and older were requested to manipulate objects, have established that children make inferences about semantic distinctions from syntactic evidence (see also Carey, 1982, Chapter 4; Soja, Carey, & Spelke, 1985). It seems then that from a very young age children utilize two imperfect sources of information for constructing conventional meanings: the linguistic and the observational.

My naturalistic production data of a much younger subject than those studied by Naigles et al. (Chapter 5) provided additional support for the claim that the linguistic design guides the young child's attempts to acquire conven

---

[7] I wish to thank Carolyn Mervis for setting the ground for the formulation of this hypothesis.

tional meanings. My results showed that Keren utilized morphological and syntactic cues in bootstrapping word meanings a few months prior to showing clear evidence of productive syntax. This was particularly obvious with regard to the acquisition of Hebrew verb forms. As soon as the first verbs entered Keren's vocabulary (during the fifth month of the study), they were extended regularly and consistently as words for actions. I speculated that linguistic rather than cognitive factors determined the ease with which the verbs were mapped by the subject. Most of the verbs used by the child took the overt morphological form of infinitive or imperative from their outset. It should be emphasized that Keren picked up the relatively complex morphological construct first and did not prefer one of the tensed forms. I propose that infinitive and imperative forms were selected by the child for two main reasons: (a) these were the forms that took constant linguistic manifestations in different nonlinguistic contexts; and (b) these forms were always modeled to the child when embedded within syntactic frames (e.g., "Do you want to eat / to drink / to go / etc.").

I assume, then, that verbs were mapped more effectively than nouns since they were modeled within syntactic frames. In the input to the child, verbs were rarely recorded in isolation, a finding which was not true for nouns or nonconventional words. As reported above, among the indeterminant and unclassified situational words, I identified mainly nouns and nonconventional Hebrew words which Keren heard occasionally in isolation or in routinized, fixed-order syntactic strings. The finding that the initial mapping of isolated nouns and nonconventional forms was problematic provided indirect support for the argument that grammatical cues (i.e., syntactic and morphological) direct the attention of the young child to specific aspects of the nonlinguistic contexts in which words are learned.

To what extent the changes observed during the second phase of the stage are related to the child's increasing sensitivity to the informative value of the language structures is a question that cries out for further investigation. In future studies, the relative significance of the linguistic and nonlinguistic contexts of word learning, and the interaction of these factors with children's age and cognitive functioning, must be seriously investigated.

Constraints on Word-Meaning Acquisition

There have been a number of recent proposals concerning the means by which linguistic constraints guide and accelerate the course of lexical meaning acquisition. Huttenlocher and Smiley (1987) argued that their finding, regarding the use of object words from the start as names of kinds of objects, supported the view that object categories are primitive conceptual notions that need not be learned. Clark (1987, 1988) elaborated her views on the role of the principles of "contrast" and "conventionality" in constraining initial word meanings, and in a sequence of experimental studies, Markman (e.g., 1987,

Chapter 3) exemplified the role of the "taxonomic" and "whole object" constraints, and the constraint of "mutual exclusivity."

How are my results interpreted with regard to the issue of linguistic constraints? The answer to this question is not so straightforward. Indeterminant uses of words across ontological categories were recorded for my subject, mainly during the first phase of the one-word stage. However, none of these words were initially successfully paired with either a single instance of a category or with a more developed object concept. Only when Keren failed to identify the referent for a novel word did she extend it across categories and/or use it as a situational word. At the same time, my records (as well as reports by others) included examples of correct applications and generalizations of meaning even during the beginning of the stage. This observation indicated that, when correct initial mapping was attained, the child followed extension rules quite successfully. Keren's mapping abilities increased throughout the stage, her categorization skills improved, and she became a much more efficient word learner. She also indicated that with time and growing linguistic experiences she became more aware of the fact that words are conventional tools for communication.

Nelson (1990) interpreted my finding that more nouns were used for actions than verbs for objects, to be clear evidence against the hypothesis that linguistic constraints are innate. Her conclusion, in my opinion, is much too strong. As we have seen, several factors can be invoked to explain why many more irregular uses were recorded at the beginning of the stage. Not all of the factors have been recognized yet, and many are still far from being adequately defined and fully understood. Much more research is needed in order to discover whether early words are learned by completely different mechanisms than are later words. As Carey (Chapter 4) pointed out, a special focus of investigation should be whether early irregular uses of words (a) are linked to a different conceptual system in which the world is not defined in terms of "kinds" of physical objects, or (b) reflect the infant's lack of understanding that words in adult language refer to "kinds" of objects.

My naturalistic production data (as well as similar data collected by others) did not allow for the direct testing of this question, as a result of the difficulty in singling out conceptual from linguistic variables when they cannot be manipulated (e.g., Chapter 6). My results indicated, however, that during the second part of the one-word stage the child is far more effective and successful at word learning. The finding that during the second part of the stage the child did not add situational words to her productive lexicon, and the observation that toward the end of the stage she did replace old nonconventional forms by conventional words, informed us that learning was more constrained in the second part of the stage than it was previously.

It is very plausible that late emergence of linguistic constraints, which guide children to correct *initial hypotheses* about what words can mean, explain why during the second phase of word learning irregular uses of words are no longer recorded. The question of exactly when, during the one-word stage, various constraints start to operate in facilitating initial mapping, and how these constraints interact with conceptual developments, is a challenge for further research. Exciting potential directions for future study involve refining and elaborating the types of constraints, as well as determining their origin. How various constraints interact with each other, and whether they are interrelated hierarchically or linearly is also an important question for future investigation.

Experiments to test whether and which particular constraints guide young children toward conventional meaning should be conducted with different linguistic stimuli (i.e., not only with object words), and in different learning situations (i.e., not only when a novel word is introduced in a clear, ostensive manner). Moreover, future research must include subjects at the onset of speech, and attempts must be directed to the development of procedures which will enable assessment of comprehension as well as production abilities in these subjects (Markman, personal communication, Summer 1988).

Some Concluding Thoughts

I began this chapter by acknowledging the potential power of intensive case-study results for revealing underlying cognitive and linguistic processes that are involved in the acquisition of early lexical meanings. On the basis of a review of my own empirical results, and comparisons with other intensive investigations of early speech, I concluded that throughout the one-word stage the child's linguistic system undergoes a major structural change as it becomes more highly differentiated, symbolic, and conventional. The acquisition of the major principles for conventional use of words is not instantaneous and not general across the board. It was argued that the child gradually learns to appreciate the fact that words convey consistent meanings; that they are attached to either object concepts or to actions and relations; that words must be conventional both in terms of their form and their underlying meaning; and that words can stand for specific referents, classes of referents, and relations even in their absence in the immediate physical context.

In the discussion sections of this chapter I dealt with four topics, which are presently at the forefront of the research on word meaning acquisition. I have made an attempt to show that, in each of these areas, considerable advancements have taken place in the last few years, but the state-of-the-art allows only for initial hypothesizing. Much more research is needed before general and pervasive conclusions can be reached regarding: (a) how the child becomes so efficient in lexical learning, (b) which conditions facilitate successful learning, and (c) when we can confidently claim that the child's and the adults' linguistic knowledge are alike. I believe that future experimental studies on production as well as comprehension abilities of very young subjects, as well as intensive research programs on caretakers' as well as children's linguistic and nonlinguistic behaviors in naturalistic contexts, will prove that much more information than we possess today is indeed necessary in order to scientifically understand the mysteries of lexical meaning acquisition.

References

Anglin, J. M. (1977). *Word, object and conceptual development*. New York: Norton.

Anisfeld, M. (1984). *Language development from birth to three*. Hillsdale, NJ: Lawrence Erlbaum.

Barrett, M. D. (1986). Early semantic representations and early word usage. In S. Kuczay & M. D. Barrett (Eds.), *The development of word meaning*. New York: Springer.

Barrett, M. D., Harris, M., & Chasin, J. (1991). Early lexical development and maternal speech: A comparison of children's initial and subsequent uses of words. *Journal of Child Language, 18,* 21–40.

Bates, E. (1979). *The emergence of symbols: Cognition and communication in infancy*. New York: Academic Press.

Bloom, L. (1973). *One word at a time*. The Hague: Mouton.

Bowerman, M. (1978). The acquisition of word meaning: An investigation into some current conflicts. In N. Waterson & C. Snow (Eds.), *The development of communication*. New York: John Wiley and Sons.

Bowerman, M. (1980). The structure and origin of semantic categories in the language learning child. In M. Foster & S. Brandes (Eds.), *Symbol as sense*. New York: Academic Press.

Braunwald, S. R. (1978). Context, word and meaning: Toward a communicational analysis of lexical acquisition. In A. Lock (Ed.), *Action, gesture and symbol: The emergence of language*. London: Academic Press.

Carey, S. (1978). The child as a word learner. In M. Halle, J. Bresnen, & G. Miller (Eds.), *Linguistic theory and psychological reality*. Cambridge, England: Cambridge University Press.

Carey, S. (1982). Semantics and development: State of the art. In E. Wanner & L. Gleitman (Eds.), *Language acquisition: The state of the art*. Cambridge, England: Cambridge University Press.

Carey, S., & Bartlett, E. (1978). Acquiring a single new word. *Papers and Reports on Child Language Development, 15,* 17–29.

Clark, E. V. (1973). What's in a word? On the child's acquisition of semantics in his first language. In T. E. Moore (Ed.), *Cognitive development and the acquisition of language*. New York: Academic Press.

Clark, E. V. (1975). Knowledge, context and strategy in the acquisition of meaning. In D. Dato (Ed.), *Twenty-Sixth Annual Georgetown University Round Table on Languages and Linguistics*. Washington, DC: Georgetown University Press.

Clark, E. V. (1987). The principle of contrast: A constraint on acquisition. In B. MacWhinney (Ed.), *Mechanisms of language acquisition*. Hillsdale, NJ: Lawrence Erlbaum.

Clark, E. V. (1988). On the logic of contrast. *Journal of Child Language, 15,* 317–337.

Corrigan, R. L. (1976). *Patterns of individual communication and cognitive development*. Unpublished doctoral dissertation, University of Denver, CO.

Dromi, E. (1982). *In pursuit of meaningful words: A case study analysis of early lexical development*. Unpublished doctoral dissertation, University of Kansas.

Dromi, E. (1984). The word context production strategy in the early acquisition of meaning. In C. L. Thew & C. L. Johnson (Eds.), *Proceedings of the second international congress for the study of child language* (Vol. II). Lanham, MD: University Press of America.

Dromi, E. (1987). *Early lexical development*. London: Cambridge University Press.

Dromi, E., & Fishelzon, G. (1986). Similarity, specificity and contrast: A study of early semantic categories. *Papers and Reports on Child Language Development, 25,* 25–32.

Farwell, C. B. (1976). *The early expression of motion and location.* Paper presented at the First Annual Boston Conference on Language Development, Boston, MA.

Farwell, C. B. (1977). The primacy of goal in child's description of motion and location. *Papers and Reports on Child Language Development, 13,* 126–133.

Ferrier, L. J. (1978). Some observations of error in context. In N. Waterson & C. Snow (Eds.), *The Development of communication.* New York: John Wiley and Sons.

Frege, G. (1892). Uber sinn und bedeutung. *Zeitschr. f. philosophie und philosoph. Kritik, 100,* 25–50. [On sense and reference. Reprinted in F. Zabeeh, E. D. Klemke, & A. Jacobson (1974). *Readings in semantics.* Urbana, IL: University of Illinois Press.]

Gelman, S. A., & Markman, E. M. (1986). Understanding natural kind terms: A developmental comparison. *Papers and Reports on Child Language Development, 25,* 41–48.

Gentner, D. (1978). On relational meaning: The acquisition of verb meaning. *Child Development, 49,* 988–998.

Gentner, D. (1982). Why nouns are learned before verbs: Linguistic relativity versus natural partitioning. In S. Kuczay (Ed.), *Language development: Language, culture, and cognition.* Hillsdale, NJ: Lawrence Erlbaum.

Gillis, S. (1986). The child's "Nominal Insight" is actually a process: The plateau-stage and vocabulary spurt in early lexical development. *Antwerp Papers in Linguistics, 45.*

Gillis, S. (1987). *Words and categories at the onset of language acquisition: Product versus process.* Unpublished manuscript, University of Antwerp, Belgium.

Gleitman, L. (1989). The structural sources of verb meaning. *Papers and Reports on Child Language Development, 28,* 1–48.

Gopnik, A. (1984). The acquisition of gone and the development of the object concept. *Journal of Child Language, 11,* 273–292.

Gopnik, A., & Meltzoff, A. N. (1985). From people, to plans, to objects. *Journal of Pragmatics, 9,* 495–512.

Gopnik, A., & Meltzoff, A. N. (1986). Relations between semantic and cognitive development in the one word stage: The specificity hypothesis. *Child Development, 57,* 1040–1053.

Greenfield, P. M., & Smith, J. H. (1976). *The structure of communication in early language development.* New York: Academic Press.

Harris, M., Barrett, M. D., Jones, D., & Brookes, S. (1988). Linguistic input and early word meaning. *Journal of Child Language, 15,* 77–94.

Huttenlocher, J., & Smiley, P. (1987). Early word meanings: The case of object names. *Cognitive Psychology, 19,* 63–89.

Landau, B., & Gleitman, L. (1985). *Language and experience: Evidence from the blind child.* Cambridge, MA: Harvard University Press.

Lucariello, J. (1987). Concept formation and its relation to word learning and use in the second year. *Journal of Child Language, 14,* 309–332.

Mandler, J. M. (1979). Categorical and schematic organization in memory. In C. R. Puff (Ed.), *Memory organization and structure.* New York: Academic Press.

Mandler, J. M. (1983). Representation. In J. H. Flavell & E. M. Markman (Eds.), *Cognitive development* (Vol. I, pp. 255–287). New York: John Wiley and Sons.

Markman, E. M. (1987). How children constrain the possible meanings of words. In U. Neisser (Ed.), *Concepts and conceptual development: Ecological and intellectual factors in categorization.* New York: Cambridge University Press.

McCune-Nicolich, L. (1981). The cognitive bases of relational words in the single word period. *Journal of Child Language, 8,* 15–34.

McShane, J. (1980). *Learning to talk.* Cambridge, England: Cambridge University Press.

Mervis, C. B. (1987). Child-basic object categories and early lexical development. In U. Neisser (Ed.), *Concepts and conceptual development: Ecological and intellectual factors in categorization* (pp. 201–233). New York: Cambridge University Press.

Nelson, K. (1973). Structure and strategy in learning to talk. *Monographs of the Society for Research in Child Development, 38* (1–2, Serial No. 149).

Nelson, K. (1985). *Making sense: The acquisition of shared meaning.* New York: Academic Press.

Nelson, K. (1988). Constraints on word learning? *Cognitive Development, 3,* 221–246.

Nelson, K. (1990). Development of meaning and meaning of development in the single word period: A review of E. Dromi. *Early lexical development: First Language, 10,* 61–73.

Nelson, K., & Lucariello, J. (1985). The development of meaning in first words. In M. D. Barrett (Ed.), *Children's single-word speech* (pp. 59–87). New York: John Wiley and Sons.

Piaget, J. (1962). *Play, dreams and imitation in childhood.* New York: Norton.

Quine, W. V. O. (1960). *Word and object.* Cambridge, MA: MIT Press.

Rescorla, L. A. (1980). Overextension in early language development. *Journal of Child Language, 7,* 321–335.

Schank, R. C., & Abelson, R. P. (1977). *Scripts, plans, goals, and understanding: An inquiry into human knowledge structures.* Hillsdale, NJ: Lawrence Erlbaum.

Schlesinger, I. M. (1982). *Steps to language.* Hillsdale, NJ: Lawrence Erlbaum.

Soja, N., Carey, S., & Spelke, E. (1985). Constraints on the meaning of words. *Paper presented at the meeting of the Society for Research in Child Development,* Toronto, Canada.

Sugarman, S. (1982a). Developmental changes in early representational intelligence: Evidence from spatial classification strategies and related verbal expressions. *Cognitive Psychology, 14,* 410–449.

Sugarman, S. (1982b). Transitions in early representational intelligence: Changes over time in children's production of simple block structures. In G. Forman (Ed.), *Action and thought.* New York: Academic Press.

Sugarman, S. (1983). *Children's early thought: Developments in classification.* New York: Cambridge University Press.

Templin, M. (1957). *Certain language skills in children: The development and interrelationship.* Minneapolis: University of Minnesota Press.

Verlinden, A., & Gillis, S. (1987). *Nouns and verbs in the input: Gentner (1982) reconsidered.* Unpublished manuscript, University of Antwerp, Belgium.

Vygotsky, L. S. (1962). *Thought and language.* Cambridge, MA: MIT Press.

Ways in Which Children Constrain Word Meanings*

Ellen M. Markman

Stanford University

According to calculations reported by Carey (1978), by age 6 children have learned 9,000–14,000 words. This works out to roughly 9 new words a day from about 18 months on. In one of the most carefully documented studies of an individual child's vocabulary acquisition, Dromi (1987) reports a point at which her child began acquiring new vocabulary at the rate of 45 words a week. It is still largely a mystery as to how children acquire language at this astonishing rate.

A traditional explanation for how children form categories and acquire category terms was to assume a kind of general, all-purpose, inductive mechanism. Inhelder and Piaget (1964) and Bruner, Olver, and Greenfield (1966) implicitly held some form of this model. This view about how categories are acquired contains many implicit assumptions about the nature of categories, about the way in which they are learned, and about how children's abilities to categorize change with development (for a more complete discussion of these issues, see Markman, 1989). For example, these theories assume that concept learning begins by the learner encountering a positive exemplar of the category. From that exemplar a tentative hypothesis is formulated as to what the criteria might be that define the category. This hypothesis must then be evaluated against subsequent information. New instances that are consistent with the hypothesis support it, while inconsistent information requires that it be revised. But reformulating hypotheses in the face of negative evidence is not a trivial problem and children up until the age of 6 or 7 have been shown to have great difficulty in dealing with all but the simplest kinds of hypotheses. In sum, even 6-year-olds have trouble solving these kinds of inductive problems, yet 2-year-olds are very successfully solving the inductive problems involved in acquiring new terms. I have argued that these young children must, therefore, acquire terms in ways that do not require sophisti-

* I thank Academic Press for permission to include Tables 1 and 2 and Figures 1–4 of Markman, E. M. and Hutchinson, J. E. (1984). Children's sensitivity to constraints on word meaning: Taxonomic vs thematic relations. *Cognitive Psychology, 16,* 1–27; and Tables 1 and 2 and Figures 1 and 2 from Markman, E. M. and Wachtel, G. F. (1988). Children's use of mutual exclusivity to constrain the meanings of words. *Cognitive Psychology, 20,* 121–157.

This work was supported in part by NIH grant HD 20382.

cated, logical-deductive, hypothesis testing (Markman, 1987, 1989; Markman & Hutchinson, 1984; Markman & Wachtel, 1988).

Another related problem with the traditional view of concept learning is that it does not face the fundamental problem of induction pointed out by Quine (1960), namely, that for any set of data there will be an indefinite number of logically possible hypotheses that are consistent with it. The data are never sufficient logically to eliminate all competing hypotheses. How is it, then, that humans so frequently converge on the same hypotheses? To take a concrete example, suppose a child hears someone label a dog as *dog*. The child could think that the label refers to a specific individual (e.g., Rover), or to one of its parts (e.g., tail), or to its substance, size, shape, color, position in space, and so on. Given that it is not possible for anyone, let alone a young child, to rule out every logically possible hypothesis, how is it that children succeed in figuring out the correct meanings of terms?

The answer is that humans are constrained to consider only some kinds of hypotheses or at least to give them priority over others. This may be especially true for children first trying to learn the concepts that their language encodes. The way children succeed in acquiring these terms so rapidly is that they are limited in the kinds of hypotheses they consider. Children do not always have to reject hypotheses on the basis of negative evidence. They can implicitly reject them by being biased against them in the first place. In this chapter, I will review the evidence for some specific constraints on hypothesis that young children may use.

The Taxonomic and Whole Object Constraints

The taxonomic assumption is one way in which children may constrain the meanings of words (Markman & Hutchinson, 1984). To see why this constraint is needed it is helpful to consider what young children confront when someone teaches them a word via ostensive definition, that is when someone points to an object and labels it. Some variant of ostensive definition makes up a large part of the way very young children acquire new words because they do not yet know enough language for one to define a new term for them or contrast it with other terms, and so on. Again suppose someone points to a dog and calls it a dog. We have just seen that *dog* could be a proper name, or it could mean *furry,* or *brown,* or any of huge number of other properties. Moreover, dog could also refer to "the dog and his bone," or "Mommy petting the dog" or "the dog under a tree." In other words, objects are often found involved in relations with other objects, so what prevents the child from thinking that the label refers to the objects that are related? These last examples of thematic relations pose a particular problem because children are very interested in such relations and often find them more salient than categorical or taxonomic relations.

On a number of tasks designed to assess children's ability to categorize objects, younger children have been found to prefer to organize objects according to thematic relations (cf. Gelman & Baillargeon, 1983; Markman & Callanan, 1983; for reviews). For example, on sorting tasks 6- and 7-year-olds often sort objects on the basis of their taxonomic category such as vehicles, buildings, animals, and people. In contrast, younger children often sort objects in groups that represent causal, temporal, spatial, or other relations among the objects. These relations emphasize events rather than taxonomic similarity. For example, children might put a boy and a dog together because the boy is taking the dog for a walk. This interest in thematic relations has been found in object sorting, oddity tasks, and studies of memory and word association (see Markman, 1981). From these studies, we can conclude that children are often more interested in the thematic relations among objects than among taxonomic relations, or that thematic relations can sometimes be easier for children to notice than taxonomic ones. Even though children may find thematic relations more salient, single nouns rarely encode thematic relations. For example, English does not have a single word for thematically related objects such as a boy and his dog, or a spider and its web, or a baby and its bottle.

To return to Quine's problem of induction, on the one hand children readily learn labels for object categories, concrete nouns such as *ball* or *dog*. On the other hand, children often notice thematic relations between objects. How is it that children readily learn labels for categories of objects if they are attending to these relations between objects instead? Hutchinson and I (Markman & Hutchinson, 1984) proposed that the solution is that children expect labels to refer to objects of the same kind or same taxonomic category. This assumption would allow them to rule out many potential meanings of a novel term, in particular many thematic meanings. Even though children consider thematic relations good ways of organizing objects themselves, they do not consider thematic relations as possible meanings for words. Thus, when children believe that they are learning a new *word,* they shift their attention from thematic to categorical organization.

Although Markman and Hutchinson (1984) refer to this constraint as "the taxonomic constraint," Carey (1988) has correctly noted that there are really two constraints being hypothesized. One is that children assume terms refer to taxonomic categories, and the second is that children are biased to interpret novel labels as referring to whole objects, rather than properties, actions, events, and so on. In other words, the taxonomic assumption applies to categories of color, substance, shape, and so on as well as to objects. Thus, to be more precise, children may be biased to treat novel labels as referring to whole objects (the whole object assumption) and to treat them as referring to objects of the same kind (the taxonomic assumption). When children do consider terms as referring to substances or colors or other properties, the taxonomic assumption should still be met. The studies of Markman and Hutchinson tested both the taxonomic assumption and the whole object assumption: Children should interpret novel labels as labels for objects of the same type rather than objects that are thematically related.

To test this hypothesis, we conducted a series of studies each of which compared how children would organize objects when they were not provided with an object label versus when the objects were given a novel label. The first study investigated whether hearing a novel word will cause 2- to 3-year-old children to shift their attention from thematic to categorical relations. Basic level categories (such as "dog" or "chair") were used with these young children rather than general superordinate-level categories (such as "animal" or "furniture") (Rosch, Mervis, Gray, Johnson, & Boyes-Braem, 1976).

There were two conditions in this study. In both conditions, children were first shown a target picture and were then shown two other pictures and had to select one of them as being the same as the target.

No-word condition. To begin, children were introduced to a hand puppet and were told to put the picture they chose in the puppet's mouth. On each trial, the puppet pointed to the target card and told the child, "Look carefully now. See this?" The two choice pictures were then placed on the table and the child told to "find another one that is the same as this."

One of the choice pictures was a member of the same basic-level category as the target: For example, the target might be a poodle and the choice a German shepherd (both dogs). We attempted to make the two category exemplars fairly dissimilar yet still readily identifiable to these young children. The other choice card was a strong thematic associate to the target, in this case, dog food. There were 10 such triads in all. They are listed in Table 3.1.

Novel-word condition. Everything about the novel-word condition was identical to that of the no-word condition, with one exception. Children in this condition were told that the puppet could talk in puppet talk. They were instructed to listen carefully to find the right picture. The puppet gave the target picture an unfamiliar name and used the same name in the instructions

Table 3.1. Triads Used in Markman & Hutchinson's (1984) First Study

Standard Object	Taxonomic Choice	Thematic Choice
Police car	Car	Policeman
Tennis shoe	High-heeled shoe	Foot
Dog	Dog	Dog Food
Straight-backed chair	Easy chair	Man in sitting position
Crib	Crib	Baby
Birthday cake	Chocolate cake	Birthday present
Blue jay	Duck	Nest
Outside door	Swinging door	Key
Male football player	Man	Football
Male child in swimsuit	Female child in overalls	Swimming pool

for picking a choice picture. For example, the puppet might say, "See this? It is a sud. Find another sud that is the same as this sud."

When children in the no-word condition had to select between another category member and a thematically related object, they often chose the thematic relation. They selected other category members a mean of only 59% of the time, which was not different from chance. In contrast, when the target picture was labeled with an unfamiliar word children were significantly more likely to select categorically. They now chose the other category member a mean of 83% of the time, which is greater than chance. This effect held up over every item. As predicted, when children think they are learning a new word they look for categorical relationships between objects and suppress the tendency to look for thematic relations. These results supported the hypothesis at least for very young children and basic-level categories.

The next study tested the hypothesis that hearing a new word will induce older preschoolers to look for taxonomic relations rather than thematic relations at the superordinate level of categorization. Four- and five-year-old children participated in this study.

No-word condition. The procedure used in this condition was very similar to that used in the no word condition of the first study, except that now superordinate-level categories were used. Associated with each of the target pictures were two choice pictures. One of the choice pictures was related in a thematic way to the target, for example, as milk is to cow. The other choice picture was a member of the same superordinate category as the target, for example, as pig is to cow. An attempt was made to use a variety of thematic relations rather than just one, so as not to limit the generality of the results. A list of the materials used is shown in Table 3.2.

On each trial in the no-word condition, the experimenter, using a hand puppet, said, "I'm going to show you something. Then I want you to think carefully, and find another one. See this? Can you find another one?"

Table 3.2. Triads Used in Markman & Hutchinson's Study with 4-Year-Olds

Standard Object	Taxonomic Choice	Thematic Choice
Cow	Pig	Milk
Ring	Necklace	Hand
Door	Window	Key
Crib	Adult bed	Baby
Bee	Ant	Flower
Hanger	Hook	Dress
Cup	Glass	Kettle
Car	Bicycle	Car tire
Train	Bus	Tracks
Dog	Cat	Bone

Novel-word condition. The materials and procedures for this condition were identical to those of the no-word condition, except that a novel word was used to describe the target picture. Children were told that the puppet could talk in puppet talk, and that they were to listen carefully to what he said. The instructions included an unfamiliar label for the target: "I'm going to show you a dax. Then I want you to think carefully, and find another dax. See this dax? Can you say dax? Can you find another dax?"

As usual, when children in the no-word condition had to choose between another member of the same superordinate category and a thematically related object, they often chose the thematic relation. They selected the other category member a mean of only 25% of the time. This was less often than would be expected by chance. When the target picture was labeled with an unfamiliar word children were much more likely than children hearing no label to select categorically. They now chose the other category member a mean of 65 percent of the time, which was greater than chance.

In sum, when young children are asked to classify things, they often classify them thematically. But hearing a new word induces children to look for categorical relationships instead of thematic relationships.

From these studies we wanted to conclude that children focus on categorical relations because of the sheer presence of the word, and not because of any particular knowledge about the meaning of the word. So we would like to make sure that the effect could not be due to children translating the novel word into a familiar word.

In this next study, pictures of artificial objects were used instead of real objects. Children were not likely to translate unfamiliar names for these objects into known words, because they did not know real word names for them. If the presence of an unfamiliar word still causes children to shift from thematic to taxonomic responding when the materials were also unfamiliar, then this would rule out translation as an explanation for the effect.

Four- and five-year-old children participated in this study. The design and procedure were essentially the same as that of the earlier studies. The main difference was that the experimenter first taught children the taxonomic and thematic relations for the artificial objects before asking them to select the picture that was like the target.

No-word condition. Children were shown eight sets of pictures. Each set included a target picture, and two choice pictures, one thematically related and one taxonomically related to the target. Before children saw a given target picture and its two choices, they were shown two training pictures that illustrated how the target picture related to each of the choice pictures. One picture showed the target object and the taxonomic choice, side by side. For these pairs, children were told a common function that the two objects shared. An example taxonomic training picture is shown in Figure 3.1.

For this example, the experimenter said, "This swims in the water" (pointing

Figure 3.1.. A taxonomically related pair of objects from Markman & Hutchinson (1984).

to the left-hand object). "This swims in the water" (pointing to the right-hand object).

A second training picture showed the target and the thematic choice in an interactive relationship. The experimenter told the children how the two objects interacted. The thematic training picture for the set just given is shown in Figure 3.2.

For this example, the experimenter said, "This catches this" (pointing to the objects she was referring to as she said the sentence). Children were asked to

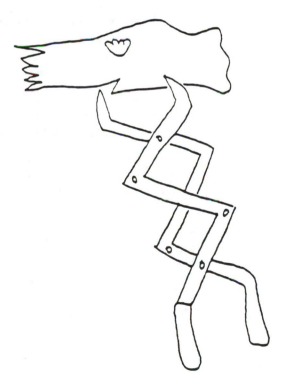

Figure 3.2.. A thematically related pair of objects from Markman & Hutchinson (1984).

repeat the spoken information, to make sure that they were paying attention. The first training picture was left on the table as the second training picture was introduced, so that children could see the connection between the target in the first picture and the target in the second picture.

A second example taxonomic training picture is shown in Figure 3.3. For this example, the experimenter said, "This pokes holes in things" (pointing to the left-hand object). "This pokes holes in things" (pointing to the right-hand object). The thematic training picture for the same set is shown in Figure 3.4. For this picture, the spoken information was "You keep this in here."

After children saw the two training pictures in a set, the pictures were removed from the table. The procedure for the rest of the trial was identical to the earlier procedures. The experimenter said, "I'm going to show you something. Then I want you to think carefully, and find another one." The experimenter then placed the target picture face up on the table directly in front of the child, and said, "See this?" She placed the two choice pictures to the left and right of the target, and then said, "Can you find another one?" Note that the choices were pictures of the individual objects as in the previous studies, rather than pictures of two objects together.

Novel-word condition. The materials and procedure for this condition were identical to those of the no-word condition, except that a novel word was used to label the target picture. After children saw the training pictures, the experimenter said, "I'm going to show you a dax. Then I want you to think carefully, and find another dax. See this dax? Can you say dax? Can you find another dax?" A different unfamiliar word was used for each set.

The results for the choices were parallel to those of the previous studies. As usual, when children in the no-word condition had to select between another

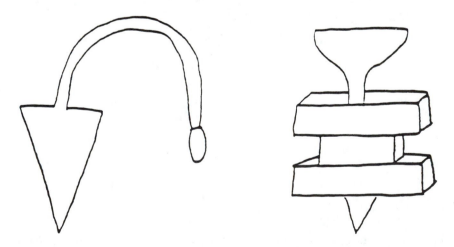

Figure 3.3.. A taxonomically related pair of objects from Markman & Hutchinson (1984).

Figure 3.4.. A thematically related pair of objects from Markman & Hutchinson (1984).

member of the same superordinate category and a thematically related object, they often chose the thematic relation. They selected the other category member a mean of only 37% of the time, which was less than chance. When the target picture was labeled with an unfamiliar word children were more likely to select categorically. They now chose the other category member a mean of 63% of the time, which was greater than chance. This effect held up over every item.

Thus, children could not have been translating in this study because they did not know what these unfamiliar objects were and had no familiar labels for them. Nevertheless, the results from this study replicated the results from the studies that used familiar objects. Again, the presence of an unfamiliar meaningless word caused children to shift from selecting objects that are thematically related to selecting objects that are taxonomically related. This suggests that children have placed an abstract constraint on what words can mean that is not mediated by the meaning of known terms.

Hutchinson (1984) has provided evidence for the generality of this labeling effect. She raised the concern that the oddity task forces children to select another object to go with the target. Although children who hear a label select taxonomically under these conditions, they may not be so likely to generalize when they are not forced to. So Hutchinson (1984) used a procedure that was designed to more closely resemble naturalistic conditions. Children were taught a novel word for the target object, as before, but were not forced to select exactly one alternative as going with that object. Children were free to select none, one, or two additional objects, one of which was related taxonomically to the target and one of which was related thematically. Hutchinson (1984) used basic-level categories for 3-year-olds and superordinate-level categories for 4- and 5-year-olds. With the exception of the 3-year-old boys, Hutchinson replicated the Markman and Hutchinson (1984) results with this procedure. That is, 3-year-old girls and 4- and 5-year-old children will spontaneously extend a term to label taxonomically related objects, even when they are free not to.

Waxman and Gelman (1986) have found that a label will induce 3-year-olds to classify taxonomically at the superordinate level, at least for superordinate categories for which the children do have a label. Moreover, they found that a novel label, actually a Japanese term, helped children organize objects taxonomically in a free classification task, instead of an oddity procedure.

Waxman and Gelman compared the effectiveness of hearing a novel label with other means of highlighting the salience of categories. In some cases, children were shown typical instances of the category and told to think about them as a group. In other cases, children were given the common English superordinate term for the categories. Four-year-olds benefited from all of these manipulations. Three-year-olds, however, were helped by the use of labels, but not by seeing typical instances. Moreover, 3-year-olds did just as well when Japanese labels were provided for these familiar superordinate categories as when the known English labels were provided.

Bauer and Mandler (1989) set out to determine whether the labeling effect would hold up for even younger children. They were particularly interested in comparing children they thought might span the age at which the naming explosion occurred. In a series of studies, they looked at 16–31-month-old children's tendency to sort thematically and whether labeling would increase the children's tendency to sort taxonomically. To their surprise, even the youngest children were sorting taxonomically from the start. That is, even with no labels children were sorting taxonomically around 75% of the time. Labeling did not increase this already high level of performance. Bauer and Mandler (1989) have thus convincingly demonstrated that quite young children are capable of sorting taxonomically and that there may not be any general preference to sort thematically. However, because of children's very high rate of sorting taxonomically in the unlabeled condition, Bauer and Mandler were unable to test whether children of this age expect labels to refer to objects of the same kind. Although children in the labeled condition sorted taxonomically as predicted so did children in the unlabeled condition. Thus, it is important to know whether in those cases where children are not sorting taxonomically from the start, that its, when they do show a thematic preference, will hearing a label cause them to shift to taxonomic sorting. This question was addressed by Backscheider and Markman (in preparation).

There are several reasons why Bauer and Mandler (1989) may have achieved such a high rate of taxonomic responding in their young children. First, they used a reinforcement procedure whereby they briefly pretrained children to select taxonomically and where this selective reinforcement of taxonomic choices was maintained throughout the testing procedure. Second, although they used thematic relations quite similar to those of Markman and Hutchinson (1984), these relations may not have been the most salient or interesting to younger children. In a control study, Bauer and Mandler reinforced children for thematic responding and found that when reinforced children could select thematic options. But this does not speak to the relative salience of the items. So Backscheider and I selected thematic items that were likely to be highly familiar to even 18-month-olds. The most important change that we made from the Bauer and Mandler procedure was that we did not differentially reinforce taxonomic responding. Our results replicated the original Markman and Hutchinson (1984) findings, even with 18- to 24-month olds. In the absence of a label, very young children selected thematically 68 percent of the time. In marked contrast, when an object was given a novel label children selected thematically only 23% of the time. That is they interpreted the novel label as referring to objects of the same taxonomic category 77% of the time. Thus the taxonomic assumption is used by children by 18 months of age.

One limitation of all of the studies described so far that provide evidence for the taxonomic and whole object assumptions is that there are not any very salient thematic relations around at the time the object is first labeled. An object is labeled and then other objects are provided such that the label could be extended to thematic or taxonomic relations. But salient thematic relations are not present at first. One question, then, is whether the taxonomic assumption is powerful enough to override children's preference for thematic relations if objects are engaged in dynamic, salient, thematic relations at the time of labeling. We have recently tested this by providing a novel label ("See this dax") at the time objects were shown engaging in a dynamic thematic relation (Backscheider & Markman, in preparation). Children were then asked to find, for example, "some more daxes." They were given four objects that could be arranged into two thematic pairs or into taxonomic sets. Here again we found that labeling greatly increased the amount of taxonomic responding compared to the no label conditions.

To summarize, there are now a number of studies using several different methodologies which together demonstrate that children from 18 months on honor the taxonomic assumption. We do not yet know whether younger babies honor the constraint (Nelson, 1988). However, if the taxonomic constraint is already in place by 18 months, that suggests that it could play a fundamental role in acquiring word meanings even in very early language learners. In particular, it is at roughly 18 months of age that children undergo the vocabulary spurt where they become capable of acquiring words at very fast rates. This is the period of time that Dromi (1987) and in this volume has documented so carefully and that may mark the beginnings of genuine language learning. This very fast form of learning is likely a highly constrained form of learning. To speculate, then, the emergence of the taxonomic constraint may be what accounts for the very young child's sudden ability to acquire words rapidly.

The Mutual Exclusivity Assumption

Another way children may constrain word meanings is to assume that words are mutually exclusive—that each object will have one and only one label.

In order for categories to be informative about objects, they will tend to be mutually exclusive, especially at the basic level of categorization. A single object cannot both be a chair and a dresser or a chair and a table. A single object cannot both be a cow and a bird or a cow and a dog. Obviously, however, there are many exceptions: Categories overlap, as in "dog" and "pet," and they are included in one another as in "poodle" and "dog." So mutual exclusivity is not an infallible assumption to make. On the other hand, it is a reasonable one and, as I hope to show, by assuming that terms are mutually exclusive, children make progress in acquiring new words, even if it is at the cost of making some mistakes along the way.

In fact, one piece of evidence in favor of the hypothesis that children assume words will be mutually exclusive is that it helps explain some errors children make. It helps explain, for example, why children find class inclusion difficult (because it violates mutual exclusivity) and why the part-whole relation of collections is simpler (because it maintains mutual exclusivity) (Markman & Wachtel, 1988; Markman, 1989). Of course, children will eventually have many violations of mutual exclusivity. To acquire class-inclusion relations, for example, children must override their initial tendency to assume terms are mutually exclusive. With enough evidence to the contrary, children will allow multiple labels for the same object. Thus violations of mutual exclusivity in children's lexicon's are not necessarily evidence against this principle. The claim is that children should be biased to assume, especially at first, that terms are mutually exclusive, and only relinquish that assumption when confronted with clear evidence to the contrary.

Mutual exclusivity is related to several other principles that have been postulated to account for language acquisition, including Slobin's (1973) principle of one-to-one mapping and Pinker's (1984) Uniqueness Principle (see Markman & Wachtel, 1988, for a discussion). A third principle, Clark's (1983, 1987) Principle of Lexical Contrast is most closely related to Mutual Exclusivity and some of Clark's evidence for lexical contrast constitutes evidence for mutual exclusivity as well.

Following Bolinger (1977), Clark states that every word in a dictionary contrasts with every other word and to acquire words children must assume that words contrast in meaning. Although mutual exclusivity is one kind of contrast, terms may contrast in meaning without being mutually exclusive. *Robin* and *bird,* for example, contrast in meaning because the meaning of *bird* is different from that of *robin,* but these terms are not mutually exclusive. Thus, although these principles are related, they are different, and evidence in favor of one is not necessarily evidence in favor of the other. Children could violate mutual exclusivity yet honor lexical contrast as just described. They also could honor mutual exclusivity without adhering to the more general principle of contrast. Clark (1983, 1987) provides an extensive review of the literatures both from linguistics and from language acquisition in support of the lexical contrast theory. She uses linguistic contrast to pull together a number of different linguistic and developmental phenomena. Some of the evidence that Clark cites is evidence for mutual exclusivity as well. I will give some examples here, but see Markman (1989) for a more complete discussion.

Clark (1983) argues that the developmental patterns seen in young children's overgeneralization of terms can be explained by the principle of lexical contrast. Children do not overextend a term to cover an object once they have another name for that object. Although Clark interprets this as evidence for lexical contrast theory, it supports the mutual exclusivity hypothesis and is a problem, rather than support, for the principle of contrast. Suppose, for example, a child overextended the term *dog* to cover four-legged mammals, including cats, and horses. Once the child acquires the word *cat,* then he or she would stop overextended *dog* to cover cats. This is exactly what would be predicted by the mutual exclusivity hypothesis. Children try to avoid accepting two category names for the same object, so they would eliminate one. But it is not what would be predicted by lexical contrast because the terms *cat* and *dog* should already contrast in meaning. The term *dog,* as used by the child, refers to dogs and cats and horses and would mean something approximating "four-legged mammal," while the term *cat* refers to cats. Because general and specific terms already contrast in meaning, the principle of contrast does not provide sufficient motivation for why overextensions should be narrowed in these cases.

Further evidence for mutual exclusivity that Clark (1987) interprets as evidence for lexical contrast is that 2- and 3-year-olds appear to reject multiple labels for things. A child told that something is a poodle might object saying that "It is not a poodle, it's a dog." Again, children's rejection of second labels does not follow from the contrastive assumption alone. Words can contrast in many different ways, not just by being mutually exclusive, and specific and general terms applying to the same object already satisfy the principle of lexical contrast.

In order for lexical contrast to explain why children narrow overextensions or reject second labels for objects, additional assumptions are needed. One way of dealing with this would be to assume that mutual exclusivity is a favored way of adhering to the contrastive hypothesis. Children may start out interpreting a novel term by trying to adhere the mutual exclusivity assumption — an extreme form of contrast. If that fails, they then may attempt an interpretation of a term that violates mutual exclusivity, but that preserves some other form of contrast.

One problem with the evidence that Clark (1983, 1987) and Markman and Wachtel (1988) cite in favor of mutual exclusivity, is that it comes almost entirely from production data. There may be many reasons why beginning language learners would be limited in the amount they can produce which would prevent them from expending valuable resources on redundant information. This limitation on production could be for very different reasons than a constraint on the lexicon. A lexical constraint should be apparent in comprehension as well as in production. In fact Markman and Wachtel (1988) argued that the best evidence for mutual exclusivity would be from comprehension not from production. They designed six experimental studies of children's comprehension of terms to investigate whether children honor mutual exclusivity. I summarize these next.

The simplest situation where the principle of mutual exclusivity could be applied is where two objects are presented, one of which already has a known label and one of which does not. If a new label is then mentioned, the child should: (a) on the taxonomic assumption, look for an object as a first hypothesis about the meaning of the label; (b) on the mutual exclusivity assumption, reject the already labeled object; and (c) therefore, assume the other object is being referred to by the novel label.

Three recent studies have found support for this hypothesis (Golinkoff, Hirsh-Pasek, Lavallee, & Baduini 1985; Hutchinson, 1986; Markman & Wachtel, 1988).

In Study 1 of Markman and Wachtel (1988), 3-year-olds were presented with six pairs of objects, where one member of each pair was an object that children could label (e.g., banana, cow, spoon) and one member was an object for which the children did not yet know the label (e.g., a lemon wedgepress, tongs).

There was a control condition where each child was shown the six pairs of objects and asked by a puppet to "show me one." This was to ensure that if children select a novel object when they hear a novel label that it is due to the labeling per se and not just a response bias to go with the novel object. In the novel label condition the procedure was identical except that the child was asked to "show me the x," where x was a nonsense syllable, randomly assigned to the object.

Children who heard a novel term applied in the presence of two objects, one of which was familiar and one of which was unfamiliar, had a striking tendency to select the novel object as the referent for the novel term. They selected the novel object in almost 5 of the 6 pairs, mean = 4.90. The tendency to select an unfamiliar object as the referent for a novel label does in fact reflect children's adherence to the mutual exclusivity principle because they do not have such a bias when no labels are provided. In the control condition, children perform at chance, selecting a mean of 3.30 unfamiliar objects out of 6.

In summary, in this very simple situation where one could map an unfamiliar word to an unfamiliar object, 3-year-old children use the principle of mutual exclusivity in figuring out the meaning of a new word. Note also that in this situation the child can simultaneously satisfy the principles of taxonomic organization and mutual exclusivity. The next study from Markman and Wachtel (1988) examined what happens when this simple mapping strategy is no longer possible, and the taxonomic assumption and mutual exclusivity may conflict.

Suppose a novel word is used to describe a single object. According to the taxonomic and whole object assumptions, a child should first hypothesize that the new word refers to the object as an exemplar of a category of similar objects, and not to the object's part, substance, and so on. Suppose, however, that the object described by the novel term is an object for which the child already has a label. In this case, in order to adhere to the principle of mutual exclusivity, the child would have to reject the novel term as a label for the object, but then may not have any clear alternative as a possible meaning for the term. That is, since there is no other object around to label, the simple novel label-novel object strategy cannot be used. Under these circumstances, there are several different options available. Children could decide to abandon mutual exclusivity in these cases and interpret the novel term as a second label for the object. Another possibility is that they could reject the term as a label for the object without coming up with an alternative meaning. Rejecting one meaning for the term, however, leaves the child with a term that is not yet attached to any referent. This in itself may motivate children to try to find some meaning for the novel term. The mutual exclusivity principle does not speak to how children select among the potential meanings, but children might analyze the object for some interesting part or property and interpret the novel term as applying to it. Such an analysis is considerably more difficult than the simple novel label-novel object matching strategy, and there may be many candidate meanings for a term. The remaining studies examine whether children can use mutual exclusivity, in this more difficult situation, to learn part and substance terms.

Study 2 of Markman and Wachtel (1988) addressed whether children can use mutual exclusivity to reject a novel term as a label for an already labeled object, and whether that would motivate them to search for another salient aspect of the object to label. In this study, we attempted to teach children labels for objects with prominent parts. In this study, children heard a novel noun attributed to either a familiar or an unfamiliar object. The term could thus refer to either the object itself or to a salient part of the object.

Three- and four-year-olds heard either familiar or unfamiliar objects labeled with a novel term and were then tested to see whether they thought the term referred to the object as a whole or to a salient part of the object. The set of familiar and unfamiliar objects along with their relevant parts is presented in Table 3.3.

Children were assigned to one of two conditions, the Familiar Condition where the object had a known label, or the Unfamiliar Condition where children did not know a label for the object. In both conditions children were taught a label applied to an object with a noticeable part. The labels used were in fact adult labels for the part. In neither condition did children already know a label for the part being taught. For example, children in the Familiar object condition were taught "boom" as the part of a (familiar) fire-truck and "dorsal fin" as the part of a (familiar) fish. Children in the Unfamiliar condition were taught "finial" as the part of an (unfamiliar) pagoda, and "trachea" as a part of an (unfamiliar) lung. The prediction is that children will interpret the label as referring to the object itself for unfamiliar objects, but to a part for familiar objects.

In order to ensure that children understood the questions about parts and wholes, children in both conditions were asked about familiar objects and their parts using known labels. All children were asked, for example, whether an eraser was the whole object or just the part, and whether a pencil was the whole object or just the part. They were asked whether a tail was the whole object or just the part and whether a cat was the whole object or just the part. These well-known objects and labels are presented in Table 3.4.

For the experimental items, the experimenter told the child what he or she was about to see, and, after the experimenter provided the label, she then placed the picture on the table. Then she asked the child: "Which one is the _____ ? This whole thing (the experimenter circled the object with her index finger), or just this part (the experimenter circled to the part)?"

Here is a summary of the predictions from this study. First, children in both conditions should understand the known labels for parts and wholes, and all children should do well on these items. Namely, they should think that known

Table 3.3. Experimental Items for Study 2 of Markman & Wachtel (1988)

		CONDITION	
Familiar		**Unfamiliar**	
Object	**Novel Label for Part**	**Object**	**Novel Label for Part**
Fish	Dorsal fin	*Current detector	Detector
Fire truck	Boom	Pipe tool	Damper
Hammer	Claw	*Ritual implement	Crescent
Camera	Focusing grip	*Pagoda	Finial
Telephone	Receiver	Microscope	Platform
Race car	Air foil	*Lung	Trachea

*These items were used in Study 3 as well.

Table 3.4. Known Objects and Parts for Study 2 of Markman & Wachtel (1988)
(Used in both Familiar and Unfamiliar Conditions)

Known Label for Whole	Known Label for Part
Cat	Tail
*Wagon	*Handle
Bird	Beak
*Flower	*Stem
*Pencil	*Eraser
*House	*Chimney

*These items were used in Study 3 as well.

terms for wholes refer to the whole object and that known terms for parts refer to the part. Most important, the predictions for the experimental items differ depending on the condition. Children hearing a label apply to an unfamiliar object should assume that the label refers to the object itself and not just its part. Thus, they should give few part responses. Children hearing a label refer to a familiar object should, on the basis of mutual exclusivity of labels, reject the term as a label for the whole and assume that it refers to the part instead. So these children should give more part responses. The obtained results in terms of number of part responses given are shown in Figure 3.5.

Children in both conditions were expected to perform quite well on the familiar baseline items, giving part responses for known part terms (e.g., "tail") and object responses for known object labels (e.g., "cat"). As can be seen in Figure 3.5, in both conditions, children performed as expected when known labels were used to refer to parts and wholes.

As predicted, children interpreted a novel term quite differently depending on whether the object was familiar or not. Children gave a mean of only 1.2 out of 6 part responses (20%) in the Familiar condition, compared to a mean of 3.4 part responses (57%) in the Unfamiliar condition. Thus, as expected by the mutual exclusivity hypothesis, children hearing a novel term in the presence of an object with a known label were less likely to think the novel term referred to the whole object than were children who heard the term in the presence of an object with no known label.

One rather stringent test of the strength of the taxonomic and mutual exclusivity assumptions is to compare children's interpretation of novel terms to their interpretation of the well-known words. The taxonomic assumption predicts that children in the Unfamiliar condition should treat the novel terms similarly to how they interpret known object labels and differently from how they interpret known part terms. Conversely, the mutual exclusivity assumption predicts that children in the Familiar condition should treat the novel terms differently from how they interpret known object labels, and similarly to how they interpret known part terms.

The results were, by and large, in accord with even this stringent test. In the

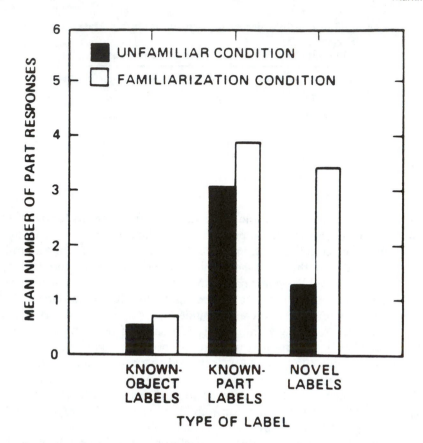

Figure 3.5.. Number of part responses (out of a maximum of 6) given by children in the Familiar and Unfamiliar Conditions to known labels for objects, known labels for parts, and novel labels, from Markman & Wachtel (1988).

Unfamiliar Condition, children treated the novel label much as they treated known labels for objects and quite differently from how they treated known labels for parts. Moreover, in the Familiar condition, children gave more part responses to novel labels (e.g., *receiver*), than to known object labels. This is what one would expect on the mutual exclusivity hypothesis. On the other hand, they gave fewer part responses to novel labels than they gave for known part terms. The bias to interpret novel labels as labels for objects (as well as the assumption of mutual exclusivity) may have been affecting children in the Familiar Condition, leading them to make an intermediate number of part responses.

    In summary, the results from this study labeling objects and parts of objects support the mutual exclusivity hypothesis. If there is an unfamiliar object around, that is, an object for which children do not yet have a label, young children interpret a new noun as a label for the object. In this study, children interpreted the new term (e.g., *trachea*) as a label for the whole object (e.g., lung) just as frequently as they interpreted known object labels (e.g., *cat*) as labels for the whole object. If the object the child views is familiar, however, then by mutual exclusivity children should reject the term as a label for the object and look for some other meaning for the term. In this study, although there was some tendency to interpret the label as labeling the object, children were less likely to interpret the new noun as a label for a familiar object and interpreted it as referring to a salient part of the object instead.

In Study 2 of Markman and Wachtel (1988), the parts and wholes that children were questioned about in the experimental items differed for the Familiar and Unfamiliar conditions. Study 3 was designed to equate the items in the two conditions. Only unfamiliar objects were used in this study, but some of the children were provided with labels for the objects before the experimental labels were taught. In this way, the identical item could be unfamiliar for some children and "familiar" or at least previously labeled for other children.

There were two conditions in the Study, the Familiarization condition and the Unfamiliar Condition. The labeling procedure and method of asking children whether the object referred to the part or the whole was virtually identical to that used in Study 2. The main difference is that in the Familiarization condition, children were first taught a label for the object. To do this children were shown a picture of the object — for example, the lung — told what it was called — for example, "This is a lung," — and given a short description of the function of the object — for example, "We all have two lungs in our chest and use them to breathe." They were given this familiarization with the experimental objects before they were then run in the standard procedure.

In both conditions children were asked about four of the six unfamiliar objects that had been used in Study 2. They were also asked about four objects whose labels were known and whose parts were known. As before, the experimenter told the children what they were about to see, for example, "Here is a finial," and then presented the picture of the object. She then asked, "which one is the finial, this whole thing (the experimenter circled the object with her index finger) or just this part (the experimenter pointed to the part)?"

In summary, the design of Study 3 was very similar to that of Study 2. The main difference is that, instead of a Familiar condition where children were taught a term for a familiar object, there was a Familiarization condition, where children were first familiarized with a previously unfamiliar object, and then were taught the new term.

As in Study 2, children's responses were scored as to whether they said that the label referred to the whole object or its part. The results are plotted in Figure 3.6.

As can be seen in Figure 3.6, the results from Study 3 replicated those of Study 2. As predicted, children interpreted a novel term quite differently in the

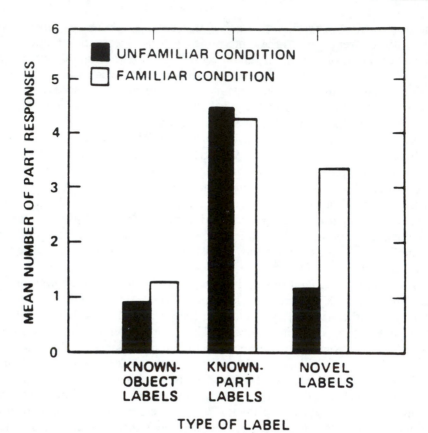

Figure 3.6.. Number of part responses (out of a maximum of four) given by children in the Familiarization and Unfamiliar Conditions to known labels for objects, known labels for parts, and novel labels, from Markman & Wachtel (1988).

two conditions. Children who heard the term (e.g., *trachea*) in the presence of an unfamiliar object (e.g., lung) more often interpreted the term as referring to the object (the lung) and not its part. They gave a mean of 1.27 part responses out of 4 (32%). In contrast, children in the Familiarization condition interpreted the novel labels as referring to parts of the object. For example, children who had just heard the picture of a lung labeled "lung" interpreted "trachea" as referring to the part (the trachea) and not the object (lung). They gave a mean of 3.4 part responses out of 4 (85%).

In summary, Study 3 again provides evidence for the mutual exclusivity hypothesis. When a novel term is used in the presence of an object that already has a label, children tend to reject another label for the object, and, in this case, assume the term refers to a part of the object instead. This was true in this study, even though the label for the (previously unfamiliar) object was provided only a few moments before another novel label was taught.

In Study 1 of Markman and Wachtel (1988), children could use a simple strategy of mapping an unfamiliar label to an unfamiliar object to preserve mutual exclusivity. Because there was only one object referred to in Studies 2 and 3, this simple strategy was precluded. Children still adhered to mutual exclusivity in this case, and used it to learn terms for salient parts of objects. Parts of objects are themselves objects or at least objectlike, however. Thus, learning parts of objects may be as close to the simple mapping strategy as one can get using a single object. The next three studies from Markman and Wachtel (1988) examined whether mutual exclusivity is used by children when the experimenter refers an object made of a salient substance, using an adjective or mass noun. There are two ways in which this situation differs from that of the studies on learning labels for parts. First, instead of depicting objects with salient parts, we selected objects with a metallic substance we thought would be salient and that young children have not yet labeled. Second, in these studies the object was referred to by an adjective or a mass noun — "See this? Its pewter." This is not the typical way, in English, of designating objects. It therefore provides a strong test of the taxonomic assumption. When an unfamiliar object is labeled, the bias to look for object labels may be strong enough to override grammatical form class information. So even when an adjective or mass noun is used to describe an object, children may interpret it as the label for the object. A commonly heard anecdote, for example, is that young children think that *hot* is the label for stoves because parents refer to stoves by the term *hot* before they label them as "stoves," for example, "Don't touch that, it's hot."

These two issues, then, are examined in Study 4. First, following the taxonomic assumption, will children interpret even a novel adjective as a label for an unfamiliar object? Second, following the mutual exclusivity assumption, will children reject a novel term as a label for a familiar object made from a salient substance.

In Study 4, 3- and 4-year-olds heard a puppet refer to an object as pewter. Half of the children heard the term attributed to a familiar object — a metal cup. Half of the children heard the term attributed to an unfamiliar object — a pair of metal tongs. To introduce the novel term "pewter," a puppet showed the child the object (either the metal cup or the metal tongs) and said: "See this? It is pewter."

If the tendency to expect an object label is strong enough to override form class cues, then children hearing "pewter" ascribed to the metal tongs should interpret "pewter" as the label for tongs. They should then agree that a different pair of tongs, made from a different substance and of a different color — a pair of wooden tongs — is also pewter. In contrast, when children hear "pewter" ascribed to a familiar object, if they try to adhere to the mutual exclusivity principle, then they should reject "pewter" as the label for the cup. They should, then, deny that a cup made from a different substance and of a different color — a ceramic cup — is pewter. The main prediction, then, is that when the children see an object that is similar in kind to the original object but that is of a different substance, they should agree that it is "pewter" when the object referred to is unfamiliar (the metal tongs) but deny that it is pewter when the object is familiar (the metal cup). Thus children should agree that a pair of wooden tongs is pewter but deny that a ceramic cup is pewter.

This prediction from the mutual exclusivity hypothesis was confirmed. Of the 12 children who were taught that a metal cup was pewter and then asked if a ceramic cup was pewter, only one child thought it was. The other 11 children denied that it was pewter. Thus, even in this more difficult situation, children adhered to the mutual exclusivity principle, denying that a new term could be a label for an object even when it might not be clear what else the term refers to. In contrast, of the 12 children who were taught that metal tongs were pewter, 7 of the 12 thought that wooden tongs were also pewter.

Another question addressed by this study is whether children would interpret even a novel adjective or substance term as a label for an unfamiliar object. The results indicate that at least to some extent 3-year-olds are willing to override form class clues in order to interpret the term as a novel label. That is, about half of the children considered "pewter" to be the label for tongs and agreed that wooden tongs were pewter.

Study 5 from Markman and Wachtel (1988) was a modified replication of Study 4 that used a within-subjects design. Each child heard one novel substance term applied to a familiar object and a different novel substance term applied to an unfamiliar object. The two substance terms were "chrome" and "rattan."

The findings from this study replicated those of Study 4. First, the bias to assume that a novel term refers to a novel object was again strong enough to override discrepancies in grammatical form class. Seventy-five percent of the children who heard the terms "chrome" or "rattan" attributed to novel objects, treated the terms as labels for the object. Second, children were less likely to think that the novel terms were labels for the objects when they already knew a label for the object. Only 40% of the children who heard "rattan" and "chrome" attributed to familiar objects treated the terms as labels for the objects; 60% rejected the terms as labels.

In Studies 4 and 5, 3- and 4-year-old children treated a novel term as a label for a novel object, but tended to reject the term as a label for a familiar object. Although we know that children are rejecting the novel term as a term for a familiar object, we do not know whether they have in fact accepted the term as a substance term. Study 6 attempted to get at children's hypotheses about the meanings of the terms more directly by giving children a forced-choice between object labels and substance labels.

In this study, we labeled an object using a novel term, for example, "See this (a metal cup)? It's chrome," as in the previous studies. Children were then shown a similar object but of a different substance (e.g., a ceramic cup). They were also shown a chunk of the substance itself — for example, an unformed piece of chrome. They are then asked "Which is chrome? This thing here or this stuff here?" This procedure is similar to that used by Soja, Carey, and Spelke (1985) in their investigation of children's acquisition of count nouns and mass nouns. The question for the present study is whether children will interpret a term as a substance term in the presence of an object as long as the object has a known label. In other words, will mutual exclusivity help children override their bias for object labels to interpret a novel term as a substance term?

As in Studies 4 and 5, children heard a familiar object (a hat) or an unfamiliar object (an odd-shaped container) labeled as rattan. They also heard a familiar object (a cup) or an unfamiliar object (tongs) labeled as chrome. The experimental test for whether children interpreted the term as a label for the object or the substance was to give children a choice between a similar object of a different substance and the substance itself.

In this study, children heard a substance term applied to an object and were then asked whether the term applied to the stuff it was made of or the object as a whole. To ensure that children understood the questions and procedure, children were asked the same kinds of questions for two familiar objects and two familiar substances before the experimental items were shown. To illustrate, a child would be shown a wooden cat and a hunk of wood and asked: "Which one is the wood, this thing here (pointing to the cat) or this stuff here (pointing to the wood)?" He or she would then be asked: "Which one is the cat, this thing here (pointing to the cat) or this stuff here (pointing to the wood)?" The same procedure was used for a sand-filled car and a pile of sand.

After these familiar pairs of items were presented, the two experimental items were presented. As each item was presented, the experimenter said "See this? It's chrome," or "See this? It's rattan," depending on the object. For the experimental forced-choice test, children were asked only one question about each pair, and it was always asking which of the choices was chrome or which was rattan. Children were questioned about one familiar item and one unfamiliar item, each of a different substance. The questioning procedure was the same as for the well-known objects. To illustrate, for the familiar rattan condition, children were shown the rattan hat and told "See this? It's rattan." They were then shown a plastic hat and a piece of rattan and asked: "Which one is rattan, this stuff here (pointing to the piece of rattan) or this thing here (pointing to the hat)?" The unfamiliar rattan condition was the same except that the crescent-shaped container substituted for the hat. For the familiar chrome condition, children were shown the metal cup and told "See this? It's chrome." They were then shown a ceramic cup and a piece of metal and asked: "Which one is chrome, this stuff here (pointing to the piece of metal) or this thing here (pointing to the ceramic cup)?" The unfamiliar chrome condition was the same except that the tongs were substituted for the cup.

When these preschool children were asked about well-known objects and substances, they were quite able to answer the questions correctly. That is, when they were asked about cats or cars they pointed overwhelmingly to cats and cars, pointing to the object rather than the substance 1.96 out of a possible 2 times. When asked about wood and sand, they pointed to wood and sand, pointing to the object only .48 out of 2 times. Since the object was in fact made of the relevant substance, pointing to the object when asked about the substance is not, strictly speaking, an error. A wooden cat, for example, is wood. Nevertheless it was relatively rare for children to use that strategy, and for the most part they clearly differentiated between the two kinds of questions they were asked.

As expected from Soja et al.'s (1985) work, 3-to-5-year-olds have no trouble understanding this kind of question, so we now can determine whether these children can use mutual exclusivity to reject a new term as an object label for a familiar object and interpret it as a substance term instead. The predictions are that when children heard a novel term applied to a novel object (the odd-shaped container or the tongs), they should have chosen the object as the referent of the term, but when they heard the term applied to a familiar object, they should have chosen the substance as the referent of the term. In other words, children should select the substance in the familiar object condition more often than in the unfamiliar condition. This prediction was supported. The mean number of object responses was .57 out of 1 for the unfamiliar condition compared to only .13 out of 1 for the familiar condition. Thus, in support of the mutual exclusivity hypothesis, when children heard a novel term applied to a familiar object, they rejected the term as a label for the object and interpreted it as a substance term instead.

In sum, these studies provided evidence that children do, in fact, assume that words tend to be mutually exclusive. The first study, along with Golinkoff et al. (1985) and Hutchinson (1986), demonstrated that when a novel object label is heard, children assume that it refers to a novel object rather than to an object whose label is already known. This finding is not due to a general preference for novel objects, as it is seen only when a novel label is mentioned. To use mutual exclusivity in this situation, children can adopt a simple strategy of mapping the novel label onto the novel object. The remaining studies explored whether children adhere to the principle of mutual exclusivity when this simple strategy can no longer be used.

If a novel label is applied to an object for which children already have a label, then they should, by mutual exclusivity, reject the new term as an object label. If that object, however, is the only one around, then children cannot interpret the term as a label for a different object. Instead they must analyze the same object for some property or attribute to label. Studies 2–6 provided evidence that 3- and 4-year-olds try to maintain mutual exclusivity of terms even in this more difficult situation. Studies 2 and 3 explored whether children could use mutual exclusivity to reject a label for an object and interpret it as a label for a part of the object instead. In this case a new noun was attributed to an object and children had to decide whether the term referred to the object itself or its part. Children interpreted a novel label as referring to the object itself when the object did not yet have a label. In contrast, as predicted, they interpreted the label as referring to the part when the label for the object was already known. Studies 3–6 examined whether children would use mutual exclusivity when taught a substance term, for example, "pewter," by showing them an object and saying "See this. It's pewter." If the object were unfamiliar, for example, a metal pair of tongs, then half or more of the children thought that "pewter" was the label for tongs. They agreed, in this case, that a pair of wooden tongs was also pewter. Even when the new term is an adjective or mass noun, then, children may still interpret it as a label for the object. In contrast, if the object were familiar, for example, a metal cup, children rejected the new term as a category label. They denied, in this case, that a ceramic cup was pewter, and selected the substance as the referent of the term.

Summary

Together, the studies reported here show how constraints such as the taxonomic and whole object assumptions and the assumption of mutual exclusivity can guide children's initial hypotheses about what words can mean, thereby, helping to solve the problem of induction that word meaning poses. Mutual exclusivity can help children acquire property terms as well as category terms. First, it provides children with grounds for rejecting a class of hypotheses about a term's meaning. Namely, the new term should not be another object label. Second, it motivates children to acquire terms other than object labels. Having rejected one meaning of a term, children would be left with a word for which they have not yet figured out a meaning. This should then motivate children to find a potential meaning for the novel term, leading them to analyze the object for some other property to label. In this way, the mutual exclusivity assumption motivates children to learn terms for attributes, substances and parts of objects.

This function of mutual exclusivity helps overcome a major limitation of the whole object assumption which leads children to look for object labels. Although the whole object assumption provides a critical first hypothesis about word meanings, children must eventually be able to learn terms for properties of objects and not just terms for objects alone. These two principles complement each other. The taxonomic and whole object assumptions clearly have priority when the object being labeled has no previously known label, since mutual exclusivity is not relevant in those cases. When one object has a known label and another has no known label, then both mutual exclusivity and the whole object assumptions can be met. The whole object and mutual exclusivity assumptions compete when a child hears a term applied to an object for which they already know a label. Here mutual exclusivity can motivate children to learn terms other than object labels.

References

Backscheider, A., & Markman, E. M. (in preparation). *Young children's use of the taxonomic assumption to constrain word meaning.* Stanford University, Stanford, CA.

Bauer, P. J., & Mandler, J. M. (1989). Taxonomies and triads: Conceptual organization in one-to-two-year olds. *Cognitive Psychology, 21,* 156-184.

Bolinger, D. (1977). *Meaning and form.* London: Longman.

Bruner, J., Olver, R., & Greenfield, P. (Eds.). (1966). *Studies in cognitive growth.* New York: John Wiley & Sons.

Carey, S. (1978). The child as word learner. In M. Halle, J. Bresnan, & A. Miller (Eds.), *Linguistic theory and psychological reality* (pp. 264-293). Cambridge, MA: MIT Press.

Carey, S. (1988). Lexical development—the Rockefeller years. In W. Hirst (Ed.), *The making of cognitive science: Essays in honor of George A. Miller* (pp 197-209). Cambridge: MA: Cambridge University Press.

Clark, E. V. (1983). Meanings and concepts. In J. H. Flavell & E. M. Markman (Eds.) and P. H. Mussen (Series ed.), *Handbook of child psychology* (Vol. 3): *Cognitive development* (pp. 787-840). New York: John Wiley & Sons.

Clark, E. V. (1987). The principle of contrast: A constraint on language acquisition. In B. MacWhinney (Ed.), *The 20th Annual Carnegie Symposium on Cognition.* Hillsdale, NJ: Lawrence Erlbaum Associates.

Dromi, E. (1987). *Early lexical development.* Cambridge, MA: Cambridge University Press.

Gelman, R., & Baillargeon, R. (1983). A review of some Piagetian concepts. In J. H. Flavell & E. M. Markman (Eds.) and P. H. Mussen (Series Ed.), *Handbook of child psychology* (Vol. 3). New York: Wiley.

Golinkoff, R. M., Hirsh-Pasek, K., Lavallee, A., & Baduini, C. (1985). *What's in a word?: The young child's predisposition to use lexical contrast.* Paper presented at the Boston University Conference on Child Language, Boston, MA.

Hutchinson, J. E. (1984). *Constraints on children's implicit hypotheses about word meanings.* Unpublished doctoral dissertation, Stanford University, Stanford, CA.

Hutchinson, J. E. (1986, April 4-6). *Children's sensitivity to the contrastive use of object category terms.* Paper presented at Stanford 1986 Child Language Research Forum. Stanford University, Stanford CA.

Inhelder, B., & Piaget, J. (1964). *The early growth of logic in the child.* New York: Norton.

Markman, E. M. (1981). Two different principles of conceptual organization. In M. E. Lamb & A. L. Brown (Eds.), *Advances in developmental psychology* (pp. 199-236). Hillsdale, NJ: Lawrence Erlbaum Associates.

Markman, E. M. (1987). How children constrain the possible meanings of words. In U. Neisser (Ed.), *Concepts and conceptual development: Ecological and intellectual factors in categorization.* Cambridge: Cambridge University Press.

Markman, E. M. (1989). *Categorization and naming in children: Problems of induction.* Cambridge, MA: MIT Press, Bradford Books.

Markman, E. M., & Callanan, M. A. (1983). An analysis of hierarchical classification. In R. Sternberg (Ed.), *Advances in the psychology of human intelligence* (Vol. 2). Hillsdale, NJ: Lawrence Erlbaum Associates.

Markman, E. M., & Hutchinson, J. E. (1984). Children's sensitivity to constraints on word meaning: Taxonomic vs thematic relations. *Cognitive Psychology, 16,* 1-27.

Markman, E. M., & Wachtel, G. F. (1988). Children's use of mutual exclusivity to constrain the meanings of words. *Cognitive Psychology, 20,* 121-157.

Nelson, K. (1988). Constraints on word learning? *Cognitive Development, 3,* 221-246.

Pinker, S. (1984). *Language learnability and language development.* Cambridge, MA: Harvard University Press.

Quine, W. V. O. (1960). *Word and object.* Cambridge: MIT Press.

Rosch, E., Mervis, C. B., Gray, W. D., Johnson, D. M., & Boyes-Braem, P. (1976). Basic objects in natural categories. *Cognitive Psychology, 8,* 382–439.

Slobin, D. I. (1973). Cognitive prerequisites for the development of grammar. In C. A. Ferguson & D. I. Slobin (Eds.), *Studies of child language development* (pp. 45–54). New York: Springer.

Soja, N., Carey, S., & Spelke, E. (1985, April). *Constraints on word learning.* Paper presented at the 1985 Biennial Convention of the Society for Research in Child Development, Toronto, Canada.

Waxman, S., & Gelman, R. (1986). Preschooler's use of superordinate relations in classification. *Cognitive Development, 1,* 139–156.

4

Ontology and Meaning – Two Constrasting Views

Susan Carey

MIT

Many researchers now believe that in limiting their hypotheses about word meaning, children make many assumptions of many different kinds (cf. Carey, 1982; Clark, 1987; Markman & Hutchinson, 1984; Markman & Wachtel, 1988; Osherson, 1978). To focus the issue, let us begin with two related sources of constraint suggested by Markman, the taxonomy assumption (Markman & Hutchinson, 1984) and the whole object assumption (Markman & Wachtel, 1988), both of which limit hypotheses about word meanings in the following situation: Suppose the child hears "that's a cup" when the speaker is indicating a brown plastic cup half-filled with coffee. Suppose further that the child knows of no word to refer to any aspect of the situation, so assumptions about mutual exclusivity (Markman & Wachtel, 1988) or contrast (Clark, 1987) cannot help. "Cup" could refer to cups, tableware, brown, plastic, coffee, being half-full, the front side of the cup and the table, the handle, any undetached part of a cup, a temporal stage of the cup (that is, the particular cup at some particular time), the number one, cup-shape, and so on for an infinitude of possibilities. The *whole object assumption* limits hypotheses of the meaning of "cup" to those that include whole cups in the extension of the word. The *taxonomic assumption* limits the hypotheses of the meaning of the "cup" to taxonomic categories including cups. Markman and Hutchinson define a taxonomic category as one in with the members are grouped together on the basis of similarity, rather than on the basis of other types of relations (e.g., causal or thematic relations). These two assumptions constitute the following procedure[1] for constraining the meaning of a newly heard noun:

Procedure 1

- Step 1: Test to see if the speaker could be talking about a solid object; if yes,

---

[1] The procedures specified in this chapter are not intended as processing models for how the child might fix the meaning of a newly heard word. Rather, they embody proposals for what the child must be taking into account. How the child represents this information and brings it to bear in the word-learning situation is left open.

- Step 2: Conclude the word refers to individual whole objects of the same type as the referent.

As stated, Procedure 1 is still far too weak to do the work Markman wants of it. Returning to the brown cup: *brown thing, plastic thing,* and *thing I like* are all categories of whole objects defined by similarity to the target object, as is *cup.* We need an analysis that picks out *cup* as the relevant taxonomic category. We will return to this issue below. Furthermore, although Procedure 1 already has many steps, it is woefully incomplete. For example, it does not specify how the learner decides what portion of the world the adult might be referring to. As stated, Procedure 1 is incomplete in quite a different way as well; it makes no reference to the age of the learner. Markman's evidence for the whole object and taxonomy assumptions is derived from studies of children over age 3 ½. Adults (and 4-year-olds) use syntactic information to decide whether Procedure 1 is invoked; that is, only if the newly heard word is a count noun would Procedure 1 apply (Brown, 1957); it is an open question whether 2-year-olds, let alone 14-month-olds, use Procedure 1, and if so, if they are so conditioned by syntactic information (see Chapter 5, for evidence that the syntactic frames in which newly heard verbs appear to constrain the meanings young 2-year-olds assign to them.)

Others have taken the opposite view of Procedure 1. Rather than being too weak, Nelson (1988), argues that constraints such as those embodied in Procedure 1 are far too strong. First, according to Nelson, the word "constraint" implies total adherence, rigid limitation of choices, and nativism, implications that are either known to be false or unproven. For these reasons, she prefers the terms "bias" or "strategy." Terminological quibbles aside, her second and important objection is that it is false that word learners obey Principle 1, at least in the earliest period of word learning. Like Dromi (1986; Chapter 2), Nelson divides the one-word period into two phases, roughly corresponding to the periods before and after the vocabulary spurt. One interpretation of the difference between the two phases is that in the first phase the child has not firmly settled on the types of conceptual entities words encode. According to Dromi, in this phase many lexical entries are unstable (words appear in one usage, disappear and then reappear in a different usage), and many appear to have nonadult meanings (i.e., to include both actions and objects, as "giddiup" used when pointing to pictures of animals or to people riding, or to include both properties and objects, as "hot" used when pointing to stoves or to hot or cold things). Others have documented patterns of word use early in the holophrastic stage that seem to reflect associative clusters of properties of salient referents of the word. Famous examples include Vygotsky's case of a child who used a baby word for dog, the equivalent of "bow-wow" for in the presence of dogs, the sound of a bark, a glass-covered clock with shiny reflections, and a fur stole (Vygotsky, 1962). More recently, Bowerman (1976) described her daughter's use of "moon" for moon-shaped objects (such as lemon slices), for shiny green leaves, and for a hangnail. And finally, another deviant pattern of word usage is the overrestricted, as in the case of Bloom's (1973) subject who used "car" only when looking at cars on the street below out of a window. After the vocabulary spurt, such unstable and nonadult uses practically vanish.

There are two questions raised by the denial that Procedure 1 plays a role in early word learning. The first is that of specifying what early word meanings *are* like. The second is that of accounting for the change between the early procedures children use and the later procedures, those similar to Procedure 1. Quine (1960), in *Word and Object,* attempted to answer both of these questions. His specification of what early word meanings are like:

> The mother, red, and water are for the infant all of a type; each is just a history of sporadic encounter, a scattered portion of what goes on. His first learning of the three words is uniformly of a matter of learning how much of what goes on about him counts as the mother, or as red, or as water. It is not for the child to say in the first case, "Hello! Mama again," in the second case, "Hello! another red thing," and in the third case "Hello! more water". They are all on a par: "Hello! more mama, more red, more water."

Quine's proposal is that all early words function most like mass nouns in the child's conceptual system—that is, "book" refers to portions of book experience or stuff, any given book being a piece of book stuff, just as "water" refers to portions of water stuff, and "red" to portions of red stuff. Even this way of putting it is spuriously precise, since the child at this stage, according to Quine, does not conceptualize "stuff" and "portion of stuff" as do adults. Quine's answer to the second question (the impetus for change) is that the child comes to conceptualize the world in terms of kinds of objects, portions of stuff, properties of objects and stuffs, individual objects, and events in the course of learning the syntax of natural languages. Thus, Quine holds that until the child learns the syntax of quantification (determiners, plurals, and quantifiers such as numbers, "some" and "another"), the child's conceptual system does not make the distinction between kinds of objects and portions of stuff.

Those, like Quine, who deny Procedure 1 to young children credit them with some version of Procedure 0.

Procedure 0

- Step 1: Conclude that the word refers to aspects of the world that share salient properties of the perceptual experience when the word is used.

Procedure 0 accommodates putative complexive meanings (as in Bowerman's "moon"), meanings in which single words are used to refer to objects, events, and properties (as in Dromi's "hot"), and overspecific meanings (as in

Bloom's "car," on the assumption that the child's being at the window was a salient feature of the adult's use of "car."). The constraints on word meanings, then, would be the weighted feature space that orders perceptual salience of aspects of the world the child is sensitive to.[2]

Many people have suggested that some version of Procedure 0 underlies the projection of word meanings early in the course of lexical acquisition. For example, Clark (1973) proposed that children's early word meanings were salient perceptual features of what the child takes the referents of the adult words to be, and recently Landau, Smith, and Jones (1988) have proposed that early in lexical learning, nouns refer to shapes.

Note that Procedure 0 is taxonomic, in the sense of being similarity based, and thus does not differ from Procedure 1 in that respect. Rather, the two differ in the ontology underlying word meanings. In Procedure 1, the child checks whether the aspect of the world being referred to can be conceptualized as a solid physical object, and if so, projects word meaning according to taxonomic category of physical object. According to Principle 1, words refer to individual whole objects of a given kind. Kind of object plays no role in Procedure 0.

There are at least two reasons infants might follow Procedure 0 rather than Procedure 1. The first is that the infant's conceptual system does not yet represent the word in terms of kinds of physical objects. The second is that the child has not yet learned that words refer to such entities. Note that an adherent of Procedure 0 is not committed to the view that infants have no conception of solid objects. Spelke (1985) demonstrated that prelinguistic infants individuate as single objects those stimuli that are bounded coherent wholes that move in a unitary fashion. They know that such entities persist when out of sight, and take them to be substantial, in the sense that one cannot pass through the space occupied by another. Thus, the infant's perceptual system analyzes the world in terms of objects. This does not mean, however, that the infant has available the conception "kind of object," nor that the infant takes words, or nouns, to refer to kinds of objects. At issue is how the infant construes objects as well as what the child thinks words mean. As Quine so eloquently points out, one could construe a given physical object (say a cup) as a cup, as a collection of undetached cup parts, as a portion of ceramic, as a temporal stage of a cup. Similarly at issue is how the infant construes portions of substances, events, properties, individuals, and the other ontological categories that are the backbone of language.

Quine's proposal differs from Nelson's in the mechanism by which strategies such as Procedure 1 come to replace those like Procedure 0. Nelson sees no role for learning English syntax, since she believes that words have come to

---

[2] Of course, adherents of the proposal that Procedure 0 underlies early word learning owe us an account of that weighted feature space. But that debt only makes the proposal incomplete, not wrong.

have adult meanings by the second period of the holophrastic period. I know of no suggested mechanism in Nelson's writings, other than "learning what words do" from experience with them. However, one could suggest a mechanism that would get us part of the way there. Suppose, upon first hearing a new word, a very young infant relies on Procedure 0, forming a representation of the entire context in which the word was heard in terms of the available feature space. Upon further experience with the word, the child learns what features are relevant to its extension. For terms like "water," texture, runniness, color, shininess, and wetness are relevant; shape, location, activities performed on water are not. For terms like "cup," shape, activities performed with it are relevant; texture, color, location, and so on are not. This could be worked out, word by word, over repeated experience with each word, and this working out could underly the inconsistent word uses early in word learning. After this had been worked out for several words, the child could notice that when the referents of terms are solid physical objects, certain features are relevant; when they are nonsolid substances other features are relevant—that is, the child could induce that there are words for objects, nonsolid substance, events, individuals, and so on.

There are two problems with this suggested mechanism. First, if the child literally does not have the conception of kind of object, portion of nonsolid substance, and so on, he could not make this induction, because he would not be able to represent the generalization that captures the regularity. This induction is possible only if the problem the child is solving is merely one of how words work, given a conceptual system already capable of construing the world in terms of the language's ontology. Second, learning the extension of a word does not guarantee the relevant conceptualization of the word's intension, as Quine so eloquently pointed out. Quine's proposal is that simultaneously learning how quantifiers, plurals, determiners, and so on, work constrains the inductions in the right conceptual space.

Quine's proposal may seem a nonstarter. After all, Nelson, Dromi, and others agree that by the end of the holophrastic period the child's word usage closely approximates that of the adult, from which they infer that the child has worked out the ontology of word meanings and learned how words work. But we do not actually know what these words mean to the toddler. Nouns could refer to shapes in the child's lexicon (e.g., "doggie" means dog-shaped, "cracker" means cracker-shaped, "book" means book-shaped), as Landau et al. suggest. The experimental evidence for the whole object constraint (Markman & Wachtel, 1988) is equally consistent with the hypothesis that the child considers the word to refer to shapes, since the objects of the same kind always shared shapes. Additionally, that children approximate adult usage in production tells us nothing about the history of learning the word's meaning, nothing about the principles that constrain the child's first hypotheses, nor whether the referent's status as a solid physical object plays a role in such principles.

To address Quine's conjecture, Soja, Spelke, and I sought to determine whether the referent's status as a physical object affects the similarity relations that determine the taxonomic category posited by the child, *on first hearing the word,* before the child commands the quantificational system of English. To address this possibility, one must compare word learning when the aspect of the world the adult indicates can be conceptualized as a physical object and when it cannot. We chose to compare objects with nonsolid substances. Nonsolid substances such as gels, liquids, and powders do not form bounded coherent wholes that move in a unitary fashion, and in the mature language, these are quantified over portions that aggregate, rather than over individuals of a kind. However, any instance of either an object or a portion of a nonsolid substance has a shape, color, texture, and so on, and so a perceptual feature space unmodulated by the ontological status of the referent could apply equally to instances of either. Two complex constraints are being compared to Procedure 0 — Procedure 1 above, and Procedure 2:

Procedure 2

- Step 1: Test to see if the speaker could be talking about a nonsolid substance; if yes,
- Step 2: Conclude the word refers to portions of the same type as the referent.

If children can be shown to follow both Procedures 1 and 2 before they command the syntax of quantification, Quine's conjecture will be falsified. Note also that if the child can be shown to follow both principles, the Landau et al. hypothesis that early nouns refer to shapes will also be falsified, for shape is irrelevant to identifying portions of substances. The $64,000 question, then, is what data can be brought to bear on deciding whether 2-year-olds follow both Procedures 1 and 2. We certainly succeeded in showing that the referent's status as a solid physical object or nonsolid substance influenced the projection of word meaning (Step 1 in Procedures 1 and 2). The argument that the child was projecting word meanings according to kind of object and portions of substance is more tenuous.

Here I will sketch only one of Soja's studies (Soja, 1987; Soja, Carey, & Spelke, submitted). We assessed whether the referent's status as a solid object or as a nonsolid substance influences the child's hypotheses about the meaning of a newly heard word, as in Procedures 1 and 2, or whether the child's hypotheses are based on a similarity space that is neutral with respect to the solid object/nonsolid substance distinction, such that words pick out referents on the basis of shape, number, and other salient perceptual properties of the original aspect of the world used to introduce the meaning of the word, as in Procedure 0. To assess Quine's conjecture, we looked at word learning by children of age 24 months, and we analyzed their speech production for count/mass syntax. Furthermore, if children command the syntax of quantification and make the syntactic distinction between count nouns and mass nouns, then they may use quantifiers and noun subcategorization as a clue to the meaning of the newly heard noun. Brown (1957) found that 4- and 5-year-old children assume newly heard mass nouns refer to substances and newly heard count nouns refer to objects (see Gathercole, 1986, for a slightly different interpretation). To see whether 2-year-olds make use of this information in our word learning situation, we contrasted two different introducing events: (a) syntax neutral (the new word appeared in neutral quantification contexts, in which both objects and nonsolid substances were introduced and referred to as "my xxx, the xxx"), and (b) informative syntax (objects introduced and referred to as "a xxx, another xxx" and nonsolid substances introduced and referred to as "some xxx, some more xxx." Sensitivity to the information in the syntactic context would lead to a greater differentiation of the object trials and the substance trials in the informative syntax condition than in the neutral syntax condition.

Children were introduced to new words by ostensive definitions; the referents were unfamiliar objects made of unfamiliar substances, or unfamiliar nonsolid substances arranged in unfamiliar shapes. If Procedure 1 limits 2-year-olds' inductions about word meaning, when they hear a new word referring to an unfamiliar object they should take it to refer to objects of that kind. We do not know, of course, how 2-year-olds might determine the relevant taxonomic category, even if they were following the procedure. For example, "plank" is a taxonomic category of solid objects defined largely by substance. Therefore, we offered a choice to the child that included one item that did not meet Spelke's test for being an object, and thus could not be an instance of an object of the same taxonomic category as the target. This item was three of four irregular pieces made of the substance of the original. The other item was made of a different substance, but shared the shape of the original (see Figure 4.1; object trial). If the child is following Procedure 1, his or her choice should be the other object of the same kind, namely the item sharing number, size, and shape with the original target. They should reject the choice sharing substance. If Procedure 2 guides 2-year-olds' inductions about word meaning, when they hear a new word referring to an unfamiliar nonsolid substance, they should take it to refer to substances of that kind. To test this hypothesis, half of the trials were nonsolid substance trials (see Figure 4.1; nonsolid substance trial). Since nonsolid substances do not form bounded, coherent, wholes, items containing multiple piles of a substance can be portions of same kind of substance as the target. That is, if subjects honor Procedure 2, they will choose the item sharing substance, ignoring the mismatch in number, size, and shape. It is the role of number in the two types of trials that supports the inference that the child is construing substances in terms of portions that aggregate and objects in terms of kinds of individuals.

OBJECT TRIAL   SUBSTANCE TRIAL

This is my blicket.   This is my stad.

Which is the blicket?   Which is the stad?

Figure 4.1. Sample trials — neutral syntax condition.

The details of the procedure and data analyses are presented elsewhere (Soja, 1987). Do note from Figure 4.1 that the nonsolid substances were arranged in more distinctive and complex shapes than were the objects (as checked by adult subject ratings). This was to ensure that greater choice based on shape on the object trials would not be due to differential salience of the shapes of the objects. The results are shown on Figure 4.2, which displays the percent choices based on shape matches. Since there were two choices on each trial, chance would be 50 percent. Performance differed from chance responding on both the object trials and the nonsolid substance trials. When the referent of a newly heard word was a physical object, 2-year-old subjects projected the word to another object of the same kind, respecting the shape and number of the original referent; when the referent was a nonsolid substance, 2-year-old subjects projected the word to another sample of the same substance, violating the shape and number of piles of the original

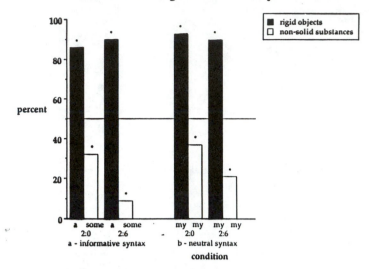

Figure 4.2. Percent choices matching target on shape and number.

referent. As can be seen from Figure 4.2, this tendency was stronger on the object trials (89% correct, overall, when correct if determined relative to Procedure 1) than the nonsolid substance trials (61% correct overall, when correct is determined relative to Procedure 2).

As also can be seen from Figure 4.2, there was no difference between the informative syntax and the neutral syntax conditions. Two-year-olds were at ceiling on the object trials, but far from ceiling on the nonsolid substance trials. Nonetheless, hearing the new word in mass noun contexts did not facilitate the induction that it referred to the substance. Also, in their spontaneous production, the children differed greatly in their command of count-mass syntax, from omission of determiners and quantifiers on all nouns to quite a bit of selective use of count noun frames with count nouns. This variation was completely uncorrelated with the individual child's adherence to Procedures 1 and 2.

Soja's studies falsify both Quine's and Landau et al.'s versions of the characterization of the word-learning system at 24 months of age. The ontological status of the referent is certainly relevant to the projection of word meaning, consistent with Procedures 1 and 2. In what remains of this chapter, I raise several issues concerning constraints on word learning at age 2:0, speculating way beyond what available data allows me to.

Syntax and Constraints on Word Meanings

These studies falsify Quine's conjecture that the child induces the ontological distinction between objects and substances through learning the syntax of individuation. These data show that the referent's status as an object or a nonsolid substance constrains the child's hypotheses about noun meanings at least from age 2:0, well before he has mastered the relevant syntactic devices. An adherent of Quine's conjecture might reply that we may have grossly underestimated the child's command of the relevant syntax, since we have looked only at production. There are now two well-documented demonstrations of syntactic distinctions not under the child's productive control being comprehended, and even constraining initial interpretations of word meaning. Katz, Baker, and Macnamara (1974) and Gelman and Taylor (1984) have shown that the 2-year-old is sensitive to the syntactic distinction between proper and common nouns, taking only the latter to refer to taxonomic categories of objects. Similarly, Naigles (1986, see also Chapter 5) has shown that young 2-year-olds take into account the syntactic context in which newly heard verbs occur in projections of verb meaning. However, if 2-year-old children comprehend the count/mass distinction, and have induced the object/substance distinction in the course of making sense of that syntactic distinction, then the informative syntax condition should have facilitated their word learning efforts. There was no hint in Soja's studies of such an effect.

We do not know whether syntactic evidence that the new words, "blicket," "stad," and so on, were nouns actually influenced the children's interpretations of their meanings, since we included no conditions in which they were not nouns. However, several considerations make it seem likely that the words being nouns played a role in the child's lexical hypotheses. First, that objects and substances are named by nouns is a linguistic universal, and bootstrapping theories of early syntactic categories agree that the noun/object-substance mapping is likely to be innately specified (e.g., Pinker, 1984). Second, the studies of Katz et al. and Gelman and Taylor, mentioned above, show that the syntactic distinction between common and proper nouns constrain hypotheses about new word meaning at this age. Be this as it may, the present studies suggest that within the linguistic category "common noun," at ages 2:0 the syntactic context — mass or count — in which a new noun occurs does not affect the child's hypotheses about its meaning. Rather, the referent's ontological status (in these studies, as an object or as a nonsolid substance) seems to determine the child's hypotheses. The correspondence between the conceptual distinction between objects and substances, on the one hand, and the syntactic distinction between count and mass nouns, on the other, is likely learned later (cf. Gordon, 1985; Gathercole, 1986; Brown, 1957).

Ontology and Constraints on Word Meanings

Landau et al. claim that adults, as well as children, ignore ontological categories in their inductive projections of noun meanings. They suggest that for adults, as well as children, noun meanings are determined by shape, irrespective of the ontological categories to which the noun's referents belong.

In support of these claims, they offer examples in which the extension of a noun includes objects that share shapes but fall into different ontological categories, in Keil's (1979) sense of different ontological categories. For example, both real bears and stuffed toy bears are called "bear." Or for another example, when asked what a Oldenberg statue of a 100-foot-high clothespin is, people do not say, "a statue of a clothespin;" rather, they reply, "a clothespin." Actually, three different claims must be unpacked here:

1. A noun's extension may include referents of different ontological types.
2. Ontological distinctions are irrelevant to noun meaning.
3. Nouns refer to shape.

We agree with the first claim, but deny the second two.

That a stuffed bear and a real bear are both called "a bear" is just one example of the profligacy with which natural languages unite different ontological types in the extension of single words (see Keil, 1979, for numerous other examples). The lexicons of natural language regularly exploit systematic relations among entities of distinct ontological types. For example, certain geographical entities (countries, states, cities) are the sites of political entities; this relation is exploited in having a single word refer to both, as in "My country is shaped like a boot," and "My country is democratic." Similarly, abstract linguistic objects are instantiated in physical tokens, and we use the same word for both the abstract object and its various types of physical tokens, as in "The sentence was loud," "The sentence was blurred," and "The sentence was elegantly constructed." Stuffed animals, mechanical monkeys, and statues are representational objects; the relation of representation is a paradigm example of those which lead to the use of a single lexical item to refer to entities of different ontological types. Thus, while we agree that nouns may well include entities from two or more distinct ontological categories in their extensions, this certainly does not imply that the extensions of nouns are united by sharing a common shape. Countries, as political entities, and sentences, as acoustic or abstract objects, do not have shapes.

Landau et al. may well have meant that when a noun refers to a physical object, shape determines the relevant taxonomic category that unites its extension. But this restatement belies their claim that ontology is irrelevant to noun meaning, since the restatement makes explicit reference to the ontological category of the referent. As Soja's studies show, 2-year-old children ignore the shape of nonsolid substances in their hypotheses about the meaning of newly heard nouns referring to them. Dickinson (1988) extended these findings to 3- to 5-year-olds and adults. Shape cannot be the *general* taxonomic basis for noun categories, for the simple reason that many types of entities named by nouns, such as substances and abstract entities are not distinguished on the basis of shape. However, it may be that for solid physical objects, and for very young children, shape determines the relevant taxonomic basis for noun meanings. In all experiments to date probing patterns of projection of noun meaning from an initial referent that is a solid physical object, the taxonomically based choices shared shape. However, shape similarity also reflects deeper similarity—similarity of shape follows similarity of parts, and thus similarity of function in the case of artifacts or similarity of evolutionary and/or genetic forces in the case of biological kinds. We do not know whether the child, even at age 2, is after a deeper source of similarity than shape similarity, but we do know that the adult is. Keil's studies of natural kind terms show that adults, and even early elementary aged children, when deciding what a given animal is, are robustly sensitive to how an animal came to get its shape. For example, adults and 10-year-olds are certain that if an antelope were to get a long neck by plastic surgery, it would not become a giraffe, even if the surgeon made it physically indistinguishable from a giraffe (Keil, 1989).

Identifying the Right Taxonomic Categories

As pointed out above, if one defines taxonomic categories simply as those categories determined by similarity relations, as opposed to causal or thematic relations, the taxonomic assumption fails to rule out many hypotheses about possible noun meaning the child would never entertain. What is needed is an analysis that distinguishes *cup* as a relevant taxonomic category from other similarity-based categories, such as *brown thing* or *thing I like* (or, for adults, even *cup-shaped*).

I know of two related proposals for distinguishing a property such as being a cup, which is a good candidate for a property that might determine the extension of a noun, from properties such as being brown or being cup-shaped, which are not. The first is Markman's (1989). She suggests that the properties that are candidates for noun meanings are those with the most inductive depth. If I know that an object is a cup, there are many inferences I can draw about its size, shape, purpose, origin, parts, material it may be made of, and so on. If I know an object is brown, very little follows. Markman suggests that the properties the child entertains as candidates for noun meanings are the inductively deep ones. The second derives from the philosophical literature on metaphysics, in which it is pointed out that to have a concept entails more than to be able to determine its extension. Knowing what a cup is entails being able to trace any given cup through time, being able to know whether one has the same cup on two different occasions, or two different cups. This literature draws (and debates) the distinction between essential and accidental properties. Any property of a given object, such that if that object ceases to have that property, it ceases to exist, is an essential property. Note that essential properties are not concerned with categorization, with what makes something a cup, or a dog. Rather, they are concerned with what makes something itself, that is, with individuation and tracing entities through time. Examples of essential properties are those of being a dog or being an animal. If Domino, my pet Labrador, ceased to be a dog or an animal, she would cease to exist (presumably, she would be dead, and/or destroyed). However, if she ceased being black, 4-legged, in Cambridge, a pet, or having an infinitude of other properties, she would still exist. Perhaps the child's first hypotheses about a newly heard noun is that it picks out a taxonomic category determined by a property essential to the referent.

These two proposals are related in that essential properties are inductively rich properties. The condition of being an essential property is stronger than the condition of having enough inductive depth to be lexicalized as a noun in the adult lexicon. "Pet," "passenger," and many other nouns pick out categories in terms of nonessential properties of their referents. Hall and Waxman (1988) have recently shown that 4- and 5-year-old children's first hypotheses about newly heard nouns that refer to objects for which no label was previously known are that they are taxonomic categories determined by a property essential to the referent, rather than by a temporal stage property such as "being a passenger." They showed their subjects a strange creature climbing a mountain, and told them, "See this, this is a blicket because it is climbing the mountain." They were then asked to indicate another blicket, given a choice of another creature of the same kind in some other context (e.g., riding in a bus) and a different kind of creature climbing a mountain. Subjects choose the new creature of the same kind, ignoring the explicit reference in the introducing event to the fact it was called a blicket because it was climbing the mountain. If however, they already knew a name for the creature, they would accept *mountain-climber* as a meaning for "blicket."

I am suggesting here that Procedures 1 and 2 should be restated; I am uncertain whether (a) or (b) is the best formulation:

New Procedure 1

- Step 1: as in Procedure 1.
- Step 2: (a) the noun picks out a taxonomic category of objects determined by an inductively rich property of the referent, or (b) the noun picks out a taxonomic category of objects determined by an essential property of the referent.

New Procedure 2

- Step 1: as in Procedure 2.
- Step 2: (a) the noun picks out a portion of some substance determined taxonomically by an inductively rich property of the referent, or (b) the noun picks out a portion of some substance determined taxonomically by an essential property of the referent.

Just what the essential properties are, or the inductively deep properties are, vary according to the ontological category of the referent. For example, I am the same person I was seven years ago, even though I do not today share a single molecule with myself of seven years ago. Apparently, being made of exactly the same stuff is not critical to being the same person. However, a portion of gold cannot be identical to another portion if they contain no molecules in common. The conditions of identity for substances are different from those for people, whereas the conditions of identity for dogs are deeply similar to those for people. For adults, at least, metaphysical commitments cannot be separated from constraints on word meanings. The present studies suggest this is true also for 2-year-olds. Of course, we do not yet know whether words such as "dog" pick out taxonomic categories determined by essential properties at that age.

Are Procedures 1 and 2 Language Specific?

Procedures 1 and 2 are stated as part of a language acquisition system; they are rules for constraining hypotheses about noun meanings. But it is certainly possible that any induction the child might make would follow these rules. For example, seeing a new object and hearing that if you shake it rattles, an adult would certainly be more likely to assume that another object of the same kind would rattle than would pieces of that object. After all, I am suggesting that what determines object kind are inductively rich properties. Therefore, other things being equal, any new property might be projected as would candidate word meanings. But for adults, it is not *any* new property, for other things are not always equal. Imagine you encounter an unfamiliar object made of an unfamiliar substance. It has an unfamiliar odor, and it is extremely heavy. In these cases, you would expect an object of a different kind to have the same odor, and also to be heavy, so long as the new object were made of the same substance. Soja (1987), Wiser (1986), and Schmidt (1987) have compared projection of word meaning with projection of odor and weight by children as young as 2 ½. These studies show that by age 3 weight is projected on the basis of solid substance kind, and by age 2 ½ odor is projected on this basis. At these ages, with the same stimuli, word meaning is projected according to object kind. That is, young children are sensitive to solid substances, and do make inductive projections based on them. Not *all* inductive projection follows Procedure 1. In this sense, Procedure 1 is part of the language acquisition device, and not simply part of the similarity space underlying all of the child's inductive inferences. As of yet, we do not know the answer for younger 2-year-olds; we have not found a technique that we can use with toddlers tapping their inductive projection of odor and weight.

Are Procedures 1 and 2 Innate?

Soja's studies show that 24-month-olds make the distinction between objects and nonsolid substances, and guide their projection of word meanings according to whether they classify the initial referent of a word as either one of these. Two-year-olds, however, are well past the vocabulary spurt, and many of her subjects were well into multiword utterances. What about younger children, children in the first phase of holophrastic speech? Are Nelson, Dromi, and others correct in their contention that there is a long period of initial forays into language before the child has worked out that words refer to individual objects of a particular kind, portions of substances, events, and so on?

The data that support this contention derive from analyses of production, and as Nelson and Dromi admit, it is very difficult to make inferences of word meaning from patterns of word use, especially in the single word phase. For example, when the child points to the cookie jar and says, "cookie," does this reflect a complexive meaning including cookies and the locations in which cookies are found, or is the child merely expressing a desire for a cookie and the knowledge that there are cookies in the jar? Huttenlocher and Smiley (1987) questions several assumptions often made in such inferences: that those aspects of context which are present during word use are assumed to be concept instances, that usage for a restricted range of instances is evidence for undergeneral meanings, that all aspects of the context in which words are used are part of their meanings. Furthermore, in an analysis of several children's production of object words during the holophrastic stage, Huttenlocher found no evidence of either complexive meanings, nor overly context-bound uses, and no evidence of a change in word use during the holophrastic stage. Huttenlocher's data, however, were drawn from 5-hour observations with a month between them; intensive observations such as Dromi's are clearly what is needed, for periods of unstable meanings may be very brief. But given the difficulty of inferring word meaning from word use, inferences from production must be supplemented by inferences from comprehension, and these by word learning studies. A good place to start would be to try to adapt Soja's methodology for use with young toddlers who have not entered the second phase of the holophrastic period.

References

Bloom, L. (1973). *One word at a time: The use of single word utterances before syntax.* The Hague: Mouton.

Bowerman, M. (1976). Semantic factors in the acquisition of rules for word use and sentence construction. In D. M. Morehead & A. E. Morehead (Eds.), *Normal and deficient child language.* Baltimore: University Park Press.

Brown, R. (1957). Linguistic determinism and the part of speech. *Journal of Abnormal and Social Psychology, 55,* 1–5.

Carey, S. (1978). The child as word learner. In M. Halle, J. Bresnan, & G. A. Miller (Eds.), *Linguistic theory and psychological reality.* Cambridge: MIT Press.

Carey, S. (1982). Semantic development: The state of the art. In E. Wanner & L. R. Gleitman (Eds.), *Language acquisition: The state of the art* (pp. 347–389). Cambridge: Cambridge University Press.

Carey, S., & Bartlett, E. (1978). Acquiring a single new word. *Papers and Reports on Child Language Development, 15,* 17–29.

Clark, E. V. (1973). What's in a word? On the child's acquisition of semantics in his first language. In T. Moore (Ed.), *Cognitive development and the acquisition of language* (pp. 65–110). New York: Academic Press.

Clark, E. V. (1987). The principle of contrast: A constraint on language acquisition. In B. MacWhinney (Ed.), *Mechanisms of language acquisition* (pp. 1–33). Hillsdale, NJ: Erlbaum.

Dickinson, D. K. (1988). Learning names for materials: Factors constraining and limiting hypotheses about word meanings. *Cognitive Development, 3,* 15–36.

Dromi, E. (1986). The one-word period as a stage in language development: Quantitative and qualitative Accounts. In I. Levin (Ed.), *Stage and structure: Reopening the debate* (pp. 220–245). Norwood, NJ: Ablex.

Gathercole, V. C. (1986). Evaluating competing linguistic theories with child language data: The case of the mass-count distinction. *Linguistics and Philosophy, 9,* 151–190.

Gelman, S. A., & Taylor, M. (1984). How two-year-old children interpret proper and common names for unfamiliar objects. *Child Development, 55,* 1535–1540.

Gordon, P. (1985). Evaluating the semantic categories hypothesis: The case of the count/mass distinction. *Cognition, 20,* 209–242.

Heibeck, T. H., & Markman, E. M. (1987). Word learning in children: An examination of fast mapping. *Child Development, 58,* 1021–1034.

Huttenlocher, J., & Smiley, P. (1987). Early word meanings: The case of object names. *Cognitive Psychology, 19,* 63–89.

Katz, N., Baker, E., & Macnamara, J. (1974). What's in a name? A study of how children learn common and proper names. *Child Development, 45,* 469–473.

Keil, F. C. (1979). *Semantic and conceptual development: An ontological perspective.* Cambridge: Harvard University Press.

Keil, F. (1989). *Concepts, kinds and cognitive development.* Cambridge, MA: MIT Press.

Landau, B., Smith, L. B., & Jones, S. S. (1988). The importance of shape in early lexical learning. *Cognitive Development, 3,* 299–321.

Markman, E. (1989). *Categorization and naming in children.* Cambridge, MA: MIT Press.

Markman, E., & Hutchinson, J. E. (1984). Children's sensitivity to constraints on word meaning: Taxonomic versus thematic relations. *Cognitive Psychology, 16,* 1–27.

Markman, E. M., & Wachtel, C. A. (1988). Children's use of mutual exclusivity to constrain the meanings of words. *Cognitive Psychology, 20,* 121–157.

Naigles, L. C. (1986). *Acquiring the components of verb meaning from syntactic evidence.* Paper presented at the Boston Child Language Conference, Boston, MA.

Nelson, K. (1988). Constraints on word learning? *Cognitive Development, 3,* 221–246.

Osherson, D. N. (1978). Three conditions on conceptual naturalness. *Cognition, 6,* 263, 290.

Pinker, S. (1984). *Language learnability and language development.* Cambridge, MA: Harvard University Press.

Quine, W. V. (1960). *Word and object.* Cambridge, MA: MIT Press.

Soja, N. (1987). *Constraints on word learning.* Unpublished doctoral Dissertation, MIT.

Soja, N., Carey, S., & Spelke, E. (1991). Ontological categories guide young children's inductions of word meanings: Object terms and substance terms. *Cognition.*

Spelke, E. S. (1985). Perception of unity, persistence, and identity: Thoughts on infants' conception of objects. In R. Fox & J. Mehler (Eds.), *Neonate cognition* (pp. 489–497). Hillsdale, NJ: Erlbaum.

Vygotsky, L. (1962). *Thought and language.* Cambridge, MA: MIT Press.

5

Children Acquire Word Meaning Components from Syntactic Evidence*

Letitia G. Naigles

Yale University

Henry Gleitman
Lila R. Gleitman

University of Pennsylvania

Common sense suggests that children acquire word meanings by noticing the external contingencies for their use. For example, the meanings of *dog* and *walk* are at least partly gleaned by observing that these words are uttered in the presence of dog objects and walking motions. However, as we discuss presently, there are difficulties in explaining all of word meaning acquisition as a straightforward projection from observed situations. Therefore, recent discussions have emphasized that the child may have another rich body of information from which to deduce the word meanings: These are the varying syntactic positions in which the meaningfully distinct words appear. For example, the facts that *dog* is a substantive and *walk* an act are inferred in part by observing that the former word occurs as a noun and the latter word as a verb, as Brown demonstrated in an elegant experiment performed 30 years ago (Brown, 1957). In this paper, we continue the line of investigation initiated by Brown, concentrating attention on the acquisition of verb meanings. We will show that children conjecture new components of verb meanings when those verbs occur in novel syntactic environments. We begin with a commentary on why a realistic procedure for acquiring word meanings, though heavily informed by extralinguistic observation, requires linguistic-structural observation as well.

---

* The authors would like to thank the children, parents, and teachers of the Swarthmore Presbyterian Day Nursery, Infant-Friendship Center, Parent-Infant Center, Children's Garden, Aardvark Nursery School, St. Faith Nursery School, Trinity Lutheran Nursery School, The Seedlings, and TLC Day Care Center, all of the Philadelphia area. We also want to thank Anna Hradnansky and Cynthia Fisher for their assistance in coding the data. Special thanks go to Barbara Landau, Kenneth Wexler, and Esther Dromi for informative discussion and commentary. This research was supported by March of Dimes Grant #12–25 to Lila R. Gleitman and Barbara Landau, and by an NSF predoctoral fellowship to Letitia G. Naigles. Some of the data presented here were reported by L. Naigles at the 11th annual meeting of the Boston University Child Language Conference, October 1986.

Learning Verb Meanings from Observation of the World

Consider the task of learning that the word *bring* encodes the concept 'bring.' The evidence is overwhelming that prelinguistic infants and very young children perceive and conceive the ambient world in the terms that might be necessary to derive such a concept, that is, as concerning objects that move from place to place in the scene in view, and affect each other's positions and movements (Acredolo & Evans, 1980; Spelke, 1982). Given these perceptual-conceptual preliminaries, a linguistic novice is in a position to notice that "bring" is often uttered when an entity$_1$ exerts force on another entity$_2$ such that both entities move from somewhere to somewhere else, that is, that the word *bring* is uttered in the presence of bringing situations. For instance, "Adam is bringing the truck to Mary" can be uttered relevantly when Adam is bringing the truck to Mary.

No one doubts that observation of ongoing scenes informs learning in much the sense just sketched, but the demonstrable usefulness of such observation should not be confused with a proof that the information it provides is sufficient. One catch is that some words encode mental states of the kind that seem to be closed to observation. For example, it's hard to envisage how one could literally observe that John is in the mental state we call thinking whenever it is asserted of him that he is *thinking* (as in "John is thinking about an elephant" or "John is thinking of an answer"). A related problem is evidenced by the fact that learners with quite different observational opportunities come to have very similar mental representations of word meaning. For instance, both sighted and congenitally blind 3-year-olds know that the verb *look* concerns perceptual observation and is distinct from such physical contact expressions as *set-eyes-on* and *touch*. Similarities of the observational circumstances do not seem to explain these effects satisfactorily (Landau & Gleitman, 1985).[1]

A third problem, which we seek to address in this paper, is that the same scene in the world — even a readily observable scene — can be represented, and thus described linguistically, in many ways. For example, the situation describable as "Adam is bringing the truck to Mary" is also describable, *inter alia,* as "Adam is moving/taking/conveying/accompanying the truck to Mary," "Mary is getting/receiving/taking the truck from Adam," "Adam and

---

[1] A less interesting, but real, problem is that often a caretaker will speak of one thing ("Time for your nap!") while the child is attending to something else (say, the toy he is playing with). The learner must take care not to attempt a mapping between this sentence and this object of attention. It has been pointed out repeatedly in the literature (Bloom, 1970; Brown, 1973) that mothers are prone to talk of the "here and now" with their offspring, a factor that surely mitigates this problem to some extent. Still, it is largely unknown how useful a constraint on interpretation this may provide. This is because there is so much latitude in what may grab one's attention, *within* the here-and-now. For example, it is just because one is not thinking of eating one's peas that one's mother says "Eat your peas!"

the truck are moving/coming to Mary," "Adam is coming to Mary with the truck," and so forth. It is puzzling how the child chooses among these several plausible and salient ways of interpreting the situation, so as to arrive at the right conjecture about the meaning of the verb item in the utterance heard.[2]

Notice that this problem cannot be resolved by assuming that the child has secure information about the thematic roles played by the entities in the discourse (namely, Adam and the truck), for this determination also is dependent on the right verb interpretation having already been chosen. That is, if the situation we have been describing is interpreted as one of bringing, then Adam would be the causal agent in this affair. But if the same situation was interpreted as one of coming, as in "Adam is coming to Mary with the truck" then Adam is an actor but no causal role is implied for him.

In short, one can fix the meaning of a verb from observing the world only if that observation is consistent with a single apposite predicate. But this is rarely if ever the case, for situations can always be construed in myriad ways, as Quine (1960), and others have discussed. Even if caretakers always speak pertinently of scenes to which the child is carefully attending (a matter independently in doubt) and speak only of what can literally be observed of such scenes (just as much in doubt), the latitude of interpretation for those scenes is so broad that extralinguistic observation appears to be inadequate to the task.

A natural response to the problem just raised is that the child learner has more than one chance to observe verbs used in context. For example, the verb *move* will be used to describe situations in which the truck moves to Mary but Adam does not change his position, while all situations in which *bring* is used require that Adam move along with the truck. If the learner adopts the principle of mutual exclusivity for word meanings (Markman & Hutchinson, 1984; see also Chapter 4) or the principle of contrast (Clark, 1987) — that is, if the child assumes that each different word has a distinct meaning — perhaps she

---

[2] After all, if the learner conjectured that bring meant come or move or get, there would be no positive evidence to dissuade her, for everytime she heard someone say bring she would observe a situation in which there was movement and in which there was coming. Then barring the systematic presentation of negative evidence (correction by adults), it is hard to see how a learner who relies solely on semantic/situational evidence could acquire the detailed distinctions among the thousands of verbs. This is a subset/superset problem analogous to that raised by Gold (1967) for the acquisition of syntax. If the child falsely conjectures the superset (larger) language, no positive evidence will arrive as a corrective just because each sentence in the real (subset) language is a sentence in the false conjectured superset language as well. In response to this problem, Wexler and Manzini (1987) have proposed that learners must always choose the subset language as their initial conjecture. But evidently this solution will not work for learning verb meanings. Consider some situation in which an animate being is locomoting across the room. Children do not seem to choose the least inclusive interpretation consistent with such a situation (e.g., 'saunter,' or 'walk in some lackadaisical fashion') or the most inclusive interpretation (e.g., 'move' or 'locomote'). Rather, they appear to select some middle-sized or "basic"-level interpretation (e.g., 'walk' cf. Rosch, 1978; Rescorla, 1980). Moreover, they learn all of these levels of description in the end, that is, they finally acquire the verbs saunter, walk, and move.

can resolve these problems: Since "move" means 'move,' "bring" must mean something else. This could lead the learner to seek an additional requirement for the use of *bring* (namely, the concomitant movement of Adam). (For a useful proposal which incorporates such ideas, see Pinker, 1987.)

It seems, then, that the problem of learning from observation poses no unsolvable logical problem, if we leave aside the acquisition of mental state verbs and the like. However, in practice the procedure just sketched may be unrealistic. Consider again the scenario we have been discussing: The child first conjectures that "bring" means 'move,' but then notices that "bring" is not used for all moving situations. Then "bring" must mean something more specific than 'move.' But what? To answer this question, the child must replay her stored examples of bringing (or add more), seeking the missing specification. This could be of manner (e.g., *run, saunter*), of direction (e.g., *approach, exit*), of causation (*bring, convey*), or of some combination of these (*push, carry*). We suggest that acquiring the word meanings solely from the observation of events would require such extensive storage and manipulation of contingently categorized event/conversation pairs as to be unrealistic as the sole method used by real children (for some empirical evidence for these difficulties, Chapter 2). Therefore, there is impetus to seek co-operative procedures that may be used by word learners.

The Potential Usefulness of Structural Information

Where are the children to find additional information to constrain their semantic conjectures? Recent linguistic theory acknowledges that the structures in which verbs appear are projections from their semantics; that is, verbs which differ in meaning differ correspondingly in their licensed syntactic environments. For example, *come* can appear in one-argument sentence frames such as *John comes* but not two-argument frames such as *Bill comes John*, while the reverse holds for *bring* (*Bill brings John*, but not *John brings*). This difference in the number of noun-phrases (NPs) corresponds to the logic of these two verbs: *Come* can be used to encode only the motion of an entity (John) while *bring* must encode also the causal agent (Bill) of such a motion. Thus, verbs which appear in transitive frames often encode a causal agent while verbs in intransitive frames cannot encode the causal agent. More to the point: A verb like *move* is noncausal in intransitive environments (*The coals move to Newcastle*) and causal in transitive environments. Evidently the structure carries a semantic value. If this is so, and if learners know these values, they could use the structural information to narrow down the range of interpretations that is available from observation of the scene.[3] This is the

---

[3] We take no stand in this chapter as to how these structural/semantic relations are to be described in a formal linguistic theory. Many have held that they are to be captured in the structure of the lexicon (which may include quasiproductive processes for word construction), but others

conjecture that we will explore experimentally in this chapter. However, quite a number of issues require to be raised before such a hypothesis could be considered seriously enough even to deserve experimental review.

Are There Stable Syntactic/Semantic Correlations?

Clearly there are plenty of counterexamples to any claim of transparency in the mapping between clause structures and semantic interpretations. For example, not all the subjects of transitive sentences are causal agents: *Adam leaves Mary* does not mean 'Adam causes Mary to leave.' Such imperfections, or complexities, in the syntactic/semantic relations do not automatically render them unusable for learners, for surely humans can profit from imperfect correlations (see Braine, 1971; Billman, 1988; and for a review of category learning from this perspective, see Smith & Medin, 1981). Still, it would be reassuring to demonstrate that the adult verb lexicon does exhibit broad and fairly reliable syntactic/semantic correlations: If these relations aren't there, the child can't hope to learn by attending to them. Extensive linguistic investigations by Jackendoff (1983), Grimshaw (1983), Levin (1985), and others do reveal reasonably consistent relationships between the clause-structural privileges and semantic interpretations of verbs, on a variety of dimensions. For example, it is characteristic in English to mark the paths and goals of objects moving through space with prepositional phrases (John goes *to France*, John heads *for the hills*). This property is marked in the syntax of many languages, though of course the particular formal device used varies from language to language (Talmy, 1975).

Recent studies by Fisher (Fisher, Gleitman, & Gleitman, 1991) document such patterning experimentally. Fisher's procedure is as follows. Judgements of grammaticality for sets of verbs in many subcategorization-frame environments were obtained from adult subjects.[4] A syntactic space defined on frame-overlap is derived from these data; that is, verbs are said to be syntactically similar insofar as they share frame privileges. From another group of subjects, judgements of semantic relatedness for the same verbs are obtained. This is done by having the subjects choose the semantic outlier for triads of verbs, following a procedure developed by Wexler and Romney (1972). A semantic space for the verbs is constructed from these data in terms

---

have argued that these relations are syntactic. (See Bowerman, 1983, and Borer and Wexler, 1987, for important proposals.) Of course, some also hold that there are no such relations at the level we are discussing, and therefore that the clause-structural privileges for each verb have to be acquired by an independent act of memorization (Fodor, 1985).

[4] For example, the verb give is offered to subjects in such sentence as John gives a ball to Mary, John gives Mary a ball, John gives, and so on; that is, in the frames NP V NP PP, NP V NP NP, and NP V. Subjects will accept some of these frames for certain verbs and reject others (e.g., they accept the first two examples but reject third). The pattern of acceptance for other verbs is different, for example, subjects accept John vanishes but not John vanishes a rabbit to Mary or John vanishes Mary a rabbit.

of the number of times that two verbs stick together in the contexts of all other verbs in the set. The semantic and syntactic spaces, so constructed, are then examined in a regression analysis, which essentially asks about the extent to which the semantic and syntactic partitionings are the same. The findings, for repeated and varied samplings of English verb sets, are that there are powerful and consistent correlations between the two sets of data. To an interesting extent, one can predict the syntactic environments from the semantic organization, and one can predict the syntactic environments (frames) from the semantic partitioning; and one can predict the semantic partitioning from the syntactic overlap data. Thus, if a learner were so disposed, she could use her knowledge of a verb's meaning to predict (part of) its syntax and she could use her knowledge of a verb's syntax to predict (part of) its semantics.

We should point out that both the linguistic work by Jackendoff and others, as well as the experiments just described, suggest that only a limited subset of semantic properties are likely to be formally encoded onto clause structures. For example, there is no evidence—least in English—that differences in manner (e.g., *tear, break, crush*; see Fillmore, 1968) or rate (e.g., *run, walk, saunter*) are exhibited as regular distinctions of clause structure. In contrast, differences having to do with such properties as 'cause', 'transfer', and 'state/act' are in many languages reflected in the clausal privileges. We seek only to show that, where the language design does offer potential semantic information, young learners will make use of this information.

Do Children Exploit the Semantic/Syntactic Correlations in Learning?: Evidence for "Semantic Bootstrapping"

Bowerman (1974, 1977, 1983) has provided compelling evidence that children make syntactic conjectures based on semantic conjectures. Given knowledge of the meaning of a verb, they are willing to make predictions about the syntactic structures in which these verbs will appear. For example, children apparently appreciate that certain verbs appear intransitively and express the motion of some entity (e.g., *The ship sinks*), but also appear transitively, in which case the entity causing the motion is also expressed (*The pirate sinks the ship*, i.e., causes it to sink). Bowerman's finding is that children will extend this relationship to new cases. If they have heard, say, "The lion falls," they sometimes will utter "The horse falls the lion" as a way of saying that the horse causes the lion to fall. Since they have heard "The baby is eating," they will utter "Don't eat the baby!" as a way of requesting that the baby not be fed. Though in the case just given the child's conjecture was false of the exposure language, the idea here is that the learner will generally be correct in such predictions. This is because word meanings are an important source of evidence as to the structure of clauses in which they can appear (see also Grimshaw, 1981, and Pinker, 1984, for important discussions of this claim about language learning, now called "semantic bootstrapping").

As advertised earlier, we are interested in testing the supposition that learners will also use the correlations, so to speak, in reverse: They will use the constructional facts about a verb as evidence for its semantic interpretation. So far, we've sketched two background facts that begin to give plausibility to this idea: (a) the semantic/syntactic correlations that are there in the language design, and (b) children appreciate this patterning to some extent, for they will guess at the syntax once they know, or think they know, the meaning. But two further background notions, to which we now turn, would have to be motivated in order to render our hypothesis viable.

Can Children Parse the Sentences so as to Render Structural Information Available?

A learning procedure for lexical semantics that exploits structural information can only be realistic if the novice learner can discriminate aspects of the syntactic structures of the utterances he encounters. Gleitman and Wanner (1982) suggested that the course of language learning in many linguistic communities was best accounted for on the hypothesis that toddlers represent input sentences as phrase-bracketed structures (see also Gleitman, Gleitman, Landau, & Wanner, 1987, for a review). Striking evidence for this view comes from the work of Hirsh-Pasek et al. (1987a,b) who showed that 8-month-old infants are sensitive to the acoustic correlates of phrase and clause boundaries in spoken sentences. They look longer at a loudspeaker if the speech that emanates from it contains appropriately marked phrase-boundary information than if it does not. A number of experimental studies with older children are consistent with the same supposition. For instance, Morgan (1986) showed that 3-year-old children can repeat prosodically organized strings of nonsense syllables far more reliably than they can repeat prosodically disorganized strings, presumably because they can hold them in memory better; see also Read and Schreiber (1982) for evidence from older children. In light of such findings, it is possible to suppose that toddlers represent input sentences as phrase-bracketed structures much before they comprehend them.

Do Children Know the Linking Rules in Time?

There is another precondition for the hypothesis that syntactic configurations are used to exact verb meaning during language learning: The young learner must have some antecedent hypotheses about the ways in which verb meanings map onto the syntactic structures. Evidence comes from various sources. Hirsh-Pasek, Golinkoff, DeGaspe-Beaubier, Fletcher, and Cauley (1985) studied 17-month-olds (many of whom could only utter single nouns) and presented them with videotaped scenes featuring Big Bird and Cookie Monster, accompanied by a disembodied voice (an audiotape) that said "Big Bird tickles Cookie Monster" or "Cookie Monster tickles Big Bird." The infants looked longer at the videotape that showed the appropriate tickler and ticklee than at its counterpart, thus demonstrating that they knew the semantic significance of subject and object position in English at a very early language-learning stage. Further information comes from the work of Bowerman (1983) that we've just discussed: Two-year-olds acknowledge—far too readily, in fact—a correlation between transitive structures and causative interpretations. They utter a novel transitive structure (Don't eat the baby) so as to add a causative component to an old verb. See also Lord (1979) who has evidence that children will sometimes play this scenario in reverse, removing a NP to render a noncausal interpretation, For example, "It can hear now," said of a clock whose ticking has just become audible.

Related results come from our own laboratory (Naigles, Hirsh-Pasek, Golinkoff, Gleitman, & Gleitman, 1987). We have been studying the influence of particular syntactic environments in directing children's attention to particular aspects of an observed scene. For instance, 24–30-month-old children are shown a pair of scenes on videotapes (e.g., Big Bird erect, forcing Cookie Monster into a squatting position and, on the other screen, Big Bird and Cookie Monster squatting together). Half the children hear a transitive sentence with a new (nonsense) verb ("Big Bird is gorping Cookie Monster") and half hear an intransitive sentence ("Big Bird and Cookie Monster are gorping," or "Big Bird is gorping with Cookie Monster"). The findings are that the children look significantly longer at the scene that matches the syntax—to causative scenes with transitive verbs and to noncausative scenes with intransitive verbs. This begins to show that children know something of the syntactic/semantic patterning in the language very early in the period when they are starting to acquire a productive verb vocabulary.

Notice that we have said nothing about how children might have acquired these quasisystematic links between clause structures and semantic interpretations. Perhaps some of them need not be learned, but may be available as default assumptions about language design (for discussion in this vein, see Pinker, 1987). Others surely must be acquired on the basis of specific exposure conditions, for they vary across the languages of the world. In the experiments that follow, we do not resolve or even address the problem of how the links are forged. We will show only that young children do conjecture partly new interpretations for verbs when these are heard in new syntactic environments. If they do so correctly, it follows that they understand something of the semantic/syntactic linkages, and make use of them in learning; though, to be sure, such findings do not answer to how the linkages were forged in the first place.

Summary and Prospectus

We have asserted that certain semantic properties are exhibited on the surface clause structures of ordinary speech. Moreover, we have reviewed the evidence that children can extract the surface structures from prosodic cues, and that— very early in the verb learning game—they recognize at least some of the correlations between the forms and the meanings. This evidence, taken together, indicates that even very young and linguistically quite uninformed learners meet the necessary preconditions for out language-learning hypothesis. It is therefore realistic to ask whether learners actually exploit this structural information in understanding the meanings of sentences. Particularly, we will ask here how a sentence which introduces a known verb into a novel syntactic environment is interpreted. That is, do children believe that new syntactic environments for verbs regularly add (or subtract) some semantic component to their interpretation?

Experiment 1

Method

Bowerman's evidence suggested that children sometimes extend the syntactic privileges for known verbs (e.g., *fall*) so as to extend their semantic properties. Our experimental question is the obverse one: Do children extend the semantic properties of known verbs in response to new evidence about their syntactic privileges? We asked whether presentation of an unattested transitive structure for an intransitive motion verb induced the learner to generate a causal interpretation; and if an unattested intransitive structure for a transitive motion verb induces the learner to remove the causal component.

For direct comparison, our test materials were designed to consist of the same semantic/syntactic structures whose spontaneous uses were investigated by Bowerman. The child subjects were asked to act out a variety of sentences containing motion verbs by manipulating toy animals, a procedure employed in many prior comprehension experiments (e.g., Roeper, 1982). Our primary interest was in sentences that violated the subcategorization requirements for the particular verbs used. Examples are *The zebra goes the lion* (an intransitive verb is placed in a transitive syntactic frame) and *The zebra brings* (a transitive verb in an intransitive frame).

Subjects. The subjects were 94 middle-class children, 42 girls and 52 boys, enrolled in preschools in and around Philadelphia. They were separated into three age groups: 51 2-year-olds, (26 boys, 25 girls, ranging from 2;4–2;11, mean of 2;9); 23 3-year-olds, (11 boys, 12 girls, ranging from 3;1–3;11, mean of 3;7); and 20 4-year-olds (15 boys, 5 girls, ranging from 4;1–4;11, mean of 4;4). All were native speakers of English.

Apparatus. The apparatus consisted of a toy Noah's ark. This ark and its contents (Noah and his wife, and a number of brightly painted wooden animals), along with a board that served as a stage, provided the medium in which the children could act out various sentences. While our primary interest was in ungrammatical sentences in which transitive verbs were placed in intransitive frames and vice versa, the children were also asked to act out

Table 5.1. Examples of Test Sentences

Frame	Grammatical	Ungrammatical
(1)NP V NP PP	The zebra brings the chicken next to the ark.	The elephant comes the giraffe towards the ark.
(2)NP V NP	The lion moves the kitty.	The zebra goes the lion.
(3)NP V PP	The zebra goes to the ark.	The lion puts in the ark.
(4)NP V	The elephant falls.	The zebra brings.

grammatical sentences using the same verbs and nouns. All of the subjects' responses were recorded on videotape.

Stimuli. The stimuli consisted of 42 sentences which the children were asked to enact. Two were pretest sentences (*The chicken rides the zebra*, and *The giraffe hits the elephant*), designed to familiarize the subjects with the situation and the task, and forty served as experimental sentences. The 40 experimental sentences were designed by fitting each of ten motions verbs into four sentences frame. Four of the verbs were transitive (*bring, take, push,* and *put*), four of them were intransitive (*come, go, fall,* and *stay*) and two (*move* and *drop*) were verbs that could legitimately appear in both transitive and intransitive frames.

The sentences were of four different structures: (1) NP V NP PP, (2) NP V NP, (3) NP V PP, and (4) NP V. Thus for the verbs *drop* and *move,* all of the sentences were grammatical; for the remaining verbs, two of the sentences were grammatical and two were ungrammatical. For example, *fall* is ungrammatical in frames (1) The lion falls the chicken onto the elephant and (2) The lion falls the chicken; and grammatical in frames (3) The lion falls off the ramp and (4) The lion falls. There was thus a total of 16 ungrammatical sentences and 24 grammatical one.[5] All sentences in the set had animate subjects (and the transitive sentences had animate direct objects as well), so as to remove the possibility that thematic roles were assigned on the basis of the animate/inanimate distinction. Table 5.1 presents examples of the test sentences, both grammatical and ungrammatical, for each frame. The complete list of sentences can be found in Naigles (1988).

All 40 experimental sentences were presented orally to the 3- and 4-year-old subjects in two sessions, each lasting about 15 minutes. The procedure had to be modified and shortened for the 2-year-olds since it proved impossible to have them return for a second session. As a result, they were run in two groups. One group ($N = 32$) was presented with 20 experimental sentences consisting of all ten verbs presented in Frames 2 and 3 (for a total of 8

---

[5] The four sentences BRING2, TAKE2. PUSH2, and PUT2 may be considered ungrammatical because of the absence of a prepositional phrase in the predicate; however, the judgment is not clear, and in any case is not central to the work described here.

ungrammatical and twelve grammatical sentences). A second group ($N = 19$) heard all 10 verbs presented in Frame 4, along with six filler sentences which were introduced to keep the total number of sentences which were introduced to keep the total number of sentences roughly equivalent to that of the first group of 2-year olds (for a total of 4 ungrammatical and 12 grammatical sentences).[6] The sentences were presented in two semi-random orders to the 3- and 4-year-olds, and in a single semi-random order to the 2-year-olds.[7]

Procedure. Each subject was tested separately, in a quiet room provided by the school. He or she was shown the ark, introduced to Noah and his wife, and asked to name each of the animals. If any animal was named incorrectly, the subject was immediately corrected; however, such mistakes were rare. Then the subject was told:

We're going to play a game, where I say something, and you show me how to do it with the animals!

The animals were placed off the stage, and the subjects were told to choose the one(s) they would need to act out each sentence. The two pretest sentences were then presented for the child to enact. These were designed to get the subjects in the "motion verb" mode; all were enacted correctly.

After this warm-up, presentation of the test sentences began. Each sentence was spoken by E and then immediately repeated by her. If there was a long pause with no action from S, E repeated the sentence once again and provided encouragement, saying "Just do what you think." Feedback after enactments was always positive (e.g., "good" or "OK"), regardless of what the child did. After each enactment, the animals were removed from the stage.

Coding

The subjects' enactments were coded upon reviewing the videotape. We should note at the outset that it would be quite paradoxical if we claimed that we could determine exactly what the stimulus sentences meant to our Ss by observing their enactments. Given our own introduction to this paper, we hold that observation of real-world events (in this case, enactments) cannot wholly or precisely determine the meanings of the verbs that the listeners have in mind (in this case, the construals of the child enactors). But our goals on the coding

---

[6] We never used Frame 1 (that is, NP V NP PNP, as in the The zebra brings the chicken next to the ark) for children in this age-group, since pilot tests showed consistent failure among two-year-olds on sentences of this type (whose three-argument structure is presumably the most complex of the ones here used).

[7] Order of presentation yielded no effect for the 3- and 4-year-olds. Owing to the well-known problems of testing and retaining 2-year-olds' data, we decided to present their sentences in only one order. This ensured that every 2-year-old who passed the "grammatical sentences" test (see Analysis section) could be used in our analysis.

are more modest than this, and are limited to what we really *can* observe: As will be described in detail just below, we coded only for whether the entities the child selected and manipulated were those mentioned in the stimulus sentences, for which among these entities seemed to be acting upon the other, and for whether the action roughly resembled the notion usually encoded by the verb. (Insofar as we — privately — believe that we know exactly how the children interpreted what they heard, our supposition is that we arrived at this belief state by observation enhanced by a little syntactic bootstrapping of our own.)

The coding scheme will first be described for enactments of the grammatical sentences and then for the ungrammatical ones. For ease of explication, examples used here are those that appear in Table 5.1.

Grammatical sentences. The enactment of each grammatical sentence was coded as either correct or incorrect according to the following criteria:

Frame 1: The zebra brings the chicken next to the ramp. To count as correct, the enactment of this sentence had to be such that the zebra was made to appear as the chicken's "bringer." The child might accomplish this by making the zebra push, carry, or move behind the chicken toward the ark; or by holding the zebra close to the chicken while only the chicken was actually moved to the ark. We coded this last action as causative because it shows that the subject has (correctly) analyzed the structure of the sentence as indicating that the patient, object of the sentence, is the one which is supposed to move.

Frame 2: The camel moves the kitty: The camel had to be displayed as the agent of the kitty's movement, with any of the same actions listed for the preceding sentences considered to be appropriate; that is, the lion being made to push, carry, move behind, or move with the kitty.

Frame 3: The zebra goes to the ark: The zebra must be made to move alone in the direction of the ark.

Frame 4: The lion falls: The lion had to be displayed as moving alone in a downward direction. The child could knock it over on the stage, or make it fall off the ramp, or off the ark itself.

Ungrammatical sentences. We classified the subjects' enactments of these sentences into three categories: (a) *Frame Compliance,* in which the subject obeys the semantic implications of the new subcategorization frame in which the verb appears rather than those of the verb itself; (b) *Verb Compliance,* in which the subject obeys the previously known semantic implications of the verb itself rather than those implied by the new frame in which the verb appears; and (c) *Other,* in which the enactment is "wrong" in some other way. Some examples will concretize these three enactment categories as they were applied to the four types of frames. (For more discussion and a complete list of the enactments that were counted as Frame Compliant, Verb Compliant, and Other, see Naigles, 1988.)

Intransitive verbs in transitive frames: Frame 1 (NP V NP PP) and 2 (NP V NP). Enactments were coded as Frame Compliant when a causative action was introduced into the motion characteristic of the verb. We considered the action as causative when the child treated the first NP of the sentence as the agent (that is, the cause) of the second NPs movement. As an example, take the ungrammatical sentence

*The elephant comes the giraffe.

This was scored as Frame Compliant if the child manipulated the elephant so as to make it push, carry, or move behind the giraffe. In all these cases, the elephant's action was such that it apparently made the giraffe move. We also scored the enactment as Frame Compliant if the child moved both animals together in the same hand, a response pattern often seen when the children enacted grammatical sentences such as *The zebra brings the chicken.*

The enactment was scored as Verb Compliant if the child manipulated the animals as that either the elephant or the giraffe moved alone, or if they both moved independently of one another (i.e., in separate hands); that is, if the relevant action was as required by come in an intransitive frame.

The enactment was coded as Other if it did not fit into either of the two preceding categories. The bulk of Other responses were enactments in which the child employed wrong movements (e.g., a vertical motion for come or no motion at all) or used the wrong animals. Occasional enactments suggested that the child misheard some part of the sentence, as when the elephant was made to stroke the giraffe repeatedly in a sentence containing *come* (that is, "come" might have been confused with "comb"). Though we coded such responses as Other, we will reconsider them in later discussion.

Transitive verbs in intransitive frames: Frame 3 (NP V PP) and 4 (NP V). Enactments of these sentences were coded as Frame Compliant when the first NP was cast as the performer of an action that was noncausative. As an example, take the sentence

*The zebra brings to Noah.

The enactment of this sentence was coded Frame Compliant if the child manipulated the zebra to make it move (alone) to Noah. In this enactment, the intransitive frame overrode the ordinary transitive meaning of the verb as such, as if "bring" were an intransitive verb such as *come*.

An enactment was coded as Verb Compliant when a new animal was introduced by the child to be the object of the action while the zebra became the agent. An example is an enactment in which the zebra was made to push a cat to Noah. Here, the transitive character of the verb (the subcategorization rules for *bring* demand a direct object) overrode the intransitive frame in which it appeared. As before, the enactment was coded as Other if neither of the two preceding categories were appropriate. In almost all cases, this was when wrong movements or wrong animals were used.

The reliability of the coding. The enactments for both the grammatical and ungrammatical sentences were initially coded by *E* (LGN). To determine the reliability of the coding procedure, another individual coded 10 percent of the videotaped enactments with the audio turned off. This sample consisted of the entire set of enactments by two 2-year-olds, two 3-year-olds, and two 4-year-olds. The reliability coder had no knowledge of the sentence to which the child responded. She coded these enactments by describing what she saw, using a detailed inventory of action descriptions (see Naigles, 1988). These descriptions were then classified into the three main categories Frame Compliant, Verb Compliant, and Other using the coding system, and compared to the original codings prepared by *E*. The results showed considerable agreement for both grammatical and ungrammatical sentences, with codings in agreement 93.3% and 88.8% of the time respectively.

Results and Discussion

Enactment of grammatical sentences. The first step in interpreting the data is to make sure that our subjects understood the task we set them. If they did, they should have been able to enact the grammatical sentences correctly, since they were all composed of nouns and verbs known to an average 2-year-old, and were all quite simple in structure. We therefore eliminated any subject who failed to enact at least 80% of the grammatical sentences correctly. Using this criterion, we eliminated no 4-year-olds, 3-year-olds, and 12 2-year-olds, thus leaving 20 4-year-olds (15 boys and 5 girls, with a mean age of 4;4), 20 3-year-olds (9 boys and 11 girls, with a mean age of 3;7), and 39 2-year-olds (20 boys and 19 girls, with a mean age of 2;9). Of the two-year-olds, 20 were in the group which heard sentences in Frame 2 and 3, while 19 were in the group which heard sentences in Frame 4 (as described in the Procedure section). The average percent correct for these subjects, for the grammatical sentences, was 93.4, 92.7, and 93.3 for the 4-, 3-, and 2-year-olds, respectively. We can thus conclude that the subjects in the final pool understood the task, and were able to carry it out correctly when structures were familiar ones.

Enactments of the ungrammatical sentences. Our major question concerns the enactment of ungrammatical sentences. If the children's interpretations of verbs are in line with the grammatical frames in which these verbs are usually heard rather than the frames of the novel test sentences, then the intransitive verbs (e.g., *come*) should be enacted noncausally and the transitive verbs (e.g., *bring*) should be enacted causally (a response pattern we have dubbed Verb

Table 5.2. Mean Percent Frame Compliant for each Age Group#

Frame	Two	Three	Four
(1) NP V NP PP	–	78.75	79.20
*The elephant comes the giraffe towards the ark.			
(2) NP V NP	69.15	70.45	71.65
*The zebra goes the lion.			

#Two-year-olds were not presented with ungrammatical sentences of the Frame 1 variety, since they were unable to enact grammatical sentences of this type. (The proportion of correct enactments by 7 2-year-olds tested during piloting on grammatical sentences of this type was 0.5.)

Compliance). But if the children derived their semantic interpretation of the verbs from the syntactic structure in which it appears in the stimulus sentence, as the syntactic bootstrapping hypothesis predicts, they should add a causal component when intransitive verbs occur in transitive frames and remove the causal component when transitive verbs occur in intransitive frames (a response pattern we have dubbed Frame Compliance).

Responses that could not be coded as either Frame Compliant or Verb Compliant, and were therefore coded as Other, were relatively rare, comprising about 11 percent of all responses. No single or systematic description can be given of these "other" responses; they did not differ as a function either of frame type or subject age. They were therefore omitted from the statistical analyses which follow. Thus all tabular presentations and analyses are based on the 89% of responses which were frame compliant or verb compliant.

Intransitive verbs in transitive frames (Frames 1 and 2) Table 5.2 presents the percentage of Frame Compliant enactments for intransitive verbs in transitive frames, collapsed across verbs, for each age group. The table shows that out of all enactments which could be coded as either causative or noncausative, at least 70% were causative, reliably more than would be predicted by chance. For Frame 1, the relevant t-values were 6.16 (df = 19, $p < .01$) and 5.07 (df = 19, $p < .01$), for the 4- and 3-year-olds, respectively (recall that 2-year-olds were not tested for this frame). The corresponding t-values for Frame 2 were 3.47 (df = 19, $p < .05$), 3.27 (df = 19, $p < .05$), and 3.27 (df = 19, $p < .05$), for the 4-, 3-, and 2-year-olds, respectively. The results were substantially the same though with somewhat lower levels of statistical significance, when the tests were conducted using verbs rather than subjects as the random variable.[8]

Inspection of Table 5.2 suggests that the probability of Frame Compliance

---

[8] Owing to the noncontinuous nature of the raw data, the statistical analyses were performed on arcsin transformations of the raw percentages. The tables, though, present the percentages in their untransformed state.

was virtually identical for all three age-groups. This suggestion is upheld by a one-way analysis of variance of the Frame 2 data for all three groups [$F(2,58) = .05$, $p = 1$]. A second analysis compared Frames 1 and 2 in the two older age-groups; while there was a suggestion of a Frame effect [$F(1,38) = 3.26$, $p < .10$], there was no trace of an effect of age [$F(1,38) = .02$, $p = 1$] or of an age/Frame interaction [$F(1,38) = 0.01$, $p = 1$].

These results indicate that children can deduce a causative semantic component for intransitive motion verbs when these are embedded in a transitive sentence frame. Moreover, they can do so when quite young—during their third year of life when they are just beginning to utter verbs in rudimentary sentences. A single presentation of a verb in a new frame—a verb which, after all, has been heard in other frames, with other interpretations, on literally thousands of previous occasions—is sufficient to produce a reliable shift in the interpretation.

Transitive verbs in intransitive frames (Frames 3 and 4). Do learners make the symmetrical shift (from a causative to a noncausative interpretation) when transitive verbs are used in intransitive frames? The findings from spontaneous speech errors are inconclusive on this point, with some investigators reporting that children will (Lord, 1979; Figueira, 1984) and others that they will not (Bowerman, 1983) overextend in this direction. The present study provides data based on the children's enactments when presented with ungrammatical sentences of the appropriate intransitive Frame types. For these sentences, the enactment was coded as Frame Compliant if the causal component of the verb was excluded. It was coded as Verb Compliant if the causal interpretation of the verb was maintained despite the intransitive frame in which it appeared.

Table 5.3 presents the percent of Frame Compliant enactments for the three age groups for Frames 3 and 4. Frame Compliance was elicited by Frame 3 (NP V PP, as in *the lion puts in the ark) but was much less clear for Frame 4 (NP V, as in *the zebra brings). Appropriate t-tests with subjects as the random variable showed that Frame 3 elicited Frame Compliance reliably more often than chance in all age-groups, yielding t-values of 3.07 (df = 19, $p < .05$), 2.32 (df = 19, $p < .05$), and 1.81 (df = 19, $p < .05$), for the 4-, 3-, and 2-year-olds, respectively. While the percent of Frame Compliant enactments for Frame 4 did not differ significantly from chance for the 3- and 4-year-olds, with t-values of -1.14 and -0.53 (df = 19, $p > .10$) respec-

Table 5.3. Mean Percent Frame Compliant for each Age Group#

Frame	Two	Three	Four
(3) NP V PP *The lion puts in the ark.	60.40	63.85	70.45
(4) NP V *The zebra brings.	65.37	40.00	44.55

tively, a significant difference was obtained for the two-year-olds (t = 2.08, df = 18, p < .05). Similar results were obtained in analogous analyses with verbs as the random variable.

A two-way analysis of variance of the data obtained for the 3- and 4-year-olds showed that Frame Compliance was significantly stronger for Frame 3 than for Frame 4 [F(1,38) = 28.39, p < .01]. There was no significant effect of Frame in the 2-year-olds, as indicated by a separate analysis of variance based on their data alone that showed essentially equal Frame Compliance for Frames 3 and 4. [F(1,37) = 0.30, p = 1]. Two additional analyses were conducted to compare the three age-groups separately in each of the two Frames. There was a suggestion of an age effect for Frame 4 [F(2,57) = 2.71, .10 > p > .05]; but no effect at all for Frame 3 [F(2,57) = 0.73, p > .10].

These various analyses provide evidence that while Frame 3 elicits Frame Compliance from all age-groups and to about the same degree, Frame 4 elicits Frame Compliance only from the 2-year-olds. The robust Frame Compliance finding for Frame 3 sentences suggest that the intransitive-Frame/noncausative-meaning link is in place in the third year of life. But the potency of this link is evidently diminishing rather than increasing as the child grows older, disappearing in the older children for Frame 4.

It appears that some frames elicit more of an effect than others, and that these effects diminish with age. To consider these factors further, we performed a second experiment, using adult subjects.

Experiment 2

The results of the preceding study suggested that the degree of Frame Compliance (that is, the willingness of the child to interpret a new form as indicating a new meaning component) depends on several factors. One is transitivity: It is easier to add a causative element to an intransitive verb (as in Frames 1 and 2) than to subtract that component from a transitive verb (as in Frame 3 and 4). Another probable factor is age, for the effect seems to diminish as the child grows older, at least for one frame. A final factor may be the degree to which the frame is elaborated. Specifically, the experimental sentences include some that contain a prepositional phrase (*PP;* that is, Frames 1 and 3), and some that do not (Frame 2 and 4).

To look at these factors more closely, we performed a second experiment using substantially the same procedure but adding a new age group: adults. We wanted to look at adult performance in this task for a number of reasons. The first is to establish what the competent user of a language does in the situation which confronted our learners; that is, how adults respond to perceived ungrammaticality in this situation. Adults' language knowledge has probably crystallized. They could not plausibly (as the children might) suppose that the new structures they are hearing are just ordinary ones that by happenstance they never heard before. Surely adults know (or think they know) what *bring* means, and they know the frames in which this verb occurs. A single discordant new sentence would be unlikely to affect their construals. By hypothesis, then, the adults would show more Verb Compliance than language-learning youngsters; that is, they would adjust the new form to fit the known meaning rather than adjusting the meaning to fit the form. In addition, adults allow us another look at what appeared in Experiment 1 to be an age effect, with 2-year-olds more Frame Compliant for one structure (Frame 4) than the older children. An adult population also allows us to take a closer look at the differential effect of the different frames. Comparisons between our 2-year-olds and the older *Ss* suffered because the 2-year-olds had to be run on a much abridged version of the experimental procedure (with fewer trials, and without Frame 1). No such problems arise for comparisons between adults and 3- and 4-year-olds. Finally, adult subjects allow a check on our interpretation of the child enactments. After all, the children were somewhat clumsy and unclear in how they moved the toys around the stage. If the coding used for their enactments was sufficient as well to describe the adult pantomimes, we would be surer of the validity of the original coding scheme.

Method

Subjects, apparatus, and stimuli. The subjects were 20 undergraduates at the University of Pennsylvania, 10 males and 10 females, who were paid for their participation in the experiment. They were run on the identical apparatus and presented with the identical stimuli as were the child subjects of Experiment 1.

Procedure. The procedure was virtually identical to that used in Experiment 1. To explain the use of the various toys, *Ss* were informed that they were to participate in an experiment that had also been conducted with children. They were told that some of the sentences might sound odd, but they were to enact them as best they could. *Ss* were specifically told to enact the sentences as they, adult speakers of English, saw fit, *not* as they suspected children might enact them (a precaustion adopted after one pilot subject enacted the sentences as he thought a schizophrenic person would). *Ss* were given the entire set of 40 sentences in one session which lasted about 15 minutes. The sentences were presented in one of two semi-random orders. As with the children, each sentence was spoken aloud by *E* after which the subject enacted it immediately. There was no need to repeat any sentences for the adults.

Coding. The adults' enactments were coded according to the same scheme described in Experiment 1. While the frequency of the various enactment types differed, there was complete overlap in the actual pantomimes. That is, every enactment produced by at least one adult was also produced by at least one child. To determine reliability, the codings of two adult subjects were checked using the same procedure described for Experiment 1. The codings were in agreement 97.5% of the time. (For further details, see the Coding section of Experiment 1.)

Results and Discussion

Table 5.4 presents the proportion of Frame Compliance for each of the four sentence types. For ease of comparison, these results are shown along with those obtained for the children in Experiment 1. Inspection of the table shows that the adults were much less Frame Compliant than were the children. For the adults, significant Frame Compliance was found only for Frame 1 [t (19) = 5.06, $p < .01$]. For Frame 2, the percent Frame Compliance was literally at a chance level, while for Frames 3 and 4, it was significantly *less* than chance (that is, the adults were reliably *Verb* Compliant) with t's of -2.38 (df = 19, $p < .05$) and -1.89 (df = 19, $p < .05$) respectively.

Our previous discussion suggested that Frame Compliance for the child subjects depends on the two factors that distinguish between the sentence frames: transitivity and prepositional-phrase elaboration. The effects of these factors for the adults is shown in Table 5.4 and highlighted by Figures 5.1 and 5.2. The role of transitivity is displayed in Figure 5.1, which shows the percent of Frame Compliance in transitive (Frames 1 and 2) and intransitive (Frame 3 and 4) frames for 3- and 4-year-olds and for adults. (The results from the 2-year-olds were excluded, since children at that age were unable to enact one of the sentence types—specifically Frame 1—even when it was presented in grammatical form.) As the figure shows, there was more Frame Compliance for transitive than for intransitive frames (with overall Frame Compliance percentages of 70.9 and 47.2 respectively).

The effect of Frame elaboration for the same three age groups is displayed in Figure 5.2, which shows the percent of Frame Compliance when a PP is (as in Frames 1 and 3) or is not (as in Frames 2 and 4) added to the frame. As the figure shows, there was more Frame Compliance when the frame was

Table 5.4. Mean Percent Frame Compliance as a Function of Frame Type and Age

Frame	Two	Three	Four	Adult
(1) NP V PP PP (*Transitive/elab.*) *The elephant comes the giraffe towards the ark.	—	78.75	79.20	75.85
(2) NP V NP (*Transitive/unelab.*) *The zebra goes the lion.	69.15	70.45	71.65	50.00
(3) NP V PP (*Intransitive/elab.*) *The lion puts in the ark.	60.40	63.85	70.45	30.40
(4) NP V (*Intransitive/unelab.*) *The zebra brings.	65.37	40.00	44.55	34.15

Frame Compliant Enactments
(Transitive and Intransitive Frames)

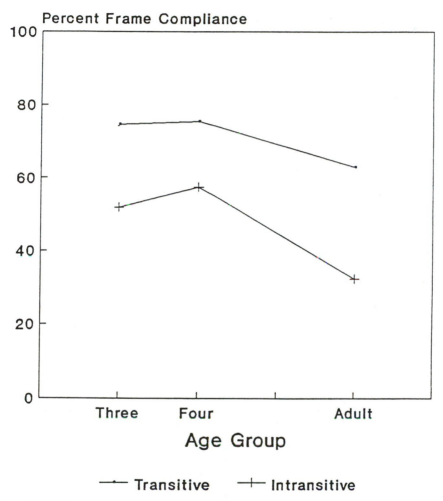

Figure 5.1. Frame Compliance for the Transitive and Intransitive Frames (Frames 1–2 and 3–4, respectively).

elaborated by the addition of a PP than when it was not (with overall frame compliance percentages of 67.0 and 51.3 respectively).

To determine the reliability of these effects, we conducted a three-way analysis of variance of the Frame Compliance results of the 3- and 4-year-olds of Experiment 1 and the adults of Experiment 2 with *age* (3,4 and adult), *transitivity* (Frames 1 and 2 vs. 3 and 4), and *frame elaboration* (Frames 1 and

Frame Compliant Enactments
(Elaborated and Unelaborated Frames)

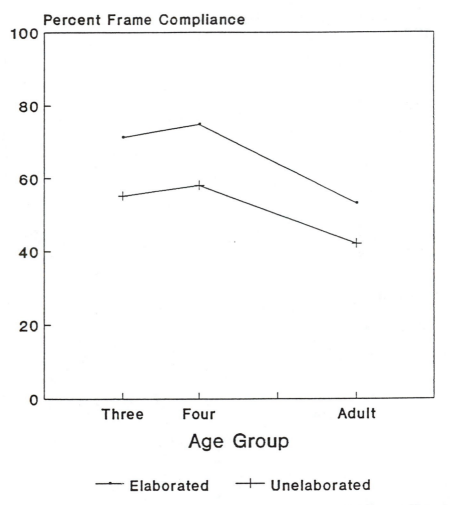

Figure 5.2. Frame Compliance for the Elaborated and Unelaborated Frames (Frames
1–3 and 2–4, respectively).

3 vs. 2 and 4) as the factors. There was a significant main effect for age
[$F(2,57) = 8.04$, $p < .001$],   for   transitivity   [$F = (1,171) = 36.37$,
$p < .001$], and for frame elaboration [$F(1,171) = 16.23, p < .001$], but there
were no significant interactions. In sum, subject age as well as two stimulus
variables (the transitive/intransitive distinction, and the presence/absence of a
PP) are reliably related to the degree of Frame Compliance.

Discussion of the Findings

We turn now to explanations of these experimental results.[9] Speaking most generally, the outcomes strongly support our general thesis: Language learners use structural properties of the speech stream as evidence for constructing the meanings of verb vocabulary items. Specifically, verbs vary in their subcategorization frames in ways that are consistent with the semantic distinctions among them. If children are sensitive to such distinctions, and expect them to be regular over the verb set, they should be inclined to conjecture a new meaning component when a verb is used in a new subcategorization environment, a procedure that we have called *syntactic bootstrapping*. To find out, we presented Ss with old verbs used in new syntactic environments. By hypothesis, these new environments imply systematic new meaning elements for these verbs. If this is so, the Ss should have interpreted the stimulus sentences in accord with the demands of the new structures (or *frames*), a behavioral style that we have dubbed Frame Compliance. This is exactly what we found. In about 70 percent of the interpretable responses, the children complied with the demands of new structures by deducing appropriate new interpretations.

Granting this overall generalization, we also found three factors that affected the Frame Compliance effect: Younger subjects were more Frame Compliant than older subjects; Frame Compliance was greater for new transitive frames than for new intransitive frames; and Frame Compliance was greater for PP-elaborated frames than for frames without PPs. We now turn to the question of how these subject and stimulus factors are related to the syntactic bootstrapping hypothesis.

The Effect of Age on Frame Compliance

Analysis of the results (and see Table 5.4) showed that Frame Compliance diminished as a function of age, with only 2-year-olds showing the effect for all frames to which they were exposed—including the shortest frame (the unelaborated intransitive, e.g., *The zebra brings)—and the adults showing

---

[9] In beginning, some apologia for the terms of explanation is perhaps in order. We will talk of our subjects, and thus of language learning and use more generally, as though the process were one of "noticing" regularities in the speech stream, "making conjectures" (or "forming hypotheses") about the system underlying these regularities, and the like. Of course, we do not mean to suggest a rational, self-conscious, explicit procedure when we do so. But it seems hard to posit a successful learning procedure for language, or a successful procedure for interpreting novel sentences, without positing that language users unconsciously do manipulate the input corpus (speech heard) and so uncover its systematic essence. Every proposal for explaining human language capacities that we know of explicitly or tacitly incorporates such a claim—whether that claim specifically is one of "relying on semantics," "organizing the observation of events," "examining the structure of sentences," and so on, and we ourselves have no way of avoiding such posits. But it should be understood that the terms that perforce we will use ("conjectures," "appreciates," "believes") are intended in their weakest and least conscious senses—and may overstate the rationality of learning procedures even so.

the effect only for the longest frame (the elaborated transitive, e.g., *The elephant comes the giraffe toward the ark).

The first response to findings in which the old behave differently from the young is to suppose that the young are lacking some relevant knowledge; that is, that what the older subjects are doing must somehow be "better" for this task setting. Yet throughout we have suggested that Frame Compliance (which *diminishes* over age) reflects a desireable stance for language learners; namely, to take syntactic information as a basis for semantic conjectures. Why then should the youngest subjects be behaving most regularly in this regard? Why should the tendency to be Verb Compliant increase over age, becoming the modal style of the adult subjects?

The decreasing potency of the frame in affecting the interpretation of the verb in fact follows directly from the syntactic bootstrapping hypothesis – and shows, in fact, that the old *do* have some information that the young do not have. As we urged in introducing this chapter, it seems likely that information from ongoing events can only partly constrain the child's conjecture about the verb meaning. Further refinements come from information about the structures in which the verb is observed to appear. At early stages of vocabulary learning, open-minded children ought to assume that not all structures have as yet been heard and therefore that certain properties of even common verbs (such as whether or not they can encode causation) may as yet be unknown to them. In this case, we hypothesized that they would make use of the structural information provided by the new frames that we gave: They would be Frame Compliant.

Even so, there must be a time in the acquisition of vocabulary when older children and adults feel warranted to believe that all the information relevant to a verb meaning – experiential and structural information – is in hand, and that therefore the construal is fixed. But if the meaning of the verb is fixed, so are its structural privileges of occurrence. This follows from the supposition that the structure is a projection of the semantic content. Thus for these more knowledgeable subjects, we hypothesized that they would perceive a novel structure for a common verb as just plain ill-formed – an anomalous usage, metaphor, or error (or experimental trick) which the listener must repair in order to understand. If the interpretation is fixed, and if the frame properties are a function of this interpretation, then the novel frame must be the locus of the anomaly, and therefore is to be repaired. This overriding of the implications of the ungrammatical frame is what we call Verb Compliance.

The beginnings of such a tendency are found in our child subjects. Though they were reliably Frame Compliant overall, they did enact a fair number of sentences Verb Compliantly (Table 5.4). Perhaps the most dramatic evidence that the children sometimes perceived, and tried to repair, anomalies were apparent mishearings of the verb uttered. These occurred only for ungrammatical (transitive) sentences containing *come* and *fall*. There were seven enactments (involving four child subjects) of these two verbs in ungrammatical (transitive) environments that were interpreted as "follow" and "comb"; and there were no such apparent mishearings of these verbs when they were presented in grammatical (intransitive) environments. It is therefore extremely likely that the "mishearing" was conditioned by the syntactic environment. Notice that by interpreting *fall* in "The lion falls the kitty" as a mispronunciation of "The lion follows the kitty" the subject is able to be Frame Compliant and Verb Compliant at the same time.

This tendency to take the stimulus sentence as frankly ungrammatical — and thus as not affecting the verb construal — becomes the dominant one for the adult subjects. They are overwhelmingly Verb Compliant. Various details of their responses suggest that their strategy is to repair what they have heard: To correct the sentence to a grammatical one, and then enact that. For example, adults often so enacted *The lion goes the kitty* as to show that they interpreted this as "The lion goes to the kitty." That is, *go* was treated Verb Compliantly as an intransitive item and the kitty was interpreted as a directional phrase — as though the speaker was assumed to have omitted the *to*. This strategy was rarely used by the child subjects. Moreover the adult Verb Compliant responses were quite variable. This same sentence was sometimes enacted by having the lion go, with the object NP (the kitty) simply ignored; or by having the lion and cat move together, ignoring the transitivity of the stimulus as presented. This inconsistancy suggests a strategy of repair (as opposed to interpretation of the stimulus "as it stands"; for fuller discussion of this characteristic response to perceived ungrammaticality, see Gleitman & Gleitman, 1970).

Supportive evidence for this interpretation of Frame Compliance in adults comes from collateral evidence on these same structures in an experiment we mentioned in earlier (Naigles et al., 1987). In that experiment, the subjects must interpret a wholly new verb ("gorp") while observing two entities either squatting together or else one causing the other to squat. Clearly, the observation (of either or both scenes) gives global information about the verb meaning. But observation cannot suffice to decide whether the verb is being used causatively or noncausatively, since both such interpretations are available from the observational evidence on one of the two screens on view. The decisive information is a spoken sentence (either "X is gorping with Y" or "X gorps Y") accompanying the scene. The finding is that both child and adult subjects in this setting make *equal* use of the syntactic information: They look at the screen which matches the syntax. In short, the clausal syntax of the verb constrains the interpretation unless (as with adults listening to "The lion comes the kitty"), subjects have rigidified prior beliefs about the verb meaning.

In sum, we believe that adults and children are alike in expecting that the structural facts about verbs line up regularly with their construals. For the child learners, the construals are not altogether fixed and therefore new structural information can lead to a revision of the construal itself: The form gives further information about the meaning. As the individual's vocabulary knowledge solidifies, it becomes less likely that somehow a component of the construal (and thus the structural constraints on use of the item) are still unknown. Hence the new structure heard is treated as anomalous, and the listener interprets the sentence Verb Compliantly, in accord with the known semantic facts.

The Effect of Frame Elaboration
Subjects in all age groups behaved Frame Compliantly more often when the frame included a locative or directional PP (e.g., *The elephant comes the giraffe toward the ark* or *The lion puts in the ark*) than when it did not (*The elephant comes the giraffe* or *The lion puts*). Why should this be so? Addition of the PP does not, strictly speaking, convert the ungrammatical instances to grammatical ones. Yet, if we are correct in our interpretations, the subject should behave Frame Compliantly only when she perceives the sentence as a grammatical one, which has to be dealt with as it stands rather than being (tacitly) repaired. How does the PP help?

One clue comes from the adult data of Experiment 2. Recall that a common strategy for adults when hearing "The zebra goes the lion" (Frame 2) was to enact 'The zebra goes to the lion' instead — as though they felt entitled to add a preposition to what they heard. This strategy accounts for many of their Verb Compliant responses to this structure. This strategy was necessarily excluded if a PP actually occurred in the stimulus (as in Frame 1 sentences such as *The zebra goes the lion toward the ark*). Restating, for this latter frame type the subject had configural information that inhibitied one false solution, and so Frame Compliance was considerably higher among adults (76%) for Frame 1 than for Frame 2 (50%).

However, the strategy just described cannot fully explain the effect that PP elaborations had in increasing Frame Compliance. Child subjects, unlike adults, rarely interpreted "The zebra goes the lion" as 'The zebra goes to the lion' (when Verb Compliant for this stimulus type, the children generally made the zebra go and ignored the lion, or they made the lion and the zebra go separately). Still, the youngsters too were more Frame Compliant when the stimulus contained a PP elaboration than when it did not.

It seems most likely that the additional semantic information in PPs simply makes it easier to take a guess at what the whole sentence might mean. These PPs, after all, characteristically express a path through space, and that path is named in the stimulus sentences (e.g., The lion comes the kitty *to/toward/next to/under/behind* the ark). This extra information certainly ought to constrain the interpretation of the whole sentence, making it a simpler matter to construct a coherent and Frame Compliant response. For one thing, the presence of path expressions secures that the verb in this awkward new environment is at least retaining its motion sense. In contrast, the bare transitive structure for *come* (*The lion comes the kitty*) allows much more latitude for doubting that even the motion component of the interpretation has been preserved.[10]

The Effect of Frame Type

Our subjects' comprehension performance suggests sensitivity to a crucial property of language design: The number of nominal phrases and the number of thematic roles in a clause must line up one-to-one (*theta-criterion;* see Chomsky, 1981). The structure of the clause follows directly from the logic of the predicate it contains. If the predicate, for example, *sneeze,* involves only its agent (the one who sneezes), then clauses containing this verb must have one and only one NP, rendering that role. Hence *John sneezes* is grammatical and interpretable, but *John sneezes a horse* is ungrammatical and takes at least some special effort to interpret. In contrast, if the predicate, for example, put, logically implicates an agent (the one who puts), an object (the thing that is put), and a place (where the thing is put), then clauses containing this verb require three NPs. Hence, *John put the book on the table* is grammatical and interpretable, but *John put* is odd and close to incomprehensible.

Sensitivity to this property by our subjects is shown by the fact that in their enactments, in effect they assigned a new thematic role to intransitive motion-verbs when these now appeared in transitive structures: If there is an extra NP, then some extra entity has to be involved in the idea expressed by the verb. Even the adult subjects were able to make this inference quite reliably (see again Table 5.4).

But the subjects' responses show more refined knowledge about the English clause than we have described thus far. Notice that, to succeed in this task, the subjects had to do more than realize *that* there was an extra NP and *that* it must be assigned some semantic role. They had to choose the correct NP (the subject NP) as agent and the correct one (the object NP) as experiencer (or theme), despite the fact that in prior hearing of these verbs it was the experiencer role that occupied subject position. That is, the experiencer in *The zebra falls* is the subject NP, but the experiencer in *The lion falls the zebra* is the object, while the subject becomes the agent. How did our *Ss* know how to make these reassignments?

The assignment of particular semantic functions (theta-roles) to particular NP positions in English sentences is systematic, especially for the kinds of motion verbs used in our experiments. To be sure, these assignments of roles to syntactic positions are not perfect (e.g., the subject NP in *John received a*

---

[10] It is also possible that the sheer structural bulk of the elaborated sentences increases their chance of being perceived as grammatical. Some data from Frazier and Fodor (1978) are informative in this regard: They found that very short sentences are often falsely judged to be ungrammatical by adult listeners. If this effect holds for our subjects, then the likelihood of Verb Compliance—by hypothesis, the response to perceived ungrammaticality—ought to be increased when the sentence is shorter (does not contain a PP) than when it is longer (does contain a PP).

letter from Mary is the goal of the action while the agent—the cause in this scenario—is the oblique object NP Mary), but they are quite regular even so. The subject of a transitive motion verb is overwhelmingly often the causal agent. Our child Ss behaved in accord with this strong probability about the semantic function to be assigned to a new NP position. When they heard "The lion falls the zebra", they assumed that the zebra fell owing to force exerted by the lion. In the elaborated frame condition (*The lion falls the zebra onto the ark*), even the adults characteristically recovered this interpretation. Overall, we have to credit Ss in our experiment, children and adults alike, with a rather subtle understanding of syntactic structure and the semantic logic that it implies.[11]

But a related finding that holds both for our child and adult subjects is not as easy to understand: the children were less Frame Compliant and adult subjects were not at all Frame Compliant—they were overwhelmingly Verb Compliant—when the stimulus sentence *removed* an argument position rather than adding an extra one. That is, *The zebra brings* and *The lion puts* in the ark were much more difficult to interpret Frame Compliantly than *The zebra goes the lion* or *The elephant comes the giraffe toward the ark*. This asymmetry has been observed in other investigations as well: Bowerman's children spontaneously and frequently uttered novel lexical causitives but rarely uttered novel intransitives (so-called "middle voice" verbs). Though not all studies achieve this result (for one exception, see Lord, 1979), most investigators of child spontaneous speech do record vastly more novel transitive-causatives than novel intransitive-noncausatives. Our comprehension findings again show such an asymmetry.

How is this perplexing asymmetry to be explained? We cannot be certain of the mechanism, but we will offer three related attempts to describe it: The first is from Bowerman (1983), the second is from Borer and Wexler (1987), and the third is our own attempt to extend the solutions of these prior investigators consequent on our experimental findings.

Word-formation rules that build structure but do not tear it down. Bowerman (1983) offers an excellent discussion of verb structures of the kinds we have been discussing, and a description of spontaneous innovations in children's speech. Roughly following Aronoff (1976), she asserts that the base ("underlying" or "deep structure") lexical description for verbs such as move and drop is intransitive, and that the transitive-causal form is derived by a quasi-productive lexical formation rule which, in effect, demotes the intran-

---

[11] Since this particular syntactic positioning of the agent phrase is nonuniversal cross-linguistically, it is rather reassuring (for the reality of the experiment as a whole) that knowledge of it seemed to vary with the subjects' age. Our 2-year-old Ss misassigned the positions of the agent and experiencer in these sentences almost 10 percent of the time (seven such errors in 80 enactments of transitive sentences), while errors of this kind were vanishingly rare for the older children (5 cases in 320 enactments) and adults (0 cases in 160 enactments).

sitive subject to object position and inserts the causal agent as subject (i.e., from a base form such as *The elephant drops*, the rule derives *The zebra drops the elephant*. This is a lexical process which *builds up* structure; that is, an NP position is added, and assigned the agent theta-role.

Why do children overgeneralize this process by applying it to new verbs for which they never heard this structure? For example, why does a child say "Don't eat the baby!" meaning 'Don't cause the baby to eat', that is, 'Don't feed the baby'? Bowerman holds that the process of building up structure in this way favored in the structure of the lexicon, that the child (tacitly, of course) realizes this, and thus feels entitled to extend the structural options in just this way.

Now how, according to Bowerman, would a new noncausal intransitive (e.g., *John knocks down*, the noncausal variant of *Bert knocks John down*) be created? The process would be more complicated. The learner would hear the causal transitive, "Bert knocks John down". He would then have to infer (correctly or not) that the lexical formation rule just discussed must have operated to create this transitive sentence; moreover, that the effects of this rule can now be undone, creating the novel intransitive by *tearing down* a part of the transitive structure. For example, the child might suppose *Someone knocked John down* had derived from an underlying intransitive *John knocked down* (meaning something like the short passive *John was knocked down*). According to Bowerman, this process of undoing the effects of a word-formation rule is relatively disfavored, accounting for the asymmetry in children's novel productions: They do exploit the word-formation rule that builds structure (adding the causative element), but they are disinclined to run the rule in reverse so as to undo its effects (deleting the causative element).

This description accounts for the observed asymmetry in lexical innovations very neatly, and by extension the asymmetry in our Frame Compliance results as well. Still, we are left with some explanatory puzzles. *Why* do children take the intransitive forms as the base, if they do? Why do they prefer building up to tearing down? Was this preference learned, or is it somehow "innate" (a part of the built-in wiring diagram for language)? Since these questions are unanswered, let us turn to another proposed solution for the asymmetry.

Two representations for intransitive sentences. Borer and Wexler's (1987) powerful solution to the observed asymmetry is technically different from Bowerman's. They relate the child's bias to an early misrepresentation of certain intransitive structures. To understand this explanation, consider the following difference in the subcategorization frames for two verb types:

Unaccusative verbs: This class of verbs, which includes such items as sneeze and giggle, appear only in intransitive structures. Their argument (theta-role), which appears as subject NP, represents the theme (the experiencer of the action or the person or thing affected by the action of the verb):

A1.   The doll giggles.
A2.   *Peter giggles the doll.
A3.   *The doll giggles Peter.

Ergative verbs: This class includes such items as *drop*, *move*, and *sink*. They represent the theme (the entity affected) in subject position when used intransitively, and in object position when used transitively. In the latter case, an agent is represented in the subject position.

B1.   The ship sinks.
B2.   John sinks the ship.
B3.   *John sinks. (on the relevant reading)

Notice that ergative verbs are the ones which add a causal reading when used transitively (B2 above), while unaccusative verbs do not (A2 is ungrammatical). According to Borer and Wexler, the distinction between the types is captured by a distinction in their underlying (D-structure) representations. Both the verb types have an intransitive (one argument) D(eep)-structure; this argument is represented in pre-verbal position for unaccusatives and in post-verbal for ergatives, thus:

> unaccusative underlying structure: NP V
> ergative underlying structure: V NP

Owing to the fact that English requires an overt subject NP, S(urface) structures for ergative verbs require either (a) moving the experiencer argument to subject position (as in B1) or (b) inserting an agent as subject (as in B2). Unaccusatives do not participate in such an operation; their D-structures are the same as their S-structures.

According to Borer and Wexler, the young child's problem arises because she has represented all intransitive verbs in the same way (as unaccusatives), so that any operation which applies to some intransitives applies to them all.[12]

---

[12] Note that we are giving capsule sketches of the Bowerman and Borer/Wexler solutions here, omitting many important technical details and some ancillary substantive assumptions about the primitive grammar and lexicon. But one detail from Borer and Wexler should be mentioned, for it gives their solution its potential power: They hypothesize that ergative representations are missing owing to the fact that young children cannot form A-chains; thus, if they had an operation moving the NP of an ergative verb, they would not be able to recover its interpretation because the NP could not be bound to its trace. We should note also that there is a third approach to understanding the child's spontaneous overgeneration of the structures we are considering, from Lord (1979). As we have mentioned, Lord's child subjects often uttered novel middle-voice verbs, and so she predicts no asymmetry. But we agree with Bowerman (1983) that novel intransitives are quite rare, and that those that do occur are generally built on another model (which we will discuss presently), For example, a child may say "I beat!", but when he does so, the context usually shows that he means "I won" (that is, *I beat some unmentioned party*), not *I was beaten*. Therefore the asymmetry in speech innovation as between lexical causatives and middle-voice intransitives, and our concordant finding for comprehension, require explanation.

Having noticed the relationship between B1 and B2 for common verbs such as *ove* and *rop*, the child postulates the same relationship between A1 and A2, just because she thinks that the intransitives are all the same. As a result, she will overgeneralize lexical causatives (for instance, saying "Daddy giggled me"). The child does not run this operation in reverse, creating novel intransitives, because while the grammar allows the addition of an agent θ-role in subject position, it prohibits the deletion of any θ-role.

As does Bowerman, Borer and Wexler bring some powerful theoretical apparatus (and internal linguistic evidence) to bear as support for their claims (see, in this regard, footnote 13). But their solution — again, like Bowerman's — requires some strong assumptions about language learning that are not self-evident. Particularly, what criterion (other than the observed asymmetry itself) shows that learners select the intransitive form rather than the transitive form as the base configuration? How do learners arrive unerringly at this solution, if they do? And how could it be demonstrated that they do?

An intolerable ambiguity. Though we cannot fully resolve the explanatory problems left open by the analyses just described, we want to suggest one further factor (also discussed by Bowerman, 1983) that may explain why children utter and understand novel causative transitives ("She fell that on me") more often than they utter and understand novel noncausative intransitives ("John knocked down"). To do so, we must consider yet another kind of verb that occurs both transitively and intransitively.

Unergative verbs (such as *see*, *read*, and *eat*), like ergatives, occur both intransitively and transitively. But whether transitive or intransitive, their subjects represent the agent. The object NP, if it occurs, represents the theme:

C1.   John eats.
C2.   John eats the frog.
C3.   *The frog eats. (on the relevant reading)

Middle-voice sentences like C3 means something close to *The frog is eaten* are marginal at best in English though they are acceptable to varying degrees if accompanied by an adverbial phrase (e.g., *This frog eats well* or *This book reads like a Gothic novel*).

Consider now the difference in entailment relations between transitive and intransitive sentences for ergatives and unergatives. Ergatives uttered in transitive contexts entail that their object NP is the one who performs the intransitive act (If *John sinks the ship*, then *The ship sinks*). Unergatives uttered in transitive contexts entail that their subject NP is the one performs the intransitive act (*If John eats the frog*, then *John eats*).

Not surprisingly, English has almost no verbs which participate in both the ergative and unergative patterns. The only counterexample we know of are the verbs of cooking, which are ambiguous as intransitives for just this reason: If one hears that *Mother is baking in the kitchen*, one doesn't know whether to wash one's hands for dessert or to open the window. To achieve something like the meaning C3, English requires an overt marker (The frog is *eaten*, The frog eats *easily*, The frog *makes good eating*). We suggest that if the language generally allowed both C1 and C3 readings for all verbs (as it does for cook and broil), with no differential marking, the level of ambiguity among spoken intransitives would be intolerable.

The question is how this idea, if true, bears on the observed paucity in youngsters' speech of novel intransitives, and the increased Verb Compliance in our studies for these same formats. Consider our experimental situation. The subject hears a transitive verb used intransitively for the first time in her experience, for example, *The zebra brings*. She is in something of a pickle if she attempts to behave Frame Compliantly. Is it an unergative, hence meaning that the zebra is bringing (something) or an ergative, meaning that zebra gets brought (somewhere)? We suggest that *Ss* tacitly recognize this problem, that is, are confused about how to interpret the structure.[13] That is, it is unclear just what the appropriate Frame Compliant response should be. Hence, the subjects are inclined to retreat to a strategy of repairing the syntax rather than accepting it. They behave Verb Compliantly by picking up some extra animal (say, the horse) and having the zebra bring *it*.

To summarize: Bowerman has reported an asymmetry in children's novel constructional behavior. They often utter novel lexical causitives but rarely utter novel noncausal intransitives. Though not all authors report this asymmetry, the evidence favoring it is pretty good. And that evidence gains more documentation from the experimental findings we have reported: Our child subjects readily understand novel transitives as causatives, and have trouble interpreting novel noncausal intransitives. Bowerman assigns this asymmetry to a postulated constraint on word-formation rules: Lexical operations build structure but do not tear it down. Borer and Wexler offer a similar (though technically distinct) proposal: that the addition of theta-roles but not deletion of theta-roles is permissible in S-structures. We accept these

---

[13] To be sure, subjects do sometimes behave Frame Compliantly for this structure, especially in the elaborated version containing a PP. Unfortunately, we cannot really tell whether they are following the ergative or accusative model when they do so, consider the stimulus The zebra put. Verb Compliance in this case is having the zebra take something else not mentioned in the sentence (say, the horse) and putting that horse somewhere. The Frame Compliant response is to deal with the sentence as involving its single overt argument (the zebra), rather than by importing a horse to serve as a second argument. For *put,* the subjects take the toy zebra in hand and move it forward in space, stopping the motion short someplace. But we do not know from this response style whether the subject has in mind 'a zebra putting' (Type C) or 'putting a zebra' (Type B). This is because we don't know whether the subject envisages himself as a part of the enactment (as the one who puts the zebra), or whether he is rendering the inalienable act of putting, performed by a zebra (since the zebra is only a toy, willy-nilly the child has to move it, whatever her conceptual intention). To be sure, subjects often asked "Puts what!?" before carrying out the enactment, suggesting that they opt for the Type C model, which is by far the more frequent in English. But we have no sure knowledge that this is so.

proposals as excellent and informative descriptions of the observed asymmetries in children's creation and appreciation of novel structures. But we remained mystified as to *why* the lexicon was organized in conformity with these postulated principles. Therefore we suggested a factor that may be prolegomenon to an explanation: Transitive verbs are not freely "intransitivized," because there are two models (unergative and ergative) for how to do so, only one of which (cooking and baking aside) is correct for any single verb. Not knowing how to make the choice, the child avoids innovative structures for these verbs and is at some disadvantage in interpreting them on first hearing.

We conclude that children as young as two years of age realize that each nominal position encodes a thematic role, and have a good deal of language-specific knowledge about which arrangements and case markings are assigned to each of these roles. They show some tendency to utter known verbs in novel syntactic environments, as a consequence of this knowledge (cf. Bowerman, 1982), though a number of factors interact to limit the frequency and scope of such spontaneous syntactical innovations. And their strong inclination is to reinterpret the meaning of verbs in compliance with new frame demands, upon a single exposure. This is despite their voluminous experience with these same verbs in other syntactic environments, and therefore with partly different interpretations.

We do not suppose that the adult subjects of Experiment 2 have somehow given up the requirement that the meanings and forms of language line up in a coherent way. They differ from the children largely by what they make of an observed mismatch of form and meaning, such as occurred in our stimulus materials. Since they are entitled to firm conviction about the construals of the simple verbs used in the experiment, they respond to the odd sentences by bringing the forms into alignment with the verb meaning rather than, like the children, bringing the verb meaning into alignment with the forms.

Conclusions

Let us return now to the main theoretical burden of this work. We hold, with many others, that the information available from inspection of the real-world contingencies for verb use, *taken alone,* is too variable and degenerate to fix the construals. Therefore there must be an additional convergent source of evidence that the child exploits in constructing a mental lexicon. One such potential source resides in the structural privileges of occurrence for the meaningfully distinct verb items. The experiments we have presented provide an initial basis for believing that learners actually exploit this evidentiary source: that they will bootstrap meaning from form ("syntactic bootstrapping") just as — as many prior investigators have shown — they will bootstrap form from meaning ("semantic bootstrapping"). Our subjects did reliably add a causative meaning-element to motion verbs on first observing that these verbs can appear in transitive structures.

Though we find these results suggestive of a syntactic-deductive procedure for amplifying and constraining observational evidence, it is important to point out that this initial result is rather narrow. For one thing, the result pertains to a single extension (the causative) for verbs whose meanings are otherwise well known to the subjects. However, other investigators have provided observational and experimental evidence for productive lexical rules pertaining to passive verbs (Pinker, Lebeaux, & Frost, 1987), dative verbs (Gropen, Goldberg, & Pinker, 1986), Figure/Ground structures (Bowerman, 1982), and S-complement verbs (roughly, the distinction between verbs of motion/location and verbs of perception/cognition; Landau and Gleitman, 1985). Thus the range within which children have been shown to appreciate syntactic/semantic relations is considerably broader than the causative structure investigated in the present experiment.

More difficult in the present context, no one, including ourselves, has a very good idea of how coarse or fine the relationship between clause structure (that is, subcategorization frames) and verb meanings may be. Many psychologists have suggested that such relationships are so refined and regular as to take the mystery out of the acquisition of language. Linguists have usually resisted this kind of claim, largely because there seem to be lots of counterexamples: There are many verbs whose meaning seem quite alike and yet which differ in their subcatorization privileges, and there are many verbs whose meanings are quite different and yet which overlap quite closely in their subcategorization privileges. Worse, cross-linguistic comparison reveals variation in the devices used to map between the syntactic forms and the conceptual structures; and some variation in the mappings as well. That is, the linking rules, if real, are not always the same ones, raising the spectre of accounting for their learning. We turn now to consideration of these inconvenient facts.

Where Could the Correspondence Rules Come From?

The weakest link in both the semantic bootstrapping and syntactic bootstrapping proposals has to do with where the appreciation of the presumed correspondence comes from. Learners in possession of the means for parsing (Gleitman & Wanner, 1982) and confronted with an utterance database with refined correspondences between the syntax and the semantics (Jackendoff, 1983; Fisher, Gleitman, & Gleitman, 1991), still can't *use* these correspondences for learning if they don't know what they are. Since some of these correspondence rules vary cross-linguistically (Talmy, 1985), it is not possible to say that the learner is provided with all of them by nature—as part of the language faculty. Along with other investigators, however, we suggest that there is sufficient cross-linguistic similarity in these linking rules to get the learning procedure started. For instance, the best guess from cross-linguistic inquiry is that, in all languages, the number of NPs in a sentence at the surface is a straightforward function of the logic of the verb concept. And as Pinker, Lebeaux, and Frost (1987) have discussed, there is an overwhelming tendency, cross-linguistically, for agents to appear as subjects and themes as direct objects, with other arguments appearing as the oblique cases. These very general tendencies across languages might be the reflexes of the default suppositions made by word and syntax learners: Those correspondence rules that are conjectured by learners, in the absence of disconfirmatory data.

No one, to our knowledge, has stated how these rudimentary presuppositions about syntax/semantic correspondences might serve as a sufficient basis for setting in motion so powerful a bootstrapping procedure as we, and others, have proposed—either for acquiring the semantics "from" the syntax or for acquiring the syntax "from" the semantics. In this chapter, we have only added to the evidence *that* the children use syntactic evidence, not for how they positioned themselves to do so. Clearly, the topic of how correspondence rules develop cries out for investigation, and has not been resolved or even addressed by us. Nevertheless, we should reiterate that evidence for use of language-specific correspondence rules *at the very inception of verb vocabulary acquisition* has been demonstrated quite conclusively in the work of Hirsh-Pasek and Golinkoff: Seventeen-month-old children know who is to be tickling whom if they hear "Big Bird tickles Cookie Monster." In the present experiment, what has been shown for 2-, 3-, and 4-year-olds is that new evidence about a verb's structure (*The lion comes the elephant*) will be evaluated in accord with such correspondence rules.

Linking the Linguistic and Extralinguistic Evidence

We have argued that the child verb learner exploits a general correspondence of syntax to semantic/conceptual structure. Specifically, we supposed that a two-argument (or two-NP, transitive) structure can encode a causal act, while a one-argument structure cannot. This is true, or close to true, but it surely doesn't follow that two-NP structures uniformly—or even most cases—encode causal events. *John sees Mary* doesn't mean that John causes Mary to see; rather, it means that John sees to (the goal of) Mary (Gruber, 1968). This path or goal interpretation is, for most verbs, encoded in the surface form by use of a PP construction (e.g., John looks *at* Mary), but is implicit for the case of *see*. So see is a counterexample both to the claim that transitive structures describe causative relations, and to the claim that paths and goals are described by PPs in English. As Gruber discussed, it is certainly possible to represent this exceptional case in a linguistic lexicon. But this should be cold comfort to learners if, as we hold, they are relying on surface evidence as a clue to interpretation. In short, the obvious existence of such counterexamples forces us to ask how these could be resolved by learners. If they really rely on syntactic information, they must be supposed to have means for recovering from the kind of error suggested by the case of see.

Part of the child's presumptive difficulty in this case can be resolved by the use of cross-cutting syntactic evidence. In order to learn, the child must examine the full range of syntactic environments in order to recover the interpretation of a verb: It is the set of frames licensed for a verb, not any one of them alone, that can help the child converge on the verb meaning. For example, as Gruber pointed out, there is considerable syntactic overlap between the verb *see* and verbs of physical motion (e.g., appearance with a wide variety of locative PP expressions), not surprising for a verb which describes a spatial perception. But there is also considerable evidence on the surface syntax that *see* is a mental-state verb. For example, mental-state verbs such as *see* and *hear* occur with sentential complements (*Let's see if Granny is home*) while verbs of physical motion do not (**Let's give if Granny is home*). It is possible to suppose that the object/theme is not the entity that moves once it is determined that the verb does not encode physical motion (though it encodes spatiality) in the first place. Thus the learner examining surface forms has ways of recovering from the (partially) exceptional encoding of verbs like see.

And of course the child has a converging source of evidence, in the external contingencies of use of each term. The child who attends to syntactic environments is certainly not ignoring the co-occuring extralinguistic environments (see Landau & Gleitman, 1985). Plausibly, learners can observe that when it is predicated by the adult speaker that *John sees Mary*, Mary does not (or need not) move.

As we see it, there is no effective procedure for learning the word meanings *solely* by inspection of syntactic environments. One reason is that many semantic properties are not and could not be syntactically encoded in the first place (e.g., manner, for discussion, see Fisher et al., 1991). Another is that, as we just discussed, there are plenty of quirks and complications in the syntactic encodings themselves. But at the same time, neither is there an effective procedure for learning the word meanings solely from observation of the extralinguistic world. This is partly because there are indefinitely many linguistic-conceptual descriptions for any single object or scene, and partly because much of what language describes — such as thoughts and wishes and causes — is closed to literal observation.

In consequence, the child confronts the problem of acquiring a verb lexicon from two imperfect databases. Both situations (extralinguistic observation) and utterances (linguistic observation) provide only probabilistic evidence for the determination of verb meanings. Yet we know that children acquire categorical (or close to categorical) knowledge of the verb lexicon. Our hypothesis is that they succeed by playing off these two imperfect databases against each other, seeking the simplest fit between them.

References

Acredolo, L. P., & Evans, D. (1980). Developmental changes in the effects of landmarks on infant spatial behavior. *Developmental Psychology, 16,* 312–318.

Aronoff, M. (1976). *Word formation in generative grammar.* Cambridge, MA: MIT Press.

Billman, D. (1988). *Clustered correlations in rule and category learning: Mastering a miniature noun subcategory system.* Unpublished manuscript, University of Pennsylvania, Dept. of Psychology.

Bloom, L. (1970). *Language development: Form and function in emerging grammars.* Cambridge, MA: MIT Press.

Borer, H., & Wexler, K. (1987). The maturation of syntax. In T. Roeper & E. Williams (Eds.), *Parameters and linguistic theory* (pp. 123–172). Dordrecht: Reidel.

Bowerman, M. (1974). Learning the structure of causative verbs: A study in the relationship of cognitive, semantic, and syntactic development. *PRCLD, 8,* 142–178.

Bowerman, M. (1977). The acquisition of rules governing "possible lexical items:" Evidence from spontaneous speech errors. *PRCLD 13,* 148–156.

Bowerman, M. (1982). Evaluating competing linguistic models with language acquisition data: Implications of developmental errors with causative verbs. *Quaderni di Semantica, 3,* 5–66.

Braine, M. D. S. (1971). On two types of models of the internalization of grammar. In D. I. Slobin (Ed.), *The ontogenesis of grammar: A theoretical symposium* (pp. 153–188). New York: Academic Press.

Brown, R. (1957). Linguistic determinism and parts of speech. *Journal of Abnormal and Social Psychology, 55,* 1–5.

Brown, R. (1973). *A first language.* Cambridge, MA: Harvard University Press.

Chomsky, N. (1981). *Lectures on government and binding.* Dordrecht: Reidel.

Clark, E. (1987). The principle of contrast: A constraint on language acquisition. In B. MacWhinney (Ed.), *Mechanisms of language acquisition* (pp. 1–34). Hillsdale, NJ: Erlbaum.

Figueira, R. (1984). On the development of the expression of causativity: a syntactic hypothesis. *Journal of Child Language 11,* 109–127.

Fillmore, C. (1968). Lexical entries for verbs. *Foundations of Language, 4,* 373–93.

Fisher, C., Gleitman, H., & Gleitman, L. R. (1991) Relations between verb syntax and verb semantics: on the semantic content of subcategorization frames. *Cognitive Psychology, 23,* 331–392

Fodor, J. D. (1985, October 25–27). *Why learn lexical rules?* Paper presented at the 10th Annual Boston University Child Language Conference, Boston, MA.

Frazier, L., & Fodor, J. D. (1978). The sausage machine: A new two-stage parsing model. *Cognition, 6,* 291–325.

Gleitman, L. R., & Gleitman, H. (1970). *Phrase and paraphrase: Some innovative uses of language.* New York: Norton.

Gleitman, L. R., Gleitman, H., Landau, B., & Wanner, E. (1987). Where learning begins: Initial representations for language learning. In F. Newmeyer (Ed.), *The Cambridge Linguistic Survey* (Vol. 3). Cambridge: Cambridge University Press.

Gleitman, L. R., & Wanner, E. (1982). Language acquisition: The state of the state of the art. In E. Wanner & L. R. Gleitman (Eds.), *Language acquisition: The state of the art* (pp. 150–193). Cambridge: Cambridge University Press.

Gold, E. (1967). Language identification in the limit. *Information and Control, 10,* 447–474.

Grimshaw, J. (1981). Form, function, and the language acquisition device. In C. L. Baker & J. J. McCarthy (Eds.), *The logical problem of language acquisition* (pp. 165–182). Cambridge MA: MIT Press.

Grimshaw, J. (1983). Subcategorization and grammatical relations. In A. Zaenen (Ed.), *Subjects and other subjects.* Indiana University Linguistics Club.

Gropen, J., Goldberg, R., & Pinker, S. (1986, October 17–19). *Constrained productivity in the acquisition of the locative alternation.* Paper presented at the Boston University Conference on Language Development, Boston, MA.

Gruber, J. S. (1968). Look and see. *Language, 43,* 937–47.

Hirsh-Pasek, K., Golinkoff, R., DeGaspe-Beaubien, F., Fletcher, A., & Cauley, K. (1985). *In the beginning: One-word speakers comprehend word order.* Paper presented at Boston University Child Language Conference, Boston, MA.

Hirsh-Pasek, K., Kemler Nelson, D., Jusczyk, P., Wright-Cassidy, K., Druss, B., & Kennedy, L. (1987a). Clauses are perceptual units for young infants. *Cognition, 26,* 269–286.

Hirsh-Pasek, K., Kemler Nelson, D. G., Jusczyk, P. W., Woodward, A., Piwoz, J., & Kennedy, L. (1987b, April). *The perception of cues to major phrasal units by prelinguistic infants.* Poster presented at the Society for Research in Child Development, Baltimore, MD

Jackendoff, R. (1972). *Semantic interpretation in generative grammar.* Cambridge: MIT Press.

Jackendoff, R. (1983). *Semantics and cognition.* Cambridge: MIT Press.

Landau, B., & Gleitman, L. R. (1985). *Language and experience: Evidence from the blind child.* Cambridge: Harvard University Press.

Levin, B. (1985). Lexical semantics in review: An introduction. In B. Levin (Ed.), *Lexical semantics in review* (Lexicon Project Working Papers, 1). Cambridge, MA: MIT Center for Cognitive Science.

Lord, C. (1979). "Don't you fall me down:" Children's generalizations regarding cause and transitivity. *PRCLD, 17,* 81–89.

Markman, E., & Hutchinson, J. (1984). Children's sensitivity to constraints on word meaning: taxonomic vs. thematic relations. *Cognitive Psychology, 16,* 1–27.

Morgan, J. (1986). *From simple input to complex grammar.* Cambridge: MIT Press.

Naigles, L. (1988). *Syntactic bootstrapping as a procedure for verb learning.* Unpublished doctoral disseration, University of Pennsylvania, Philadelphia, PA.

Naigles, L., Hirsh-Pasek. K., Golinkoff, R., Gleitman, L. R., & Gleitman, H. (1987, October 23–25). *From linguistic form to meaning: Evidence for syntactic bootstrapping in the two-year-old.* Paper presented at the 12th Annual Boston University Child Language Conference, Boston, MA.

Pinker, S. (1984). *Language learnability and language development.* Cambridge: Harvard University Press.

Pinker, S. (1987). *Resolving a learnability paradox in the acquisition of the verb lexicon* (Working Paper 17). Cambridge, MA: MIT Lexicon Project.

Pinker, S., Lebeaux, D., & Frost, A. (1987). Productivity and constraints in the acquisition of the passive. *Cognition, 26,* 185–267.

Quine, W. V. O. (1960). *Word and object.* Cambridge: MIT Press.

Read, C., & Schreiber, P. (1982). Why short subjects are harder to find than long ones. In E. Wanner & L. R. Gleitman (Eds.), *Language acquisition: The state of the art* (pp. 78–101). Cambridge: Cambridge University Press.

Rescorla, L. (1980). Overextension in early language development. *Journal of Child Language, 7,* 321–36.

Roeper, T. (1982). The role of universals in the acquisition of gerunds. In E. Wanner & L. R. Gleitman (Eds.), *Language acquisition: The state of the art* (pp. 267–289). Cambridge: Cambridge University Press.

Rosch, E. (1978). Principles of categorization. In E. Rosch & B. Lloyd (Eds.), *Cognition and categorization.* Hillsdale, NJ: Erlbaum.

Smith, E., & Medin, D. (1981). *Categories and concepts.* Cambridge: Harvard University Press.

Spelke, E. (1982). Perceptual knowledge of objects in infancy. In J. Mehler, E. C. T. Walker, & M. Garrett (Eds.), *Perspectives on mental representations.* Hillsdale, NJ: Erlbaum.

Talmy, L. (1975). Semantics and syntax of motion. In J. Kimball (Ed.), *Syntax and semantics* (Vol. 4). New York: Academic Press.

Talmy, L. (1985). Lexicalization patterns: Semantic structure in lexical forms. In T. Shopen (Ed.), *Language typology and syntactic description* (pp. 57–149). Cambridge: Cambridge University Press.

Wasow, T. (1985). Postscript. In P. Sells (Ed.), *Lectures on contemporary syntactic theories.* Stanford: CLSI.

Wexler, K., & Romney, A. K. (1972). Individual variations in cognitive structures. In *Multidimensional scaling: Theory and applications in the behavioral sciences, Vol. 2, Applications.* New York: Seminar Press.

Wexler, K., & Manzini, R. (1987). Parameters and learnability in binding theory. In T. Roeper & E. Williams (Eds.), *Parameters and linguistic theory* (pp. 41–76). Dordrecht: Reidel.

6

Competence and Performance in Child Language*

Stephen Crain

University of Connecticut and
Haskins Laboratories

Janet Dean Fodor

Graduate Center
City University of New York

Introduction

This chapter presents the results of our recent experimental investigations of a central issue in linguistic theory: Which properties of human language are innately determined? There are two main sources of information to be tapped to find the answer to this question. First, universal properties of human languages are plausibly (even if not necessarily) taken to be innately determined. In addition, properties that emerge in children's language in the absence of decisive evidence in their linguistic input are reasonably held to be innate. Clearly, it would be most satisfactory if these two diagnostics for what is innate agreed with each other. In some cases they do. For example, there is a universal principle favoring transformational movement of phrases rather than of lexical categories, for example, topicalization of noun phrases but not of nouns. To the best of our knowledge children abide by this principle; they may hear sentences such as *Candy, you can't have now,* but they don't infer that nouns can be topicalized. If they did, they would say things like *Vegetables, I won't eat the.* But this is not an error characteristic of children. Instead, from the moment they produce topicalized constructions at all, they apparently produce correct NP-topicalized forms such as *The vegetables, I won't eat.*

In recent years, this happy convergence of results from research on universals and research on acquisition has been challenged by experimental studies reporting various syntactic failures on the part of children. The children in these experiments are apparently violating putatively universal phrase structure principles or constraints on transformations. Failure to demonstrate early knowledge of syntactic principles is reported by Jakubowicz (1984), Lust (1981), Matthei (1981, 1982), Phinney (1981), Roeper (1986),

* This research was supported in part by NSF Grant BNS 84–18537, and by a Program Project Grant to Haskins Laboratories from the National Institute of Child Health and Human Development (HD-01994). The studies reported in this chapter were conducted in collaboration with several friends and colleagues: Henry Hamburger, Paul Gorrell, Howard Lasnik, Cecile McKee, Keiko Murasugi, Mineharu Nakayama, Jaya Sarma, and Rosalind Thornton. We thank them for their permission to gather this work together here.

Solan and Roeper (1978), Tavakolian (1978, 1981), and Wexler and Chien (1985). Some explanation is clearly called for if a syntactic principle is respected in all adult languages but is *not* respected in the language of children.

Assuming that the experimental data accurately reflect children's linguistic competence, there are several possible responses to the unaccommodating data. The most extreme would be to give up the innateness claim for the principle in question. One might look for further linguistic data which show that it isn't universal. Or one might abandon the hypothesis that all universal principles are innate. For instance, Matthei (1981) obtained results that he interpreted as evidence that universal constraints on children's interpretation of reciprocals are learned, not innate. However, this approach is plausible only if one can offer some other explanation (e.g., functional explanation) for why the constraints should be universal. But this is not always easy; as Chomsky (1986) has emphasized, many properties of natural language are arbitrary and have no practical motivation.

A different response to the apparent failure of children to respect constraints believed to be innate is to argue that the constraints are as yet inapplicable to their sentences. The claim is that as soon as a child's linguistic analyses have reached the level of sophistication at which a universal constraint becomes relevant, then that constraint will be respected. For example, Otsu (1981) has argued that children who give the appearance of violating a universal constraint on extraction may not yet have mastered the structure to which the constraint applies; they may have only some simpler approximation to the construction, lacking the crucial property that engages the constraint. We will discuss the evidence for this below.

A different approach also accepts the recalcitrant data as valid, but rejects the inference that the data are inconsistent with the innateness hypothesis. It is pointed out that it is possible for a linguistic principle to be innately encoded in the human brain and yet not accessible to the language faculty of children at early stages of language acquisition. The principle in question might be biologically timed to become effective at a certain maturational stage. Like aspects of body development (e.g., the secondary sex characteristics), linguistic principles might lie dormant for many years. One recent proposal invoking linguistic maturation, by Borer and Wexler (1987), contends that a syntactic principle underlying verbal passives undergoes maturational development. They maintain that before a critical stage of maturation is reached, children are unable to produce or comprehend passive sentences (full verbal passives with *by*-phrases).

It may eventually turn out that the innateness hypothesis must be augmented by maturation assumptions in certain cases. But such assumptions introduce new degrees of freedom into the theory, so its empirical claims are weakened. Unless some motivated predictions can be made about exactly *when* latent knowledge will become effective, a maturational approach is compatible with a much wider range of data than the simplest and strongest version of the innateness hypothesis, namely, that children have access to the same set of universal principles at *all* stages of language development. This more restricted position is the one to be adopted until or unless there is clear evidence to the contrary, for example clear evidence of a period or a stage at which all children violate a certain constraint, in all constructions to which it is applicable, simple as well as complex, and in all languages. So far, no such case has been demonstrated.[1]

Our research has taken a different approach. We argue that the experimental data do *not* unequivocally demonstrate a lack of linguistic knowledge. We do not deny that children do sometimes misinterpret sentences. But the proper interpretation of such failures is complicated by the existence of a variety of potentially confounding factors. Normal sentence comprehension involves lexical, syntactic, semantic, pragmatic, and inferential abilities, and the failure of any one of these may be responsible for poor performance on an experimental task. It is crucial, therefore, to develop empirical methods which will distinguish between these various factors, so that we can determine exactly where a child's deficiencies lie. Until this has been done, one cannot infer from children's imperfect performance that they are ignorant of the grammar of their target language.

In fact it can be argued in many cases that it is nonsyntactic demands of the task which are the cause of children's errors. We propose that task performance is weak at first and improves with age in large part because of maturation of nonlinguistic capacities such as short-term memory or computational ability, which are essential in the efficient practical application of linguistic knowledge. This does not deny that many aspects of language must be learned and that there is a time when a child has not yet learned them. But our interpretation of the data does make it plausible that young children know more of the adult grammar than has previously been demonstrated, and also, most significantly, that their early grammars do abide by universal principles.

In support of this nonlinguistic maturation hypothesis, we have reexamined and supplemented a number of earlier experimental findings with demonstrations that nonsyntactic factors were responsible for many of the children's errors. The errors disappear or are greatly reduced when these confounding factors are suitably controlled for. In this chapter, we report on a series of experimental studies along these lines concerned with three kinds of nonsyntactic factors in language performance: parsing, plans, and presuppositions. We will argue that these other factors are crucially involved in the experimental tasks by which children demonstrate their knowledge, and that they impose

---

[1] Carey has pointed out (BU Conference, 1988) that the linguistic maturation hypothesis predicts that knowledge of a linguistic principle should correlate with gestation age rather than with birth age in children born prematurely. Unfortunately, variability is probably such that no clear correlation could be expected to show itself by age 4 or 5, when passives and other relevant syntactic constructions are claimed to emerge.

significant demands on children. If we underestimate the demands of any of these other components of the total task we thereby underestimate the extent of the child's knowledge of syntax. As a result, the current estimate of what children know about language is misleading.

Children's Errors in Comprehension

In this section we attempt to identify and isolate several components of language-related skills, in order to gain a better understanding of each, and to clarify the relationship between the innateness hypothesis and early linguistic knowledge. Very little work has been done on this topic. The majority of language development studies seem to take it for granted that the experimental paradigms provide a direct tap into the child's linguistic competence. An important exception is a study by Goodluck and Tavakolian (1982), in which improved performance on a relative clause comprehension task resulted from simplification of other aspects of the syntax and semantics of the stimulus sentences (i.e., the use of intransitive rather than transitive relative clauses, and relative clauses with one animate and one inanimate noun phrase rather than two animates). The success of these manipulations is exactly in accord with our general hypothesis about the relation between competence and performance. As other demands on the child's performance are reduced, greater competence is revealed.

Our experiments focus on three factors involved in many child language experiments which may interfere with estimation of the extent of children's linguistic knowledge in tasks which are designed to measure sentence comprehension. These factors — parsing, presupposition, and plans — are of interest in their own right, but have received very little attention in previous research on syntax acquisition. In this section we will review our recent work on these topics. In the following section we will turn to an alternative research strategy for assessing children's knowledge, the technique of elicited production.

Parsing: Sentence parsing is a complex task which is known to be governed (in adults) by various decision strategies that favor one structural analysis over another where both are compatible with the input word sequence. Even adults make parsing errors, and it would hardly be surprising, given the limited memory and attention spans of children, to discover that they do too. These parsing preferences must somehow be neutralized or factored out of an experimental task whose objective is the assessment of children's *knowledge* of syntactic rules and constraints.

Plans: The formation of an action plan is an important aspect of any comprehension task involving the manipulation of toys or other objects. If the plan for manipulating objects appropriately in response to a test sentence is necessarily complex to formulate or to execute, its difficulty for a child subject may mask his correct comprehension of the sentence. Thus we need to develop a better understanding of the nature and relative complexity of such plans, and also to devise experimental paradigms in which their impact on performance is minimized.

Presuppositions: A variety of pragmatic considerations must also be taken into account, such as the contextual fixing of deictic reference, obedience to cooperative principles of conversation, and so forth. In particular, our research suggests that test sentences whose pragmatic presuppositions are unsatisfied in the experimental situation are also unlikely to provide results allowing an accurate assessment of a child's knowledge of syntactic principles. It is necessary to establish which kinds of presuppositions children are sensitive to, and to ensure that these are satisfied in experimental tasks.

Parsing

Subjacency. One universal constraint which should be innate is Subjacency. Subjacency prohibits extraction of constituents from various constructions, including relative clauses. However, in an experimental study by Otsu (1981), many children responded as if they allowed extraction from relative clauses in answering questions about the content of pictures. For example, children saw a picture of a girl using a crayon to draw a monkey who was drinking milk through a straw. They were then asked to respond to question (1).

1. What is Mary drawing a picture of a monkey that is drinking milk with?

Otsu found that many children responded to (1) in a way that appeared to violate Subjacency. In this case, the answer that is in apparent violation of Subjacency is "a straw." This is because "a straw" is appropriate only if the *what* has been moved from a position in the *monkey drinking milk* clause as shown in (2a), rather than from the *Mary drawing picture* clause as shown in (2b).

2. (a) *What is Mary drawing a picture of a monkey [that is drinking milk with __ ?
    (b) What is Mary drawing a picture of a monkey [that is drinking milk] with __ ?

But the *monkey drinking milk* clause is a relative clause, and Subjacency prohibits the *what* from moving out of it. Thus the only acceptable structure is (2b), and the only acceptable answer is "a crayon." If these data are interpreted solely in terms of children's grammatical *knowledge,* then the conclusion would then have to be that knowledge of Subjacency sets in quite late in at least some children.

As we noted earlier, Otsu suggested that the innateness of Subjacency could be salvaged by showing that the children who appeared to violate Subjacency had not yet mastered the phrase structure of relative clauses (of sufficient complexity to contain an extractable noun phrase). When he conducted an independent test of knowledge of relative clause structure, he found, as predicted, a correlation between phrase structure and Subjacency application in the children's performance. However, the children's performance was still surprisingly poor: 25% of the children who were deemed to have mastered relative clauses gave responses involving ungrammatical Subjacency violating extractions from relative clauses.

We have argued (Crain & Fodor, 1984) for an alternative analysis of Otsu's data, which makes it possible to credit children with knowledge of *both* phrase structure principles *and* constraints on transformations from an early age. We claim that children's parsing routines can influence their performance on the kind of sentences used in the Subjacency test; in particular, that there are strong parsing pressures encouraging subjects to compute the ungrammatical analysis of such sentences. Until a child develops sufficient capacity to override these parsing pressures, they may mask his syntactic competence, making him look as if he were ignorant of Subjacency.

A powerful general tendency in sentence parsing by adults is to attach an incoming phrase low in the phrase marker if possible. This has been called Right Association; see Kimball (1973), Frazier and Fodor (1978). In sentence (3), for example, the preferred analysis has *with NP* modifying *drinking milk* rather than modifying *drawing a picture,* even though in this case both analyses are grammatically well-formed because there has been no WH-movement.

3.   Mary is drawing a picture of a monkey that is drinking milk with NP.

To see how strong this parsing pressure is, note how difficult it is to get the sensible interpretation of (3) when *a crayon* is substituted for NP. This Right Association preference is still present if the NP in (3) is extracted, as in (1). The word *with* in (1) still coheres strongly with the relative clause, rather than with the main clause. The result is that the analysis of (2) that is most immediately apparent is the ungrammatical (2a) in which *what* has been extracted from the relative clause. Since this "garden path" analysis is apparent to most adults, it is hardly surprising if some of Otsu's child subjects were also tempted by it and responded to (1) in the picture verification task by saying "a straw" rather than "a crayon."

We conducted several experiments designed to establish the plausibility of this claim that the relatively poor performance of children on sentences like (1) is due to parsing pressures rather than to ignorance of universal constraints. In the first experiment, we tested children and adults on complement-clause questions as in (4). Subjacency does not prohibit extraction from complement clauses, so if there were no Right Association effects this sentence should be fully ambiguous, with both interpretations equally available.

4.   What is Bozo watching the dog jump through?

That is, given a picture in which Bozo the clown is looking through a keyhole at a dog jumping through a hoop, it would be correct to say either "the keyhole" or "a hoop." Intuitively, though, the interpretations are highly skewed for adults, with a strong preference for the Right Association interpretation ("hoop") in which the preposition attaches within the lower clause. Our experiment showed that the same is true for children. We tested 20 3- to 5-year-olds (mean age 4;6) on these sentences using a picture verification task just like Otsu's, and 90% of their responses were in accord with the Right Association interpretation.[2]

Thus children and adults alike are strongly swayed by Right Association. This is an important result. To the best of our knowledge the question of whether children's parsing strategies resemble those of adults has not previously been investigated. But children certainly should show the same preferences as adults, if the human sentence parsing mechanism is innately structured. And the parsing mechanism certainly should be innately structured, because it would be pointless to be born knowing a lot of facts about language if one weren't also born knowing how to use those facts for speaking and understanding. It is satisfying, then, to have shown that children exhibit Right Association. And the fact that they do offers a plausible explanation for why so many of them failed Otsu's Subjacency test—they were listening to their parsers rather than to their grammars.

Our other experiments in support of this conclusion were designed to show that even people whose knowledge of Subjacency is not in doubt—that is, adults—are also tempted to violate Subjacency when it is in competition with Right Association. We ran Otsu's Subjacency test on adults just as he did with the children. The adults gave Subjacency-violating low attachment responses to 21% of these questions. This was not quite as high a rate as for the children, but as we have noted, adults surely have a greater capacity than children do for checking an illicit analysis and shifting to a less preferred but well-formed analysis before they commit themselves to a response. In an attempt to equalize adult self-monitoring capacities with those of children, we reran the Subjacency experiment with an additional distracting task (= listening for a designated phoneme in the stimulus sentence). Under these conditions the adults gave Subjacency violating responses to 29% of the relative clause constructions, a slightly higher rate than the 25% for Otsu's child subjects.

Escalating still further, we changed the sentences so that the grammatically well-formed analysis was semantically or pragmatically anomalous, as in (5).

---

[2] For full details of procedure and results of this experiment, and of all other studies reported in this chapter, we refer readers to the original publications.

5.   What color hat is Barbara drawing a picture of an artist with?

Under these circumstances, where the semantics clearly favored the Subjacency-violating analysis, 75% of adults' responses violated Subjacency. This makes it very clear that linguistic competence may not always be revealed by linguistic performance.

   Finally, we ran another study, in which we asked adults to classify sentences as ambiguous or unambiguous. The sentences were spoken in turn with only a few seconds between them, and there were 72 of them, so the task was fairly demanding. The materials included complement questions like (4) and relative clause questions like (1), as well as ambiguous and unambiguous control sentences of many varieties. The results showed a 62% ambiguity detection rate for the ambiguous control sentences, with a 16% "false alarm" rate for the unambiguous control sentences. Thus the subjects were able to cope with the task tolerably well, though not perfectly. What was interesting was that the ambiguity of the complement questions was detected only 48% of the time, in line with our claim that Right Association obscures the alternative reading with the prepositional phrase in the main clause. And most interesting of all was that 80% of the relative clause'questions were judged to be ambiguous, even though Subjacency prohibits one analysis and renders them unambiguous. Our explanation for this extraordinary result is that the subjects first computed the Right Association analysis favored by their parsing routines, then recognized that this was unacceptable because of Subjacency, and so rejected it in favor of the analysis with the prepositional phrase in the main clause. We assume that it was this rapid shift from one analysis to the other that gave our subjects such a strong impression that these sentences were ambiguous. Note that if this misanalysis-with-revision occurs 80% of the time for adults, only a slight handicap in children's ability to revise would be sufficient to account for their errors.

   To sum up: We still have no positive proof that Subjacency is innate, but at least now there is no evidence against it. Our experiments make it plausible that children as young as can be tested are like adults *both* with respect to their knowledge of this universal constraint *and* with respect to their parsing routines — they are just not very good yet at coping with conflicts between the two.

Backward pronominalization. A fundamental constraint on natural language is the structure dependence of linguistic rules. The innateness hypothesis implies that children's earliest grammars should also exhibit structure dependence — even if their linguistic experience happens to be equally compatible with structure-independent hypotheses. However, it has been proposed that children initially hypothesize a structure-independent constraint on anaphora, prohibiting all cases of backward pronominalization (Solan, 1983).[3] Backward pronominalization consists of coreference between a noun phrase and a preceding pronoun, as indicated by the indices in (6).

6.   That he$_i$ kissed the lion made the duck$_i$ happy.

We will argue that children do in fact permit backward pronominalization, subject to structure-dependent constraints. We contend that the appearance of a general restriction against backward pronominalization is due to a parsing preference for the alternative "extrasentential" reading of the pronoun in certain comprehension tasks. The results of a new comprehension methodology show that children as young as 2;10 admit the same range of interpretations for pronouns as adults do.

Two sources of evidence have been cited as evidence that children up to 5 or 6 years uniformly reject backward pronominalization. First, children who are asked to repeat back a sentence such as (7) often respond by converting it into a forward pronominalization construction, as in (8) (Lust, 1981).

7.   Because she was tired, Mommy was sleeping.
8.   Because Mommy was tired, she was sleeping.

The fact that these children took the trouble to exchange the pronoun and its antecedent certainly indicates that they disfavor backward pronominalization in their own productions. But it does not show that the backward pronominalization interpretation is not compatible with the child's *grammar,* as suggested by Solan (1983). To the contrary, the conversion of (7) to (8) shows that children do accept backward pronominalization in comprehension; for they would think of (8) as an acceptable variant of (7) only if they were interpreting the pronoun in (7) as coreferential with the subsequent lexical noun phrase (Lasnik & Crain, 1985).

Second, it has been found that when the acting-out situation for a sentence like (6) includes a potential referent for *he* other than the duck (e.g., a farmer), this unmentioned object is usually favored by the children as the referent of the pronoun (Solan, 1983; Tavakolian, 1978). In contrast to the prevailing view, we would attribute this to a parsing preference for the extra-sentential interpretation of the pronoun; it does not have to be taken as evidence that children have a grammatical prohibition against backward anaphora. Our

---

[3] As far as is known at present, no natural language exhibits this blanket prohibition against backward pronominalization; see discussion in Lasnik and Crain (1985). This suggests that it is not a possible constraint in a natural language grammar, in which case it should not be entertained by children at any age or stage of acquisition (unless one assumes linguistic maturation).

suggestion, then, is that children's *knowledge* might be comparable to that of adults, even if their performance differs.

It is particularly important to keep this distinction in mind for potentially ambiguous constructions such as these. When a sentence has more than one possible interpretation, the interpretation that children select can tell us which interpretation they prefer; it *cannot* show that others are unavailable to them. After all, adults also exhibit biases in connection with ambiguous constructions, but this does not lead us to accuse them of ignorance of alternative interpretations. To establish how much children actually do know, we should look for the factors that might be biasing their interpretations, and also for ways of minimizing this bias so that interpretations which are less preferred but nevertheless acceptable to them have a chance of showing through.

The most likely general source of bias against backward pronominalization is the fact that interpretation of the pronoun would have to be delayed until the antecedent is encountered later in the sentence. This retention of uninterpreted items may strain a child's limited working memory. There is some evidence for this speculation. Hamburger and Crain (1984) have noted that children show a tendency to interpret adjectives immediately, without waiting for the remainder of the noun phrase, even in cases where this leads them to give incorrect responses. And Clark (1971) has observed errors attributable to children's tendency to act out a clause immediately without waiting for other clauses in the sentence. The only way to interpret the pronoun immediately in a sentence like (6) is to assign it an extrasentential referent, as children typically do.

If this proposal is correct, it should be that children will accept backward pronominalization in an experimental task that presses subjects to access *every* interpretation they can assign to a sentence. Crain and McKee (1985) used a true/false paradigm in which subjects judge the truth value of sentences against situations acted out by the experimenter. The sentences were as in (9), where either a coreferential reading or an extrasentential reading of the pronoun is possible.

9.   When he went into the barn, the fox stole the food.

On each trial, a child heard a sentence following a staged event acted out by one of two experimenters, using toy figures and props. The second experimenter manipulated a puppet, Kermit the Frog. Following each event, Kermit said what he thought had happened on that trial. The child's task was to indicate whether or not the sentence uttered by Kermit accurately described what had happened. Children were asked to feed Kermit a cookie if he said the right thing, that is, if what he said was what really happened. In this way, "true" responses were encouraged in the experimental situation. But sometimes Kermit would say the wrong thing, if he wasn't paying close attention. When this happened, the child was asked to make Kermit eat a rag. (In pilot work without the rag ploy, we had found that children were reluctant to say that Kermit had said something wrong.)

To test for the availability of both interpretations of an ambiguous sentence like (9), children judged it twice during the course of the experiment, once following a situation in which a fox stole some chickens from inside a barn (for the backward pronominalization interpretation), and once following a situation in which the fox stole some chickens while a man was in a barn (for the extrasentential interpretation).

Children accepted the backward anaphora reading for all the ambiguous sentences 73% of the time. The extrasentential reading was accepted 81 percent of the time, but the difference was not significant. Much the same results were obtained even for the 7 youngest children, whose ages were from 2;10 to 3;4. Only two of the 62 subjects consistently rejected the backward anaphora reading. Thus most children find the backward anaphora reading acceptable, although it might not be preferred if they were forced to choose between interpretations, as in previous comprehension studies.

We should note that a variety of control sentences were also tested to rule out other, less interesting, explanations of the children's performance. For example, the children rejected sentence (10) following a situation in which Strawberry Shortcake did eat an ice cream, but not while she was outside playing. This shows that they were not simply ignoring the subordinated clauses of sentences in deciding whether to accept or reject them.

10.   When she was outside playing, Strawberry Shortcake ate an ice cream.

Sentences like (11) were also tested in order to establish that subjects were not merely giving positive responses to all sentences, regardless of their grammatical properties.

11.   He stole the food when the fox went into the barn.

The difference between (11) and the acceptable backward pronominalization in (9) is that in (11) the pronoun is in the higher clause and c-commands *the fox,* while in (9) the pronoun is in the subordinate clause and does not c-command *the fox.* (A node A in a phrase marker is said to c-command a node B if there is a route from A to B which goes up to the first branching node above A, and then down to B. Note that c-command is a structure-dependent relation.) There is a universal constraint that prohibits a pronoun from c-commanding its antecedent. And indeed the children did reject (11) 87% of the time. Note that this positive result shows that the children have early knowledge not only of the absence of linear sequence conditions on pronominalization, but also of the existence of structural conditions such as c-command (see also Lust, 1981, and Goodluck, 1986).

Subject/Auxiliary inversion. Another study (Crain & Nakayama, 1987) also explored the tie between children's errors in acquisition tasks and sentence processing problems. This study was designed to test whether children give structure-dependent or structure-independent responses when they are required to transform sentences by performing Subject/Auxiliary inversion. As Chomsky (1971) pointed out, transformational rules are universally sensitive to the structural configurations in the sentences to which they apply, not just to the linear sequence of words.

The procedure in this study was simply for the experimenter to preface declaratives like (12) with the carrier phrase "Ask Jabba if . . . ," as in (13).

12.   The man who is running is bald.
13.   Ask Jabba if the man who is running is bald.

The child then had to pose the appropriate yes/no questions to Jabba the Hutt, a figure from *Star Wars* who was being manipulated by one of the experimenters. Following each question, Jabba was shown a picture and would respond "yes" or "no."

The sentences all contained a relative clause modifying the subject noun phrase. The correct structure-dependent transformation moves the first verb of the main clause to the front of the sentence, past the whole subject noun phrase, as in (14). An incorrect, structure-independent transformation would be as in (15), where the linearly first verb in the word string (which happens to be the verb of the relative clause) has been fronted.

14.   Is the man who is running bald?
15.   *Is the man who running is bald?

For simple sentences with only one clause such as (16), which are more frequent in a young child's input, both versions of the transformation rule give the correct result.

16.   Ask Jabba if the man is bald.
17.   Is the man bald?

It is only on the more complex sentences that the form of the child's rule is revealed.

The outcome was as predicted by the innateness hypothesis: children never produced an incorrect sentence like (15). Thus, a structure-independent strategy was not adopted in spite of its simplicity and in spite of the fact that it produces the correct question forms in many instances. The findings of this study thus lend further support to the view that the initial state of the human language faculty contains structure-dependence as an inherent property.

The children did make some errors in this experiment, and we observed that most of them were in sentences with a long subject noun phrase and a short main verb phrase, as in (18).

18.   Is the boy who is holding the plate crying?

By contrast, there were significantly fewer errors in sentences like (19), which has a shorter subject noun phrase and a longer verb phrase.

19.   Is the boy who is unhappy watching Mickey Mouse?

This kind of contrast is familiar in parsing studies with adults. In particular, Frazier and Fodor (1978) showed that a sequence consisting of a long constituent followed by a short constituent is especially troublesome for the (adult) parsing routines;[4] a short constituent before a long one is much easier to parse. The distribution of the children's errors in the Subject-Auxiliary Inversion task may therefore be indicative not of inadequate knowledge of the inversion rule, but of an adult-like processing sensitivity to interactions between structure and constituent length.

A follow-up study to test this possibility was conducted by Nakayama (1987). Nakayama systematically varied both the length and the syntactic structure of the sentences to be transformed by the children. The children made significantly fewer Subject-Auxiliary Inversion errors in response to embedded questions with short relative clauses (containing intransitive verbs) as compared to those with long relative clauses (containing transitive verbs). With length held constant, the children had more difficulty with relative clauses that had object gaps, as in (20), than with relative clauses that had subject gaps, as in (21) (although this effect was not quite significant).

20.   The ball the girl kicked is rolling.
21.   The boy who was slapped is crying.

The ease of subject gap constructions, as compared to object gap constructions, has been found in a number of other studies in language development, in language impaired populations, and in experiments on adult sentence processing (where the question of syntactic competence is not in doubt). It seems reasonable to interpret these results as confirming that children's error rates in language tests are highly sensitive to the complexity of the sentence parsing that is required.

---

[4] The awkwardness of the prosodic contour for (18), with its heavy juncture before the final word, may indicate that this kind of construction is also an unnatural one for the sentence production routines.

Presupposition

Syntactic parsing is not the only factor that has been found to mask knowledge of syntactic principles. Test sentences whose pragmatic presuppositions are unsatisfied in the experimental situation have been found to result in inaccurate assessments of children's structural knowledge. In this section we consider two experiments that point to the relevance of presuppositional content in sentence understanding.

The structures we discuss here are relative clauses and temporal adverbial clauses. A word of clarification is needed before we proceed. Up till now we have restricted the scope of the innate hypothesis to universal constraints (like Subjacency, and structure-dependence), which could not *in principle* be learned from normal linguistic experience (i.e., without extensive corrective feedback). But now we want to extend the innateness hypothesis to a broader class of linguistic knowledge, knowledge of universal types of sentence construction. We cannot plausibly claim that every aspect of these constructions is innate. Rather, every construction will have some aspects that are determined by innate principles, and other aspects that must be learned. And the balance between these two elements varies from construction to construction. So it is perfectly acceptable on theoretical grounds that some constructions should be acquired later than others. However, the innateness hypothesis is not compatible with just *any* order of acquisition. It predicts early acquisition of constructions that Chomsky calls "core" language, that is, the constructions that have strong assistance from innate principles with just a few parameters to be set by learners on the basis of experience. It would be surprising to discover that knowledge of *these* constructions was significantly delayed once the relevant lexical items had been learned. In the absence of a plausible explanation, this would put the innateness hypothesis at risk.

We noted in the Introduction to this chapter a range of possible explanations of apparently delayed knowledge of linguistic facts. In the present case they would include the following:

- the construction does not, after all, belong to the core but is "peripheral" and hence *should* be acquired late
- children don't hear this construction until quite late in the course of language development and so could not be expected to know it exists
- the core principles in question undergo maturation and so are not accessible at early stages of acquisition
- the experimental data are faulty and children do indeed have knowledge of this construction.

We will argue for this last alternative. And just as in the previously described studies of innate constraints, we will lay the blame for the misleading experimental data on the fact that traditional experimental paradigms do not make sufficient allowance for the limited memory and computational capacities of young children. Once again, our story is that nonlinguistic immaturity can create the illusion of linguistic immaturity.

Relative clauses. Children typically make more errors in understanding sentences containing relative clauses (as in 22) than sentences containing conjoined clauses (as in 23), when comprehension is assessed by a figure manipulation (act-out) task.

22.   The dog pushed the sheep that jumped over the fence.
23.   The dog pushed the sheep and jumped over the fence.

The usual finding that (22) is more difficult for children than (23) up to age 6 years or so has been interpreted as an instance of late emergence of the rules for subordinate syntax in language development (e.g., Tavakolian, 1981). However, though coordination may be innately favored over subordination, it is also true that subordination is ubiquitous in natural language; relative clause constructions are very close to the "core." So ignorance of relative clauses until age 6 would stretch the innateness hypothesis.

Fortunately this is not how things stand. Hamburger and Crain (1982) showed that the source of children's performance errors on this task is *not* a lack of syntactic knowledge. By constructing pragmatic contexts in which the presuppositions of restrictive relative clauses were satisfied, they were able to demonstrate mastery of relative clause structure by children as young as 3 years. There are two presuppositions in (22): (a) that there are at least two sheep in the context, and (b) that one (but only one) of the sheep jumped over a fence prior to the utterance. The reason why previous studies failed to demonstrate early knowledge of relative clause constructions, we believe, is that they did not pay scrupulous attention to these pragmatic presuppositions. For example, subjects were required to act out the meaning of a sentence such as (22) in contexts in which only one sheep was present. The poor performance by young children in these experiments was attributed to their ignorance of the linguistic properties of relative clause constructions. But suppose that a child did know the linguistic properties, but that he also was aware of the associated presuppositions. Such a child might very well be unable to relate his correct understanding of the sentence to the inappropriate circumstances provided by the experiment. Adult subjects may be able to "see through" the unnaturalness of an experimental task to the intentions of the experimenter, but it is not realistic to expect this of young children.

Following this line of reasoning, Hamburger and Crain (1982) made the apparently minor change of adding two more sheep to the acting out situation for sentence (22), and obtained a much higher percentage of correct responses. The most frequent remaining "error" was failure to act out the event described by the relative clause, but since felicitous usage presupposes that this event has already occurred, this is not really an error but is precisely the kind of response that is compatible with perfect comprehension of the sentence. This interpretation of the data is supported by the fact that there was a positive correlation between incidence of this response type and age.[5]

We have conducted another series of studies on relative clauses, trying several other techniques for assessing grammatical competence. In one study, we employed a picture verification paradigm to see if children could distinguish relative clauses from conjoined clauses, despite the claim of Tavakolian (1981) that they systematically impose a conjoined clause analysis on relatives. In this study, 17 3- and 4-year-olds responded to relative clause constructions like (24).

24.   The cat is holding hands with a man who is holding hands with a woman.
25.   The cat is holding hands with a man and is holding hands with a woman.

This sentence was associated with a pair of pictures, one that was appropriate to it and one that was appropriate to the superficially similar conjoined sentence (25). Seventy percent of the 3-year-olds' responses and 94% of the 4-year-olds' responses matched sentences with the appropriate picture rather than with the one depicting the conjoined clause interpretation.

A second technique we tried used a "silliness" judgment task (see Hsu, 1981) to establish whether children can differentiate relative clauses from conjoined clauses. Ninety-one percent of the responses of the 12 3- and 4-year-olds tested categorized as "silly" sentences such as (26), although sentences such as (27) were accepted as sensible 87% of the time.

26.   The horse ate the hay that jumped over the fence.
27.   The man watched the horse that jumped over the fence.

Notice that sentence (26) would not be anomalous if the *that* -clause were misinterpreted as an *and* -clause, or if it were interpreted as extraposed from the subject NP; in both cases, *the horse* would be the understood subject of the relative clause. The results therefore indicate that most children interpret the *that*-clause in this sentence correctly, that is, as a subordinate clause modifying *the hay*. Informal testing of adults suggests that the only respect in which children and adults differ on the interpretation of relative clauses is that

---

[5] In reviewing the literature on relative clauses, de Villiers and de Villiers (1986) suggest that if earlier work had counted the assertion-only response as correct, children would have been seen to perform better there too. This objection is unwarranted, for two reasons. First, responses of this type did not appear in other studies, presumably because these studies failed to meet the presuppositions of the restrictive relative clause. More important, in the Hamburger and Crain study this response was not evinced by any of the 3-year-old children, and accounted for only 13% of the responses of the 4-year-olds. Nevertheless, even the 3-year-olds acted out sentences with relative clauses at a much higher rate (69%) of success than in earlier studies.

the adults are somewhat more likely to accept the extraposed relative analysis *as well,* though even for adults this analysis is much less preferred.

A third experiment, on the phrase structure of relative clause constructions, indicates that children, like adults, treat a noun phrase and its modifying relative clause as a single constituent, inasmuch as they can construe it as the antecedent for a pronoun such as *one.* In a picture verification study, 15 3- to 5-year-olds responded to the instructions in (28).

28.   The mother frog is looking at an airplane that has a woman in it. The baby frog is looking at one too. Point to it.

Ninety-three percent of the time the subjects chose the picture in which the baby frog was looking at an airplane with a woman in it, in preference to the picture in which the baby frog was looking at an airplane without a woman in it. That is, the relative clause was included in the noun phrase assigned as antecedent to the pronoun.

In short: The weight of evidence now indicates that children grasp the structure and meaning of relative clause constructions quite early in the course of language acquisition, as would be expected in view of the central position of these constructions in natural language.

Temporal terms. Another line of research has yielded support for the claim that presupposition failure is implicated in children's poor linguistic performance. These studies employed sentences containing temporal clauses with *before* and *after,* as in (29).

29.   Push the red car to me before/after you push the blue car.

Clark (1971) and Amidon and Carey (1972) have claimed that most normal 3- to 5-year-olds do not understand these sentences appropriately. Since Amidon and Carey established that the children were familiar with concepts of temporal sequence (e.g., as expressed by words like *first* and *last*), the implication is that the structure of these adverbial clauses is beyond the scope of the child's grammar at this age.

However, the acting-out tasks employed in these studies were once again unnatural ones which ignored the presuppositional content of the test sentences. Felicitous usage of sentence (29) demands that the pushing of the blue car has already been contextually established by the hearer as an intended, or at least probable, future event; but this was not established in these experimental tasks. It is very likely, then, that these studies underestimated children's ability to comprehend temporal subordinate clauses. For example, Amidon and Carey reported that 5- and 6-year-old children who were not given any feedback frequently failed to act out the action described in the subordinate clause. Johnson (1975) found that 4- and 5-year-old children correctly acted out commands such as those in (30) only 51% of the time; again, the predominant error was failure to act out the action described in the subordinate clause.

30. a. Push the car before you push the truck. (S1 before S2)
    b. After you push the motorcycle, push the bus. (After S1, S2)
    c. Before you push the airplane, push the car. (Before S2, S1)
    d. Push the truck after you push the helicopter. (S2 after S1)

Crain (1982) satisfied the presupposition of the subordinate clause by having the subordinate clause act correspond to an intended action by the subject, and observed a striking increase in children's performance. To satisfy the presupposition, children were asked, before each command, to choose a toy to push on the next trial. The child's intention to push a particular toy was incorporated into the command that was given on that trial. For instance, sentence (30d) could be used felicitously for a child who had expressed his intent to push the helicopter. Correct responses (i.e., responses in which both the main clause and subordinate clause action were performed, and in the correct order) were produced 82% of the time. Crain's interpretation of these results was that the children's improved performance was due to the satisfaction of the presupposition of the subordinate clause.

However, we now note that the results of that study are open to another interpretation. It may be that improved performance was not due specifically to the contextual appropriateness of the sentence, but to the fact that the child's task was simplified because he was provided with more advance information concerning what his task would be. In the act-out or "do-what-I-say" paradigm applied to temporal terms, the child must discern two aspects of the command: (a) which two toys to move, and (b) in which order to move them. If the child has established his intent to move a particular toy, his task involving (a) is simplified. Thus, improved performance may be due to the satisfaction of presuppositions or it may be due to the additional information the child possesses.

Another study was conducted to disentangle these two factors (Gorrell, Crain, & Fodor, 1989). In this study, there were four groups of subjects. One group, the Felicity Group (F), was given commands containing *before* and *after* with prior information about the subordinate clause action, just as in the previous experiment. A second group, the Information Group (I) received prior information about the main clause action; note that this does not satisfy the presupposition of the sentence. There was also a third group, the No Context Group (NC), who received no advance information at all, and a fourth group, the Felicity plus Information Group (FI), who received information over and above what would satisfy the felicity conditions since they chose both actions in advance. Consider, for example, a subject in the F group. He would be asked to choose a toy to push. If he chose the bus, for example, a typical command would be (31).

31. Push the car before you push the bus.

On the other hand, a subject in the I group who had chosen the bus would be given the command (32).

32. Push the bus before you push the car.

Fifty-six children participated in the study, ranging in age from 3;4 to 5;10 (mean = 4;5). Each child was assigned to one of the four groups, which were of equal size and approximately matched for age. The "game" equipment consisted of 6 toy vehicles arranged in a row on a table between the child and the experimenter. The stimulus set consisted of 12 commands spoken by the experimenter which the child was to act out. There were three sentences of each of the four types illustrated in (30) above. We were careful to balance order of choice with order of action and assignment to clause type.

The results showed a significant difference between the F and FI groups on one hand, and the I and NC groups on the other. Table 6.1 shows the percentages of correct responses, where a correct response consisted of performing both actions in the sequence specified by the sentence.

Note that the relevant factor is whether subordinate clause information was provided in advance. An analysis of variance confirmed that the mere *amount* of information provided makes no significant difference. The FI group performed better than the F group by only 6 percentage points, which does not approach statistical significance. And the I group performed just a little worse (non-significantly again) than the NC group.

Although our study was not specifically designed to assess age differences, we performed a post hoc breakdown of correct responses by two age groups: under 4;4, and 4;4 and over. The older group, as one would expect, performed somewhat better than the younger group. What is perhaps most interesting is that the younger group appear to be even more sensitive than the older group to the proper contextual embedding of utterances.[6]

A breakdown of the types of errors that occurred reveals that the predominant errors are (a) acting out the main clause only, and (b) reversing the correct order of the actions. As noted above for relative clause constructions, acting out the main clause only is a quite reasonable response given that the context failed to satisfy the subordinate clause presupposition. And in fact

---

[6] These results should be interpreted with caution due to the small and unequal number of subjects in each subgroup leading to rather uneven data. For example, the older F Group performed relatively poorly compared to the younger F Group, though closer analysis reveals that this is due to the poor performance of just one child (4;4) in the F Group.

Table 6.1.

		Main Clause Information		mean
		+	−	
Subordinate	+	FI 80%	F 74%	77%
Clause Information	−	I 51%	NC 59%	55%
	mean	65%	66%	

most of these errors were found in the I and NC groups.[7] Reversals were the most frequent error type in the study though they constituted only 19% of all responses. These errors may reflect a genuine lack of comprehension of either the temporal terms or the relevant syntactic structure. However no child in either the F or FI Groups produced a consistent response pattern which would indicate that this was the case, so it seems more likely that these errors were due primarily just to occasional inattention.

The main conclusion we draw from these results is that children, from a very young age, are indeed sensitive to the proper contextual embedding of language. Their performance is facilitated by satisfying the presuppositions of temporal subordinate clauses, and information which does not satisfy the presuppositions does not result in facilitation.

A secondary conclusion is that children do construct the appropriate syntactic structure for sentences with embedded clauses. If the children in our study had failed to distinguish main from subordinate clauses (e.g., by assigning a "flat" conjunction-type structure to the experimenter's commands), we would not expect to find the difference between the F and I groups we observed. Nor is it plausible to suggest that the children relied upon a structure-independent formula of "old information precedes new information." For example, for the F group, the new information was always in the main clause. If children were assuming that old information would be first, we would have expected relatively poor performance from the F Group on sentences in which the main clause preceded the subordinate clause. In fact, no such effect was observed.

In sum: Once again, the linguistic knowledge of young children, when freed of interfering influences, appears to be quite advanced. Adults have the ability to set aside contextual factors in an unnatural experimental situation, but children, with their more limited cognitive and social skills, apparently do not have this ability. Consequently, they are highly sensitive to pragmatic infelicities. And therefore their linguistic knowledge can be accurately appraised only by tests which include controls to insure that they are not penalized by their knowledge of pragmatic principles.

---

[7] There were no main-clause-only errors in the FI Group. For the F Group, 12 of the 16 main-clause-only errors (out of 168 responses) were due to one child.

Plans

Another possible source of poor performance by children is in formulating the action plans which are needed in order to obey an imperative, or act out the content of a declarative sentence which they have successfully processed and understood. As we use the term, a plan is a mental representation used to guide action. A plan may be simple in structure, consisting of just a list of actions to be performed in sequence; or it may be internally complex, with loops and branches and other such structures now familiar in computer programs.

Formulating a plan is a skill that makes demands on memory and computational resources. In certain experimental tasks, these demands may outweigh those of the purely linguistic processing aspects of the task. So when children perform poorly, it is important to consider the possibility that formulating, storing or executing the relevant action plan is the source of the problem, rather than imperfect knowledge of the linguistic rules or an inability to apply them in parsing the sentence at hand.

Prenominal modifiers. The first study on plans that we conducted was in response to the claim by Matthei (1982) and Roeper (1972) that 4- to 6-year-olds have difficulty in interpreting phrases such as (33) containing both an ordinal and a descriptive adjective.

33.   the second striped ball

Confronted with an array such as (34), many children selected item (ii), that is, the ball which is second in the array and also is striped, rather than item (iv) which is the second of the striped balls (counting from the left as the children were trained to do).

34.   **Array for "the second striped ball"**

The empirical finding, then, appears to be that children assign an interpretation that is not the same as an adult would assign to expressions of this kind. This difference is attributed by Matthei to children's failure to adopt the hierarchical phrase structure internal to a noun phrase that characterizes the adult grammar. This structure is shown in (35). Instead, Matthei argues that children adopt a 'flat structure' for phrases of this kind, with both the ordinal and the descriptive adjective modifying the noun directly as in (36).

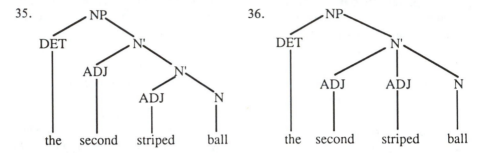

35.

36.

Any divergence between children's and adults' grammars poses a problem from the standpoint of language acquisition theory; namely, explaining how the child ultimately converges on the adult grammar without correction or other "negative" feedback. Fortunately, there is no need to assume an error in the children's grammar in this case, for there is an alternative component of the language processor in which the errors might have arisen. In a series of experiments, Hamburger and Crain (1984) show that most children do assign the adult phrase structure and do understand the phrase correctly as referring to the second of the striped balls. The difficulty that children experience arises when they attempt to derive from this interpretation a procedure for actually identifying the relevant item in the array. An analysis of the logical structure of the necessary procedure shows it to be quite complex, significantly more so than the procedure for "count the striped balls," the kind of phrase Matthei used in a pretest in an attempt to show that children were able to cope with the nonsyntactic demands of the task.

This procedural account of the children's errors is supported by the sharp improvement in performance that results from three changes in method. One change is the inclusion of a pretask session in which the children handle and count homogeneous subsets of the items which are subsequently used in an array. This experience is assumed to prime some of the procedural planning required in the main experimental task. A second change in method is to withhold the display while the sentence is being uttered, so that formation and execution of the plan are less likely to interfere with each other. A dramatic improvement in performance on a phrase like (33) also results from first asking the child to identify the *first* striped ball, which forces him to plan and execute part of the procedure he will later need for (33). Facilitating the procedural aspects of the task thus makes it possible for the child to reveal his mastery of the syntax and semantics of such expressions.

Hamburger and Crain also found quite direct evidence that children do not assign the "flat structure" analysis. The standard assumption in linguistics is that proforms corefer with a syntactic constituent. In the correct structure

(35), the words *striped* and *ball* form a complete constituent, but in the incorrect structure (36) they do not. Thus the children should permit the proform *one* to corefer with *striped ball* only if they have the correct hierarchical structure. To find out whether they permit this coreference, they were tested on the instructions in (37), with the array in (38).

37.   Point to the first striped ball; point to the second *one*.

38.

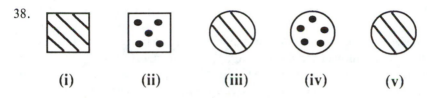

   (i)   (ii)   (iii)   (iv)   (v)

Hamburger and Crain found that the children consistently responded to the second instruction by pointing to (v) rather than (iv), showing that they took the proform *one* to corefer with expressions like *striped ball*. Thus it appears that they do know the structure (35).

Finally, we note two experiments by Hamburger and Crain (1987). The purpose of these experiments was to provide empirical support for our claim that response planning is an important factor in psycholinguistic tasks, independently of syntax and semantics.

The first experiment attempts to show that children's ability to comprehend a phrase is inversely related to the complexity of the associated plan. For this purpose we compare phrases that are arguably equal to each other in syntactic complexity but differ in plan complexity. Examples are shown in (39), in increasing order of complexity of plans.

39.   i. John's biggest book
      ii. second green book
      iii. second biggest book

Planning complexity can also be deconfounded from the complexity of semantic constituent processing. Note that semantic considerations lead to the prediction that (39i), would be hardest, because its word meanings have to combine in a way contrary to the surface sequence of words (= the biggest of John's books).

The pattern of children's responses supports the predictions of our procedural account, and does not conform to the account based on syntactic or semantic constituency. Children responded correctly to phrases like (39i) 88 percent of the time. They gave correct answers only 39% of the time for examples like (39ii), and they were only 17% correct for phrase like (39iii). Thus, this experiment provides clear evidence that plans, not linguistic structures (syntactic or semantic) can determine processing success and failure for young children.

The second experiment addresses the cognitive difficulty of planning by prefacing the test with a sequence of exercises designed to alleviate the planning difficulty. This activity does not provide any extra exposure to the phrases tested; nevertheless, we anticipate a reduction in errors on these phrases. Consider a phrase such as "the second tallest building." This plan requires the interpreter to identify its referent. The child must integrate sequential pairwise comparisons of relative size. In the pretest activity the child would be shown a display of several objects of one type (say boxes), but of different sizes, and asked to hand the experimenter the biggest one. Then, once this object was removed from the array, the experimenter asked the child to perform the task again, saying, "Now, find the biggest box in *this* group." In this way the child would identify the second biggest box without ever hearing the phrase "the second biggest box" uttered. Children's comprehension of the phrase was tested before and after the preparatory task. They gave significantly more correct responses (46%) following the preparatory task than before it (8% in this experiment). This result suggests that their difficulty with phrases of this sort stems from the complexity of the response plans.

Sentence Production

To acquire a language is to learn a mapping between potential utterances and associated potential meanings. Successful mastery should reveal itself in both comprehension and production. In the previous section we were concerned with studies of children's comprehension, in which their knowledge is tested by presenting utterances and observing the interpretations that they assign. We now turn to tests of children's competence which proceed in the other direction: the input to the child is a situation, which has been designed to suggest a unique sentence meaning, and the behavior we observe is the utterance by which the child describes that situation.

It would have been reasonable to expect that the sorts of nonsyntactic problems that present obstacles for children in comprehension tasks might prove to be as hard or even harder for them to overcome in production tasks. But we have not found this to be the case. The results of recent elicited production studies are dramatically better than those of comprehension studies directed to the same linguistic constructions. For example, Richards (1976) elicited appropriate uses of the deictic verbs *come* and *go* from children age 4;0–7;7, while Clark and Garnica (1974) reported that even 8-year-olds didn't consistently distinguish between *come* and *go* in a comprehension task.

The disparity between production and comprehension studies is particularly striking because it is the reverse of what one would expect. To find production superior to comprehension in children's language is as surprising as it would be to find production superior to comprehension in adult second-language learning, or to find recall superior to recognition in any psychological domain. It is plausible to argue, therefore, that the superiority of production is only apparent, and is due to differences in the sensitivities of production tests and comprehension tests. And the logic of the situation suggests that it is the comprehension tests that are deficient. After all, success is hard to argue with. With suitable controls, successful production by children is a strong indicator of underlying linguistic competence, as long as their productions are as appropriate and closely attuned to the context as adult utterances are. Because there are so many ways to combine words incorrectly, consistently correct combinations in the appropriate contexts are not likely to come about by accident. On the other hand, *failure* on any kind of psychological task cannot be secure evidence of *lack* of the relevant knowledge, since the knowledge may be present but imperfectly exploited.

As we saw in the previous section, comprehension studies seem to be particularly susceptible to problems of parsing, planning, and so forth which impede the full exploitation of linguistic knowledge. Production tasks appear to be less hampered by these extragrammatical factors. This is probably because production avoids nonverbal response planning, which we have seen is a major source of difficulty in act-out comprehension tasks. It is worth noting also that in constructing contexts to elicit particular utterance types, we have no choice but to attend to the satisfaction of the presuppositions that are associated with the syntactic structures in question, because otherwise the subjects won't utter anything like the construction that is being targeted. In elicited production it is delicate manipulations of the communicative situation that give one control over the subject's utterances.

Relative Clauses

Earlier we presented evidence of young children's competence with relative clauses. Further confirmation was obtained by Hamburger and Crain (1982), using an elicited production methodology. Pragmatic contexts were constructed in which the presuppositions of restrictive relatives were satisfied. It was discovered that children as young as three reliably produce relative clauses in these contexts.

A context that is uniquely felicitous for a relative clause is one which requires the speaker to identify to an observer which of two objects to perform some action on. In our experiment, the observer is blindfolded during identification of a toy, so the child cannot identify it to the observer merely by pointing to it or saying *this/that one*. Also, the differentiating property of the relevant toy is not one that can be encoded merely with a noun (e.g., *the guard*) or a prenominal adjective (e.g., *the big guard*) or a prepositional phrase (e.g., *the guard with the gun*), but involves a more complex state or action (e.g., *the guard that is shooting Darth Vader*). Young children reliably produce meaningful utterances with relative clauses when these felicity conditions are met. For example:

40.   Jabba, please come over to point to the one that's asleep. (3;5)
      Point to the one that's standing up. (3;9)
      Point to the guy who's going to get killed. (3;9)
      Point to the kangaroo that's eating the strawberry ice cream. (3;11)

Note that the possibility of imitation is excluded because the experimenter takes care not to use any relative clause constructions in the elicitation situation. This technique has now been extended to younger children (as young as 2;8), and to the elicitation of a wider array of relative clause constructions, including relatives with object gaps (e.g., *the guard that Princess Leia is standing on*).

Passives

Borer and Wexler (1987) have argued that A-chains, which are involved in the derivation of verbal passive constructions, are not available to children in the first few years.[8] Borer and Wexler maintain that knowledge of A-chains is innate, but becomes accessible only after the language faculty undergoes maturational change. We were not convinced, however, that this maturation hypothesis is necessitated by the facts. Rather, the facts seem to be consistent with A-chains being innate and accessible from the outset.

The main source of data cited in support of the maturation hypothesis is the absence of full passives in the spontaneous speech of young children. But this of course is not incontrovertible evidence that children's grammars are incapable of generating passives. Full passives are rarely observed in adults' spontaneous speech either, or in adult speech to children. But their paucity is not interpreted in this case as revealing a lack of grammatical knowledge. Instead, it is understood as due to the fact that the passive is a marked form which it is appropriate to use only in certain discourse contexts; in most contexts the active is acceptable and more natural, or a reduced passive without a *by*-phrase is sufficient. That is, the absence of full verbal passives in adult speech is assumed to be a consequence of the fact that it's only in rare situations that the full passive is uniquely felicitous. But the same logic that explains why adults produce so few full passives may apply equally to children. Perhaps they too have knowledge of this construction, but do not use it except where the communicative situation is appropriate.

We have tested this possibility in an experiment with 32 3- and 4-year-old children (Crain, Thornton, & Murasugi, 1987). One experimenter asked the child to pose questions to another experimenter. The pragmatic context was carefully controlled so that questions containing a full verbal passive would be fully appropriate. The following protocol illustrates the elicitation technique:

---

[8] An A-chain is the association of a trace with a moved noun phrase in an A-position (= argument position such as Subject). For example, in *The bagel was eaten by Bill* there is an A-chain consisting of *the bagel* and its associated trace after *eaten*.

Adult: See, the Incredible Hulk is hitting one of the soldiers. Look over
                        here. Darth Vader goes over and hits a soldier. So Darth Vader is
                        also hitting one of the soldiers. Ask Keiko which one.
Child to Keiko: Which soldier is getting hit by Darth Vader?

Note that the child knows what the correct answer is to his question, and
that he cannot expect to elicit this answer from his interlocutor (Keiko) unless
he includes the *by*-phrase. In fact, exactly 50% of responses were passives with
full *by*-phrases). Of course, active constructions are also felicitous in this
context (e.g., *Which soldier is Darth Vader hitting?*), even though the
contextual contrast with another agent (the Incredible Hulk) may tend to favor
the passive stylistically. And indeed 31% of responses were active questions
with object gaps. The other 19% of responses included mostly sentences that
were grammatical but not as specific as the context demanded (e.g., passives
lacking *by*-phrases).

Using this technique, we were able to elicit full verbal passives from all but
3 of the 32 children tested so far, including ones as young as 3;4. Some
examples are shown in (41).

41.   She got knocked down by the Smurfie. (3;4)
       Which girl is pushing, getting pushed by a car? (3;8)
       He got picked up from her. (3;11)
       It's getting ate up from Luke Skywalker. (4;0)
       Which giraffe gets huggen by Grover? (4;9)

Note that these utterances contain a variety of morphological and other errors,
but they all nevertheless exhibit the essential passive structure (underlying
subject in pre-verbal position; agent in post-verbal prepositional phrase).[9] It
might be argued that the children's passives elicited in this experiment do not
involve true A-chains. However, since they are just like adult passives
(disregarding morphological errors), the burden of proof falls on anyone who
holds that adult passives involve A-chains and children's passives do not. No
criterion has been proposed, as far as we know, which distinguishes adult's and
children's passives in this respect. For example, it is true that the children
almost always use a form of *get* in place of the passive auxiliary *be,* but *get* is
acceptable in adult passives also. (*Get* is more regular and phonologically more
prominent than forms of *be,* and this may be why it is more salient for
children.)

Children's considerable success in producing passive sentences appropriate
to the circumstances (i.e., their correct pairing of sentence forms and

---

[9] The proper reversal of underlying subject and object order occurred even when the task was
complicated by an implausible scene to be described. For example, the sentence *One dinosaur's
being eated from the ice cream cone* was used to describe a situation in which the dinosaur was
indeed being eaten by the ice cream, not vice versa.

meanings) constitutes compelling evidence of their grammatical competence with this construction. Comparison of these results with the results of testing the same children with two comprehension paradigms (act-out and picture-verification) confirms that, like spontaneous production data, these measures underestimate children's linguistic knowledge.

The finding that young children evince mastery of the passive obviates the need to appeal to maturation to account for its absence in early child language. Maturation cannot of course be absolutely excluded; but a maturation account is motivated only where a construction is acquired surprisingly late – where this means later than would be expected on the basis of processing complexity, pragmatic usefulness in children's discourse, and so forth. (Also, as noted in section 1, some important cross-language and cross-construction correlations need to be established to confirm a maturational approach; see Borer & Wexler, 1987, on comparison of English passives with passive and causative constructions in Hebrew.) The elicited production results suggest that the age at which passive is acquired in English falls well within a time span that is compatible with these other factors, and so maturation does not need to be invoked.

Wanna Contraction

Another phenomenon that can be shown by elicitation to appear quite early in acquisition is *wanna* contraction in English. The facts are shown in (42) and (43).

42. a. Who do you want to help?
     b. Who do you *wanna* help?
43. a. Who do you want to help you?
     b. *Who do you *wanna* help you?

Every adult is (implicitly) aware that contraction is admissible in (42b) but not (43b). However, on the usual assumption that children do not have access to "negative data" (i.e. are not informed of which sentences are ungrammatical) it is difficult to see how this knowledge about the ungrammaticality of sentences like (43b) could be acquired from experience (at any age). So this is yet another candidate for innate linguistic knowledge. (What is known innately would be that a trace between two words prevents them from contracting together. The relevant difference between (42b) and (43b) is that in (43b) the *who* is the subject of the subordinate clause and has been moved from a position between the *want* and the *to*. The trace of this noun phrase that is left behind blocks the contraction. In (42b), by contrast, the trace is in object position after *help,* and therefore is not in the way of the contraction.)

Crain and Thornton (1991) used the elicited production technique to encourage children to ask questions that would reveal violations like (43b) if these were compatible with their grammars. The target productions were evoked by having children pose questions to a rat who was too timid to talk to grown-ups. The details of the procedure are illustrated in the following scenarios:

Protocol for Objects Extraction
Experimenter: The rat looks hungry. I bet he wants to eat something. Ask him what.
Child: What do you wanna eat?

Protocol for Subject Extraction
Experimenter: One of these guys gets to take a walk, one gets to take a nap, and one gets to eat a cookie. So one gets to eat a cookie, right? Ask Ratty who he wants.
Child: Who do you want to eat the cookie?

Using this technique, questions involving both subject and object extraction were elicited from 21 children, who ranged in age from 2;10 to 5;5, with an average age of 4;3. The preliminary findings of the experiment are clearly in accord with the expectations of the innateness hypothesis, although we must verify our own subjective assessment of these data using a panel of judges.[10] In producing object extraction questions (which permit contraction in the adult grammar), children gave contracted forms 59% of the time and uncontracted forms 18% of the time. (There were 23% of other responses not of the target form, such as *What can you eat to see in the dark?*) By contrast, children's production of subject extraction questions (where contraction is illicit) contained contracted forms only 4% of the time and uncontracted forms 67% of the time (with 29% of other responses).

The systematic control of this subtle contrast could perhaps have been shown on the basis of spontaneous production data, but the crucial situations (particularly those that call for subject extraction questions) probably occur quite rarely in children's experience, just as they do in the case of the full passive. So it is not easy to gather data in sufficient quantity for statistical analysis. By contrast, the elicitation technique is obviously an efficient way of generating data, and thus facilitates testing for early acquisition of a variety of constructions relevant to the innateness hypothesis.

Conclusion

In this chapter we have reviewed a great many empirical studies. The thread that ties them together is the idea that, when performance problems are minimized in testing situations, children show early knowledge of a wide range of basic constructions. As early as 1965, Bellugi suggested that children's errors on Wh-questions were due, not to a lack of knowledge of the two

---

[10] In preliminary evaluation of the audio tapes, we have found it unexpectedly easy to distinguish children's contracted and noncontracted forms in most cases.

relevant transformations (Wh-movement and Subject/Auxiliary Inversion), but to a not yet fully developed capacity to apply both rules in the same sentence derivation. Our work extends this general idea to a broader set of linguistic phenomena. Our particular emphasis has been constructions which linguistic theory predicts should require little or no learning because they involve principles which are universal and hence innate. Our findings suggest that the innateness hypothesis for language is still secure even in its simplest form (in which different innate principles are not timed to mature at different developmental stages). Maturation of nonlinguistic abilities appears to be sufficient to account for the time course of linguistic development.

References

Amidon, A., & Carey, P. (1972). Why five-year-olds cannot understand *before* and *after*. *Journal of Verbal Learning and Verbal Behavior, 11,* 417–423.

Bellugi, U. (1965). The development of interrogative structures in children's speech. In K. Riegel (Ed.), *The development of language functions* (Rep. No. 8). Ann Arbor, MI: University of Michigan Language Development Program.

Borer, H., & Wexler, K. (1987). The maturation of syntax. In T. Roeper & E. Williams (Eds.), *Parameter setting.* Dordrecht: D. Reidel Publishing Company.

Chomsky, N. (1971). *Problems of knowledge and freedom.* New York: Pantheon Books.

Chomsky, N. (1986). *Knowledge of language: Its nature, origin, and use.* New York: Praeger.

Clark, E. V. (1971). On the acquisition of the meaning of *before* and *after*. *Journal of Verbal Learning and Verbal Behavior, 10,* 266–275.

Clark, E. V., & Garnica, O. K. (1974). Is he coming or going? On the acquisition of deictic verbs. *Journal of Verbal Learning and Verbal Behavior, 15,* 559–572.

Crain, S. (1982). Temporal terms: Mastery by age five. *Papers and Reports on Child Language Development, 21,* 33–38.

Crain, S., & Fodor, J. D. (1984). On the innateness of Subjacency. In *Proceedings of the Eastern States Conference on Linguistics* (Vol. I). Columbus, OH: The Ohio State University.

Crain, S., & McKee, C. (1985). Acquisition of structural restrictions on anaphora. *Proceedings of the North Eastern Linguistic Society, 16.* Amherst, MA: University of Massachusetts.

Crain, S., & Nakayama, M. (1987). Structure-dependence in grammar formation. *Language, 63,* 522–543.

Crain, S., & Thornton, R. (1991). Recharting the course of language acquisition: Studies in elicited production. In N. Krasnegor, D. Rumbaugh, R. Schiefelbusch, & M. Studdert-Kennedy (Eds.), *Biobehavioral foundations of language development.* Hillsdale, NJ: Lawrence Erlbaum Associates.

Crain, S., Thornton, R., & Murasugi, K. (1987). *Capturing the evasive passive.* Paper presented at the 12th Annual Boston University Conference on Language Development, Boston, MA.

Frazier, L., & Fodor, J. D. (1978). The sausage machine: A new two-stage parsing model. *Cognition, 6,* 291–325.

Goodluck, H. (1986). Children's interpretation of pronouns and null NPs: Structure and strategy. In P. Fletcher & M. Garman (Eds.), *Language acquisition: Studies in first language development* (2nd ed.). Cambridge: Cambridge University Press.

Goodluck, H., & Tavakolian, S. (1982). Competence and processing in children's grammar of relative clauses. *Cognition, 8,* 389–416.

Gorrell, P., Crain, S., & Fodor, J. D. (1989). Contextual information and temporal terms. *Journal of Child Language, 16,* 623–632.

Hamburger, H., & Crain, S. (1982). Relative acquisition. In S. Kuczaj (Ed.), *Language development* (Vol. II, pp. 245–274). Hillsdale, NJ: Erlbaum.

Hamburger, H., & Crain, S. (1984). Acquisition of cognitive compiling. *Cognition, 17,* 85–136.

Hamburger, H., & Crain, S. (1987). Plans and semantics in human processing of language. *Cognitive Science, 11,* 101–136.

Hsu, J. R. (1981). *The development of structural principles related to complement subject interpretation.* Doctoral dissertation, The City University of New York.

Jackendoff, R. (1977). *X-bar syntax: A study of phrase structure.* Cambridge, MA: MIT Press.

Jakubowicz, C. (1984). On markedness and binding principles. *Proceedings of the Northeastern Linguistic Society.* Amherst, MA.

Johnson, H. (1975). The meaning of *before* and *after* for preschool children. *Journal of Experimental Child Psychology, 19.*

Kimball, J. (1973). Seven principles of surface structure parsing in natural language. *Cognition 2,* 15–47.

Lasnik, H., & Crain, S. (1985). On the acquisition of pronominal reference. *Lingua, 65,* 135–154.

Lust, B. (1981). Constraint on anaphora in child language: A prediction for a universal. In S. Tavakolian (Ed.), *Language acquisition and linguistic theory* (pp. 74–96). Cambridge, MA: MIT Press.

Matthei, E. M. (1981). Children's interpretations of sentences containing reciprocals. In S. Tavakolian (Ed.), *Language acquisition and linguistic theory* (pp. 97–115). Cambridge, MA: MIT Press.

Matthei, E. M. (1982). The acquisition of prenominal modifier sequences. *Cognition, 11,* 301–332.

Nakayama, M. (1987). Performance factors in Subject-Aux Inversion by children. *Journal of Child Language, 14,* 113–125.

Otsu, Y. (1981). *Universal grammar and syntactic development in children: Toward a theory of syntactic development.* Unpublished doctoral dissertation, MIT, Cambridge, MA.

Phinney, M. (1981). The acquisition of embedded sentences and the NIC. *Proceedings of the North Eastern Linguistic Society, 11.* Amherst, MA: University of Massachusetts.

Richards, M. M. (1976). Come and go reconsidered: Children's use of deictic verbs in contrived situations. *Journal of Verbal Learning and Verbal Behavior, 15,* 655–665.

Roeper, T. W. (1972). *Approaches to a theory of language acquisition with examples from German children.* Unpublished doctoral dissertation, Harvard University, Cambridge, MA.

Roeper, T. W. (1982). On the importance of syntax and the logical use of evidence in language acquisition. In S. Kuczaj (Ed.), *Language development* (Vol. II, pp. 137–158). Hillsdale, NJ: Erlbaum.

Roeper, T. W. (1986). How children acquire bound variables. In B. Lust (Ed.), *Studies in the acquisition of anaphora* (Vol. I). Dordrecht, Holland: D. Reidel Publishing Company.

Solan, L. (1983). *Pronominal reference: Child language and the theory of grammar.* Dordrecht, Holland: D. Reidel.

Solan, L., & Roeper, T. W. (1978). Children's use of syntactic structure in interpreting relative clauses. In H. Goodluck & L. Solan (Eds.), *Papers in the Structure and Development of Child Language. UMASS Occasional Papers in Linguistics, Vol. 4,* pp. 105–126.

Tavakolian, S. L. (1978). Children's comprehension of pronominal subjects and missing subjects in complicated sentences. In H. Goodluck & L. Solan (Eds.), *Papers in the Structure and Development of Child Language. UMASS Occasional Papers in Linguistics, Vol. 4,* pp. 145–152.

Tavakolian, S. L. (1981). The conjoined-clause analysis of relative clauses. In S. Tavakolian (Ed.), *Language acquisition and linguistic theory* (pp. 167–187). Cambridge, MA: MIT Press.

de Villiers, J. G. & de Villiers, P. A. (1985). The acquisition of English. In D. Slobin (Ed.), *The cross-linguistic study of language acquisition Volume I: The data.* Hillsdale, NJ: Erlbaum.

Wexler, K. & Chien, Y. (1985). The development of lexical anaphors and pronouns. In *Papers and reports on child language development.* Stanford, CA: Stanford University.

7

The Development of Language Use: Expressing Perspectives on a Scene*

Ruth Berman
Tel Aviv University

Introduction

In acquiring a language, children also acquire a variety of expressive options. This study examines children's developing ability to use different linguistic means to describe the same referential content depending on the particular perspective that is expressed. Some linguists have discussed perspective taking in terms of the distinction between foreground and background in narrative discourse (e.g., Hopper, 1979; Reinhart, 1982; Tomlin, 1987) and the related notions of figure and ground (Talmy, 1978, 1985; Wallace 1982). Others have focused on questions of predicate-argument configurations and thematic role structure from various points of view (e.g., Foley & Van Valin, 1985; Jackendoff, 1987; Levin, 1986). The present study considers issues of predicate-argument array as a facet of how children vary perspectives in talking about a particular scene in the course of a picture-based narrative.

Compare these ways a speaker might talk about an event in the neighborhood.

1. a. They're putting up a new overpass where I live. It took them long enough to get started.
    b. A new overpass is going up where I live. It's gonna make a big difference to us.
    c. The new overpass where I live is being worked on. I can't wait!

In these three versions, pragmatic, semantic, and syntactic factors interact in the kind of information the speaker chooses to present, as well as how he or she selects to encode this information linguistically. For instance, the noun "overpass" functions as syntactic direct object and as semantic patient or theme of an accomplishment verb, the two-place predicate "put-up" in (1a); as surface subject with an undergoer relation to the one-place activity verb "go up" in (1b); and as surface subject and thematic patient of the passive predicate "be worked on" in (1c). The lead-in sentences also differ in degree of agency and patient-affectedness: Only (1a) is syntactically transitive but the subject is not necessarily referential, while the subject in (1b) is more actively involved in the event than in (1c). The follow-on sentences each present a different response on the part of the speaker to the information conveyed in the first sentence. And the subject of each follow-on sentence involves different anaphoric reference to what precedes: The pronoun "it" is expletive in (2a), but could have an expletive or a referential sense in (2b), while "I" is deictically anchored and would be interpreted in the same way even if there were no antecedent "I" in the first sentence in (2c).

In adopting a perspective on situations, speakers are free to choose both the linguistic material they wish to deploy — lexical items and grammatical forms — and the way these are arrayed together so as to focus on a particular participant, to highlight or blur the contrast between participants as dynamic agents or inert undergoers, to package several component parts of an event into one predicate or to spread them out analytically, and so on. There is nothing inherently correct or preferred in one form of expression compared with another. Rather, they represent the speaker's point of view, and so depend on the speaker's choice of how he or she will talk about some state of affairs in the real world, not simply on the external facts about that state of affairs itself. To this end, speakers have recourse to, and children must acquire: (a) a repertoire of linguistic means for expressing these different options, (b) knowledge of the functions which these means can serve in their language,[1] and (c) a cognitive basis and affective motivations for deciding among the options on any given occasion.

The child thus needs to acquire a wide array of optional devices and to learn how to alternate these felicitously to express particular perspectives. One

---

[1]I use the term "function" in a deliberately vague sense, without commitment to a particular functionalist view of linguistic analysis or language acquisition (for instance, Silverstein 1987, Van Valin 1989, or other orientations discussed in Nichols, 1984). In the present context, the "function" of linguistic forms includes: knowledge of discourse-sensitive factors such as maintaining and shifting reference, focus, and contrast; level of informativeness as well as organization and structuring of information in the text; interclause linkage and connectivity (Ariel, 1991; Berman, 1988, Giora, 1985); and also conditions governing the pragmatics of assertion and presupposition at the level of a single sentence (Crain & Hamburger, 1985). It further involves the more generalized semantic function served by an array of superficially distinct formal constructions. For instance, the function of object-specification is served by nominal modifiers such as adjectives, adjunct nouns in compounds, relative clauses, and prepositional phrases; while temporal notions of simultaneity and retrospection in ongoing discourse are expressed by morphological markers of verb aspect, by lexical adverbials, and by clause sequencing. Yet another facet to the term is the functionality of a certain construction within a language to achieve goals of the kind noted above (Slobin, 1987a). For instance, Demuth (1985) suggests that young Sesotho speakers use relative clauses very early in part because their language lacks a rich system of adjectives to achieve the same purpose; and I have argued that although passives are syntactically quite productive in Hebrew, they are relatively little used by speakers because the language has a wide range of other, more favored devices for downgrading the agent and focusing on the patient of an action (Berman, 1979). The morphological means available to a language for processes of new-word formation can likewise be shown to differ in their relative "productivity" from the point of view of speaker preferences (Berman, 1987b).

plausible hypothesis is that, initially, children adopt only a single perspective on events, and so do not vary the way they refer to situations. But in fact this is *not* the case, from very early on. Even before age 2, children distinguish between the two major temporal perspectives of result versus process. Slobin (1985) further argues that across languages, the "basic child grammar" of 2-year-olds allows them to select between highly transitive manipulative activity scenes and at least one kind of intransitive figure-ground scene in talking about events. This claim is supported by findings for early comprehension of the difference between syntactically transitive and intransitive formulations of an event — for example, "the frog is turning the bird" vs. "the frog is turning" (Naigles, Hirsch-Pasek, Golinkoff, Gleitman, & Gleitman, 1987). And detailed longitudinal studies of individual English-speaking children have shown them to distinguish different perspectives in reference to self (Budwig, 1985) as well as in the selection of verb forms in different discourse and interactional contexts (Gerhardt, 1988; Gee-Gerhardt & Savasir, 1985).

An alternative claim would be that children lack the required linguistic devices to express alternate perspectives on a situation. And indeed strings like those in (1) sound rather different than what one would expect from a 2- to 3-year-old speaker of English. Yet this argument, too, is not entirely correct. It has been demonstrated for numerous languages, including Hebrew, that by age 3 children make use of a wide range of grammatical functors and inflectional markers of categories such as number, gender, person, mood, and tense. This is also true of morphological marking of verb-aspect, as a typically grammaticized device for representing perspectives or viewpoints on a situation (Chung & Timberlake, 1985; Smith, 1983; Smith & Weist, 1987).[2] For example, among the youngest children included in the crosslinguistic collection of picturebook narratives of which the Hebrew database described below forms a part, ages 3;0–3;11, the English speakers use past simple and past progressive, present simple and present progressive on the verb, while Spanish children use past perfective and imperfective, past progressive, present simple, present progressive, and also present perfect (Slobin, 1986b). In acquiring syntax, too, 3- to 4-year-olds are capable of producing complex constructions;

---

[2]The grammar of English, for example, makes it possible to morphologically contrast all the following perspectives on a single real-world state of affairs, since speakers can distinguish durative vs. nondurative aspect by progressive marking, and present relevance or relative tense by perfect aspect (and Spanish grammaticizes even more options, through the distinction between perfective/imperfective aspect). The grammar of Hebrew, in contrast, provides only a single present vs. past tense for all these options. Compare the following comment of one friend to another watching a young boy they both know doing laps in a swimming pool:

(i) He *swims* really well	Heb. *soxe* — Present
(ii) He *is swimming* really well	*soxe* — Present
(iii) He is a really good *swimmer*	*saxyan* — Agent
(iv) He *has been swimming* really well lately	*soxe* — Present
(v) He *has* never *swum* so well	*saxa* — Past
(vi) He *swam* much better last season	*saxa* — Past

this is shown in elicited production tasks conducted by Crain and his associates (Hamburger & Crain, 1985; Crain & Nakayama, 1987, Chapter 6), as well as by the occasional relative clauses in the Hebrew 3-year-old picture book narratives discussed below, and the common use of relative clauses by Sesotho-speaking children at an even younger age (Demuth, 1983).

Thus children are able to express different perspectives linguistically, and they deploy a rich set of linguistic devices from an early age, irrespective of their particular native tongue. However, the range of functions served by these forms (in all or any of the senses of "function" noted in fn. 1 above) is elaborated and enriched across time. For instance, English-speaking children's early use of the -*ing* ending on serves to mark any kind of durative activity, not necessarily to express genuine aspectual contrast between, say, attributive "he's a really good swimmer," habitual "he swims really well," or iterative "he's swimming better than ever" (see fn. 2). Relatedly, children first acquire the unmarked use of the progressive, as behavioral (or "phenomenal" as compared with "structural") and transitory, for example, "he's hitting me," rather than its more marked use where it is construed as relatively enduring, for example, "The statue . . . is standing at the corner of Kirkland and College" (Goldsmith & Woisetschlaeger, 1982, and see also Smith, 1983).

The analysis reported on below relates to children's developing *use* of language, on the assumption that they will not necessarily use the same options for the same purposes as adults. This study differs from research which traces the developmental history of a particular linguistic construction such as progressive aspect in English, or children's use of devices such as pronouns (Budwig, 1985), verb inflections (Gerhardt, 1988), or subjectless impersonals (Berman, 1987b) to alternate perspective. Instead, I consider how children describe the contents of a single episode, to demonstrate that making inferences about a situation, overall thematic organization of verbal output, as well as command of the necessary morphosyntactic and lexical devices all combine in the developing ability to talk about events.

Perspectives on a Scene in Narrative

To address these questions, I examined a selected excerpt from Hebrew children's narratives and analyzed what perspectives speakers take on a *scene* in the sense of the events depicted on a single page of a picture storybook.[3] The

[3]The booklet in question, "Frog Where Are You" by Mercer Mayer (New York, The Dial Press, 1969), consists of pictures without words, and was used as part of a large-scale cross-linguistic project conducted in conjunction with Dan Slobin and others on the development of temporality in narrative (Berman, 1988, 1990; Berman & Slobin, 1987; Slobin, 1986, 1987b). Collection and analysis of the data were supported by grants from the United States–Israel Binational Science Foundation (BSF), Jerusalem, Israel, the Linguistics Program of the National Science Foundation, and the Sloan Foundation Program in Cognitive Science at the University of California at Berkeley.

picture shows the bedroom of a little boy and his dog, the central protagonists in the story. In the preceding picture, the boy and dog are lying awake on the boy's bed, gazing at an empty glass jar. It had held a pet frog, which crept out and got away during the night while the boy and dog were sleeping. In the picture to be analyzed, the boy is shown standing barefoot, on the floor are his slippers and a large boot, and he is holding the other boot up high—evidently looking inside it to see if his missing frog is there. The dog is to the right with his head tightly inside the glass jar of the frog, which is lying on its side.

The scene selected for analysis allowed narrators to switch perspectives between this picture in isolation or in relation to the search as a whole, between different perspectives on the dog's entry into and being caught in the jar, and between the boy and his boot and the dog and jar. The relative complexity of describing this scene was revealed by the fact that it incurred several instances of ungrammaticalities in the narratives of children whose usage was generally grammatically well formed. The scene also gave rise to rather more hesitations, repairs and backtrackings than did other parts of the narrative. This is illustrated below for some English children's narratives in (2) and for the Hebrew database of the present study in (3). In (2) and (3) below, as in subsequent examples, figures in square brackets give the children's age in years and months, for example, [5;11] refers to a child aged 5 years, 11 months, while [Ad] refers to an adult narrator.[4]

2.   a. And then the dog f . . . sticks his . . . head in and he
         gets caught   [5;11]

     b. Then—the dog he—he g—he gets stuck in the bowl.   [9;3]

     c. er . . . The dog had got a—got the jar stuck on his head.   [9;11]

3.   a. *ve ve—ha-kelev nixnas btox ha-tsinsenet*   [4;3]
         and and—the-dog enters inside the jar

     b. *ve . . . ve ha-kelev hu lakax et ha-ke'ara shel ha-tsfardea*   [5;1]
         ve sam ota al ha-xalon . . . ve sam ota al harosh shelo
         and . . . and the-dog he took ACC the-bowl of the-frog
         and put it on the-window . . . and put it on-his head

     c. *ha-kelev xipes e . . . hixnis et ha-rosh shelo ltox hakli*   [9;6]
         the-dog searched er . . . inserted his head into the-vessel

---

[4]A dash separated by spaces indicates a short pause, while three dots indicate a longer pause within a single utterance. Throughout the text, Hebrew forms are represented in broad phonetic description, without regard for historical accuracy or conventional orthography. The letter "x" stands for the velar fricative at the end of the words *Bach, loch*. In Hebrew, words are usually stressed on the final syllable. A hyphen marks bound morphemes which are separate words in English—for example, *ha-*"the," *be-*"in," *ba-*"in-the." The translations are free, unless accompanied by an additional morpheme-by-morpheme gloss. Verbs are cited in the morphologically simple form of third person, masculine singular past tense, irrespective of what was used in the texts.

Figure 7.1. Enlarged version of the fourth picture-frame (out of total 24) in the picturebook _Frog, Where Are You?_ written and illustrated by Mercer Mayer, New York, The Dial Press, 1969.

    d.   _ve ha-kelev nixnas — ve ha-rosh shel hakelev nixnas betox_ . . . [11;4]
       and the-dog went-in — and the-head of the-dog went into the jar

The database is a set of 84 Hebrew narratives based on the same picture
booklet and elicited by a standard set of procedures from a population of

native Hebrew-speaking, middle-class Israelis aged from 3 years to adulthood. Subjects were instructed as follows, with slight changes in wording depending on age group: "This is a book that tells a story about a boy and a frog. First look at all the pictures, look through the whole book, and afterwards you will tell me the story." When they had gone through the entire booklet of 24 pictures, they were told: "Now go back to the beginning, and you tell the story." The picture book remained open all the time, and the younger children were helped in turning the pages. Only minimal verbal prompts were given throughout the task. The material analyzed below is from 12 narrators at each of the following ages: 3–4, 4–5, 5–6 years (a total of 36 preschoolers), 7–8, 9–10, and 11–12 years (a total 36 schoolchildren in 2nd, 4th, and 6th grade, respectively); as well as 12 adults, all with high school or some college education.

Findings for the adults represent endstate versions of task performance. Yet the adult narratives do not constitute a unified "norm," but show great variation in content and style. They range from 35 to 160 clauses in length, and include concisely encapsulated, closely packaged narratives, on the one hand, and complexly elaborated narratives with fine details of plotline events and specification of background circumstances, on the other. In other words, adults selected different perspectives in performing the task at hand. For instance, the situation could be construed either as one of picture description and hence rendered in the present tense or anchored in the past tense in more typically narrative style. The large majority of children from age 4 up opted for the latter (85% used past tense in telling their stories), whereas the adult narratives were fairly equally divided between present and past-tense anchoring (Berman, 1988).

Analysis of the scene in question was facilitated by the fact that there were no appreciable differences with age in the number of overt *mentions* of some connection between the dog and the jar.[5] In other words, the situation was considered equally noteworthy by all respondents (even if presumably for different reasons). The "dog in/with jar" motif was mentioned by three-quarters of the adults (9/12);[6] it was also mentioned by three-quarters of the preschoolers (27/36–10, 8, and 9 mentions by children aged three, four, and five years respectively); and by nearly 90 percent of the schoolage children

---

[5]This is in marked contrast to amount of mention accorded other scenes in the same story. For instance, the contents of the preceding picture, showing the boy's awakening to discover that the jar is empty, was mentioned by only one-third of the preschoolers, by all schoolage children, and by all but one adult (Berman, 1988).

[6]The three adults who failed to do so all generalized across the specifics of the scene, thus: "(He) searched for it all over the house and his dog helped him"; "he dresses in a great hurry and decides to run and search for the frog"; "right away (he) went out to search for it." This more global presentation of events is reflected in another count: two-thirds (17/24) of the 2nd- and 4th-graders mention both the boy plus boot and the dog plus jar elements of this scene, compared with only one-third (8/24) of the 6th graders and adults.

(32/36–10, 12, and 10 mentions by children aged 7, 9, and 11 respectively). The bulk of the respondents thus referred to at least one facet of the contents of the picture in question (68 out of 84 = 81%).

The picture selected for analysis was suited for discussion of perspective taking from several points of view. First, this scene depicts the beginning of the search which constitutes the central theme of the plot as a whole. It thus was a good point for comparing local, single-picture based descriptions with a more global perspective on this scene as the onset of a larger sequence of events. Second, analysis of perspectives speakers adopt with respect to the dog getting stuck inside the jar served as a point of departure for questions having to do with (a) *argument-array* — what is selected as syntactic subject, direct object, and/or oblique object; (b) *transitivity* — for instance, does the dog stick its neck into the jar, or does it get its head stuck, or does its head get stuck; and (c) *grammatical voice:* active — the dog sticks its head in, passive — the dog is caught by/in the jar, or middle — the dog is/gets stuck in the jar. And third, since the picture depicts both the boy and the dog in a particular situation, it was also possible to examine how speakers *shift* perspective from one protagonist to another (the boy and the dog) or focus on the two protagonists together as sharing a joint searching activity.

Children's descriptions of the scene are analyzed in terms of these three aspects of marking perspective in discourse, thus: (a) *Local vs. global organization of elements:* I assumed that younger children would take a more local view of the scene. They tend to treat the task as describing a group of isolated pictures rather than as an integrated storyline with an onset, a consequence, and a conclusion, and so will not characterize the scene as the first steps in a general search for the frog. (b) *Perspectives on a single event:* I expected younger children to mention fewer components of a single event, and that they would favor an actor perspective in describing what the dog did in relation to the jar. On the other hand, different expressive options might be selected by even the youngest narrators; that is, there would be some variety in the way individual 3-year-olds choose to describe the dog's entering the jar. (c) *Perspectives on related events:* Again, even the youngest children may adopt varying perspectives on different events; for instance, they could shift from one protagonist to another as they proceed. But only older children will switch perspectives within a single scene, and they will do so by more appropriate linguistic devices of cohesion.

Local vs. Global Presentation of Events

As noted, narrators could relate to the scene by either a local description which treats it as a self-contained situation or by a global perspective in which it forms part of a larger narrative context. The picture represents the initiation of the boy and his dog's search for their missing frog, a search which forms the central motif of the story, and covers the bulk of the book (72% of its 24 pictures). That is, the search-for-frog motif is much more extensive than the scene-setting which precedes, showing that the boy has a frog and that it escapes from the jar, and the denouement which follows where the boy recovers his lost frog (in fact finds another one to take its place). Speakers have several options in relating this scene to the macrolevel theme of the search. They can adopt an "umbrella-like" perspective taking the search motif as the frame that unifies all the elements of the story, in which case (a) they need not relate to this scene at all — for example, (4a) below; (b) they can generalize across the picture by simply saying "they started searching," then go on to the next step in the story without further detail — for example, (4b); alternatively, (c) they might combine the boy's looking in the boots and the dog's looking inside the jar as both search-activities, then specify what the two protagonists did — for example, (4c); or (d) they may not express a search perspective at all, either because they do not realize that this is at issue or because they choose to detail each element in the scene rather than to generalize — an option selected by several preschool children aged 3 to 6 years but by no schoolage children aged 6 to 12 or adults. The following translations from Hebrew adult narratives illustrate the first three possibilities:

4. a. *YONA, woman aged 21 — Clauses #7–13 out of a total 37:*
    When Danny got up in the morning, (he) dressed, and found the frog was gone. Right away (he) went out to look for it. He went out towards the-forest to-look-for it.
    b. *DAFNA, woman aged 22 — Clauses 11–14 out of a total 50:*
    In the morning he awoke, and he did not find it. (He) looked for it all over the house, and the dog helped him.
    c. *SHAY, man aged 24 — Clauses 12–14 out of a total 51:*
    Danny and Yoye started looking-for . . . the frog. Danny searched inside the boot, Yoye searched inside the jar of glass and his head got stuck there.

In selecting different options for relating the "dog-in-jar" scene to a global search theme, the 12 adults divided up as follows: (a) one said nothing at all about this scene; (b) three mentioned it as the start of a general search; (c) eight started with a general statement about searching, then provided more detail about this picture (the favored option among adults); while (d) none ignored the search theme. A very different breakdown emerges on this matter among the younger storytellers in the sample.

Two criteria determined whether narrators treated this scene as initiation of the search. The first was use of a relevant verb — minimally the general activity verb for visual perception *histakel* meaning "look = look at," used alone or with an object governed by the preposition *be-* "at" or *al* "on," but more typically the verb *xipes* meaning "look for, search, seek," which takes a direct object. These are translated in (5) below as *look* and *search,* respectively. The latter is semantically more specialized, and children learn it later than *histakel* "look at," yet it is an everyday colloquial term, not of a higher register like English *search, seek*. A second criterion for reference to search-initiation was how generalized it was across (a) this particular picture, and (b) what precedes or follows in the plotline. Mentions of the search-motif were ranked on a 6-point scale of explicitness, by the criteria of lexical specificity in verb-use combined with generality of thematic plotline reference. Points on the scale are defined and illustrated in (5) below, followed by a quantitative breakdown for each age-group in Table 7.1.

5. *Types of reference to search motif, in ascending order of explicitness:*
    1. General verb for *look* in relation to boots or jar; indicates motivation of the actor to interact with the object:
        a. *And then the dog looks in . . . in . . . the jar*   [4;6]

    2. Specific verb for *search* in boot or in jar; connects event to the previous scene, showing that frog has left jar:
        b. *And the boy searches, whether it's inside his boot*   [4;3]
        c. *And the dog looked meanwhile whether a frog is in the jar*   [5;3]

    3. Verb meaning *look/search* used for both boy looking in boot, dog in jar; the two participants are described as engaged in a similar kind of event:
        d. *And the dog—looked from [sic] the jar. The boy peeped from the window*   [5;0]
        e. *And the boy looked inside the boot and the dog looked through er . . . the open jar*   [5;3]

    4. Both protagonists are combined in a single search, or boy is specified as searching and dog ignored or treated as side-issue—with or without subsequent comment summing up results of looking:
        f. *So they searched very hard inside the hat and maybe inside the jar and they didn't find (it), so they looked outside and the dog got into the jar*   [5;9]
        g. *They search (for) the frog, the dog inside the jar, the boy inside the shirt, and they don't find it*   [7;3]

    5. Same as #4, but including initial prospective comment; reference to the fact that they were both searching and/or that they searched all over the place, that is, a single inclusive search:
        h. *So they searched (for) it in the shoes and in all kinds of places, and the dog, suddenly he searched (for) it inside the jar, and got-caught*   [7;5]
        i. *And they searched (for) it, and the dog that tried to smell the jar got himself inside of that . . . utensil*   [9;6]
        j. *He searched (for) it all over the entire house, among the clothes, in the shoes, he turned the whole house upside down. The dog*

> *searched in the vase where the frog was a few moments ago, and
> found . . .* [11;5]

6. Same as #4, but including a summary statement; reference to a search
in progress, or begun, i.e. initiation of longer search:
   k. *They go to search (for) it. At first they search all over the house,
   and in the course of searching, the dog sticks its head . . .* [Ad]
   l. *Danny and Yoye started to search (for) . . . the frog. Danny
   searched inside a boot, Yoye searched inside the glass pail, and got
   stuck* [Ad]

Table 7.1 gives the raw numbers of respondents in each age group who
referred to the search-motif, ranked on the scale delineated in (5).

The table shows a clear stepwise progression from preschool to schoolage
compared with adults' reference to the search-motif. The adults overwhelmingly
note this as the onset of a generalized "searching-expedition" (Hebrew
masa xipusim), as an entire chain of events that is triggered by what preceded
(ranked as #6 above), and so do half the 6th graders, and a third of the 4th
graders, but no younger children. By early school-age (7-year-olds), reference is nearly always made to the search as an inclusive activity (rank #5), but
rarely before then; and the 5-year-olds, but not the younger children, describe
both boy and dog as both looking or searching for something. In other words,
none of the 3- and 4-year-olds, only some of the 5-year-olds, but all of the
school-age and adult respondents relate this scene to the overall frame of the
story.

Developmental differences in the perspectives of local vs. global, picture-

**Table 7.1. Number of references to search-theme, by age and type of reference
[N = number of respondents in each group who mentioned the picture]**

Age	N	1 X or Y looks in A or B	2 X or Y seeks in A or B	3 X looks in A, Y seeks in B	4 X (and Y) search for frog	5 Inclusive search (all over)	6 Inception of general search	Tot
3s	10	–	–	–	–	–	–	0
4s	9	1	1	–	–	–	–	2
5s	11	1	1	1	5	1	–	9
7s	11	–	–	–	1	10	–	11
9s	12	–	–	–	4	4	4	12
11s	11	–	–	–	–	6	5	11
Ads	9	–	–	–	–	1	8	9

description vs. story-telling, frame-by-frame vs. overarching discourse organization have been noted for narratives based on this picturebook in different languages, from various research perspectives (Bamberg, 1987; Berman, 1988; Slobin, 1986b). The present analysis further demonstrates that these distinctions affect how speakers present the contents of a particular scene, and serve to delimit the range of options available to them for this purpose. Thus, all (although not necessarily only) the children who organize their narratives around the three critical plotline elements of (a) the discovery that the frog is gone, (b) sustained search for the missing frog, and (c) recovery of frog or finding a substitute for it, will mention the search motif in describing this scene. Moreover, the way they refer to the search motif interacts with how they describe the contents of this scene. All the 3- and 4-year-olds, and many of the 5-year-olds present its component events, the boy interacting with the boot and the dog with the jar, as two separate, unrelated activities. They have no recourse to an organizing conceptual frame — linguistically expressed as a common predication, the search theme; or by means of a common point of reference — either locative, for example, *in the bedroom, inside the house* or temporal, for example, *in the meanwhile, at the same time, after they found the frog was gone, before they went outside.*

Perspectives on a Single Event

The scene depicts animate beings — the boy and his dog — or part of these beings — their head or neck — interacting with an inanimate object — a big boot and a glass jar, respectively. Descriptions of the dog's interaction with the jar demonstrate that people of similar educational and linguistic background use language to describe the same external situation in different ways. Compare, again, such excerpts as the following, translated from some Hebrew adult narratives.

6. a. *Avishai, male aged 20:*
   And the dog has the glass jar on his head.

   b. *Nir, male aged 24:*
   They search and search, the dog searches inside the jar, the boy inside the boot . . .

   c. *Shay, male aged 23:*
   Yoye [=the dog] searched inside the pail of glass, and his head got stuck there. . . . .

Children, too, rely on a variety of linguistic options to express the same external situation from the youngest age group tested (three years). In developmental terms, however, certain perspectives are favored by older children compared with younger. This is shown by analysis of clauses describing this scene in terms of (a) number and array of arguments, (b) type of predicate—with verbs divided according to the categories specified by Vendler (1967) and elaborated by Dowty (1979) and Van Valin (Foley & Van Valin, 1984; Van Valin, 1987), and (c) prepositional markers of different types of complements—arguments and adverbial adjuncts—as set out in (7).

7. *Notation for Representing Arguments, Predicates, Prepositions:*
   (see fn. 4)
   (i) ARGUMENTS: **kelev** = dog: standing also for names (e.g. *Yoye* in (6c above), nouns like *klavlav* "puppy," *kalbon* "doggy," and pronouns, e.g. *hu* "he, it," *ze* "it, this"

   dli = pail: standing for words like *tsint-senet* "jar," *agartal* "vase," *kufsa* "can," *kli* "utensil," *davar* "thing," and pronouns like *oto* "it," *betoxa* "inside-it"

   rosh = head: including words for neck, throat, and pronouns

   tsfar(dea) = frog: including words for animal, and pronouns

   (ii) VERBS: **STA** stands for verbs denoting *states,* i.e. temporally unbounded static situations—here, being or remaining (stuck) inside the jar;
   ACT stands for *activities,* i.e., temporally unbounded dynamic situations—here, going or entering into the jar, or looking inside the jar; ACH and ACC are two subclasses of activities:
   ACH stands for *achievements,* i.e., the moment of termination or the process leading up to it when an undergoer enters into a state or an activity—here, getting caught in the jar; and
   ACC stands for *accomplishments,* where an action brings about a change of state—for example, sticks his head inside the jar.[7]

---

[7]These classes refer to perspectives taken on events by choice of a predicate representing a particular kind of *Aktionsarten* or inherent lexical aspect, in contrast to grammatical aspect of the type noted in fn. 2 above. The present analysis disregards this important linguistic device for perspective-taking: First, it is not applicable to Hebrew and, second, the event in question is basically punctual and does not invite a durative/punctual contrast, as do other scenes in the story (Slobin, 1986).

Root	Form	Class	Glosses
h-l-x	*halax*	ACT	go, walk
k-n-s	*nixnas*	ACT	go/get/come-in(to) = enter
	hixnis	ACC	put/take/shove-in(to) = insert
s-y-m	*sam*	ACC	put
l-k-x	*lakax*	ACC	take
s-k-l	*histakel*	ACT	look (at)
x-p-s	*xipes*	ACT	look-for, search (for), seek
h-y-y	*yesh, haya*	STA	be = (there's), is, was . . .
sh-?-r	*nish'ar*	STA	say, remain
t-p-s	*nitpas*	ACH	get-caught
	tafus	STA	be-caught
t-q-'	*taka*	ACC	stick-into
	nitka	ACH	get-stuck
	takua	STA	be-stuck

(iii) RELATIONS: are manifested by the following prepositionals:

et	=	Accusative	Direct Object marker
be-, btox	=	in, at; inside	Stative Locative
le-, ltox	=	to; into	Goal Directional marker
lo	=	to/for-him/it	Dative marker of affectee[8]
shel	=	of, 's	Possessive, Genitive marker

This range of options was analyzed for each age group in the Hebrew narratives, starting with the 3-year-olds, aged 3;0–3;11, as presented in (8). below. As before, the bracketed numbers stand for the child's age, and position in the year-group: [3k] is the eleventh child in the 3-year-old group, and older than the ninth child [3i], both of whom are older than the third child, [3c]. The clauses outlined schematically in (8) show that 10 (out of a total 12) 3-year-olds mentioned the dog-jar situation, and that they chose no fewer than eight different ways to do so.[9] (In the examples that follow, numbers in parentheses refer to the number of children in each age group who gave that response.)

8.   *Ages 3;0–3;11:*
   a. *kelev (haya) btox dli*   STA   dog (was) in jar   (1)

---

[8]An example would be *ze nitka lo ba-rosh* "it got-stuck to-him on-the-head," where the dative *lo* "to-him" indicates that "he" was the being affected by this event. This use of dative pronouns in Hebrew is analyzed in Berman (1982).

[9]This analysis ignores reference to the content of subsequent pictures, where the dog is shown leaning from and then falling out the window with his head stuck in the jar, as noted on pp. 186–187.

b. *kelev . . . er rosh shel kelev*	STA	dog . . . er head of dog	(1)
c. *kelev nixnas ltox dli*	ACT	dog entered = went into jar	(1)
d. *kelev lakax dli*	ACC	dog took jar	(1)
e. *kelev hixnis rosh*		dog inserted = put-in head	(1)
f. *kelev hixnis rosh btox dli*		dog inserted head inside jar	(3)
g. *kelev sam dli al rosh*		dog put jar on head	(1)
h. *ve po kelev nitka*	ACH	and here dog got-stuck	(1)

Six out of the ten 3-year-olds who mentioned this event gave it a causative-agent orientation, with the dog doing something to the jar in two cases, and to its head in the other four; only one described it as a noncausative (intransitive) activity with the dog as patient — example (8c) — while two gave a verbless stative description — (8a, 8b) — and the remaining child used an inchoative verb — example (8h). The child who used the verb for *get-stuck* was the only 3-year-old who described this scene with a single argument; five specify two arguments, and the other four specify three arguments. Not one mentioned the frog as a potential fourth argument, since none of these 3-year-olds related the content of this picture thematically to preceding events. Thus even these young children were able to use straightforward locative type propositions to describe this event, with no recourse to prior events or the fact that the jar belonged to or had been associated with the frog. Moreover, by adopting a basic perspective of Theme-Location or Actor-Action in all but one case (the last example, (8h) above), these younger children were able to avoid the difficult decisions made by older narrators in choosing more complex perspectives — for instance, whether the dog deliberately stuck its head inside or got stuck there by accident, whether the dog looked inside and so got caught, or went inside and then could not get out, and so on. They simply said the dog is in the jar, the dog has gone into the jar, or the dog has put his head into the jar.

Eight of the twelve 4-year-olds mention the dog's interaction with the jar, as set out in (9) below. They present a more homogeneous perspective on this event than the threes, all eight taking an ACTIVITY orientation, seven from the point of view of the dog as actor, and one — example (9g) — taking the dog's head as focus. Four-year-olds clearly possess the linguistic means for adopting an accomplishment perspective. For instance, two of the children in this group use the causative verb *hixnis* "cause-to-enter = put in, insert" in describing subsequent scenes (e.g., "and here also he *put-in* his head, the-dog") to describe the next picture, where the dog is leaning out of the window with the jar on his head; [4j] "he fell out and he *put-in* his head (in)to . . ." two pictures later where the dog has fallen out of the window with the jar on his head.

They simply choose not to use this perspective when first describing the dog-in-jar.

9. *Ages 4;0–4;11:*

a. *kelev halax btox dli shel tsfar*	dog went inside jar of frog	(1)
b. *kelev histakel be-dli*	dog looked at/in jar	(1)
c. *kelev rotse nixnas letox dli*	dog wants enter into jar	(2)
d. *kelev nixnas letox dli shel tsfar*	dog enters into jar of frog	(1)
e. *kelev nixnas letox dli shel tsfar, ve xipes*	dog entered into jar of frog, and searched	(1)
f. *kelev nixnas le-dli be-rosh*	dog entered (in)to jar in head (ambiguous *be-* = in ~ with, unclear)	(1)
g. *rosh shel kelev nixnas le-dli*	head of dog entered (in)to jar	(1)

These descriptions are more varied than the 3-year-olds' from one point of view: They range from the juvenile reliance — in example (9a) — on a general-purpose motion verb *halax* "go" (Clark, 1978) to explicit mention of the search motive — in (9c). Some of the 4-year-olds also display a more thematic organization: three children in this group (in examples 9a, 9d, and 9e) as against not a single 3-year-old, mention the frog in relation to the jar, taking a perspective which relates this situation to an earlier one (two pictures back). One child in this age group suggests that the entry into the jar was accidental; she says the dog did it *be 'acimat'enayim* "with closing-of eyes = closing his eyes," and in this way weakens the actor-oriented perspective of the dog as voluntary agent. Downgrading of agency is also suggested by child who says that it was the dog's head, rather than the dog himself, that entered the jar — example (9g). That is, although the 4-year-olds all take a shared ACTIVITY perspective, they temper it in ways not attempted by the younger group.

This contrasts, too, with the 5-year-olds who refer to the dog plus jar in this picture (9 out of 12). They provide the most varied descriptions of the three preschool-age groups: two children talk about the dog looking in the jar; two talk about the dog going into the jar; another four take a transitive-accomplishment perspective with the verbs meaning "take, put, insert"; while one child — who also refers to the search motif explicitly for both the boy and the dog — takes a patient-achievement perspective, thus: *ve axarey ze ha-kelev nitka ha-kufsa im ha-rosh* "and after that the-dog got-stuck the-jar with his-head." But his description is illformed, as was that of the 4-year-old who had a more complex argument-array in (9f) above. This 5-year-old's formulation breaks down in relation to all three arguments: If the noun for dog is left-dislocated, then there should be a dative case-marked pronominal trace of this; if the feminine noun *kufsa* "can = jar" is the nominative grammatical subject, it requires feminine marking on the verb *nitka* "get-stuck"; and if jar is nominative then the noun *rosh* "head" should be marked for locative *be-* "on, over" and not instrumental or comitative *im*. That is, the child should have said either *ha-kelev, nitke'a lo ha-kufsa ba-rosh* "the dog, got-stuck + Fem to-him the-jar + Fem on-(his)-head" or *ha-kelev nitka ba-kufsa im ha-rosh* "the-dog + Masc got-stuck + Masc in-the-jar with its-head." This example suggests that when preschoolers opt for something other than a simple actor-activity perspective on this event, they may limit the number of other arguments they mention — as was done by child the 3-year-old in (8h) above — or else they will produce errors in formulating the interrelations between the arguments and their functions.

An age-related finding is the distinct rise in choice of *patient perspective* by means of an inchoative achievement verb (e.g., *nitka, nitpas* "get-stuck, get-caught" — in a typically intransitive verb-pattern). A quarter of the school-children, aged 7 to 12 years, who mentioned this event (8/32) express this orientation, compared with only 2 out of the 29 preschoolers (aged 3 to 6 years). The examples in (10) are from the youngest school-age children, 7-year-old second-graders, and account for 5 out of 10 descriptions of the scene given by this age group.

10.   *Ages 7;0–7;11 [second grade]:*
   a. *dli nixnas lo [=kelev] ltox rosh*
                              jar entered to-him [=dog] into head
   b. *kelev xipes btox dli ve nitpas*
                              dog searched inside jar and got-caught
   c. *kelev nitka btox dli shel tsfar*
                              dog got-stuck inside jar of frog
   d. *kelev, nitka lo [=kelev] dli al rosh*
                              dog, got-stuck to-him [=dog] jar on head
   e. *kelev, nitka lo [=kelev] rosh btox dli*
                              dog, got-stuck to-him head inside jar

The effect of *agent downgrading* is also achieved by specifying an affectee perspective on the dog through use of the dative pronoun *lo*, coreferential with the dog (examples 10a, 10d, 10e above). Moreover, 7-year-olds, but not the younger children, use left-dislocation appropriately to establish the dog as topic, then describe what happened to him as patient — as shown by correct use of gender concord in examples (10d and 10e). This evidence for development of an undergoer-perspective with respect to the dog among the 7-year-olds is supported by findings for other languages, and for other events in this story. For instance, in describing a scene where the boy gets entangled in the antlers of a deer, younger children typically selected an Actor-Activity perspective in describing the boy having climbed or gotten onto the deer (Berman & Slobin, 1987; Slobin, 1986b).

Another difference between the descriptions of preschoolers and older children reflects an increasing ability at *event-packaging*. This is expressed as (a) elaboration—by adjoining several argument and adjunct phrases within a single clause or by embedding clauses within a single sentence; or as (b) restriction—by coalescing several events into a single predication.

Examples of intraclause elaboration by children from three different school-age groups are given in (11).

11. a. *ve kelev shel-o [=yeled] nixnas im rosh btox dli*   [7;7]
        and his dog [=the boy's] entered with head inside jar

     b. *az be-dli shel tsfar, kelev hixnis rosh shel-o [=kelev]*   [9;6]
        then in-jar of frog, dog inserted his head [=dog's]

     c. *kelev nixnas—rosh shel kelev, kelev hixnis rosh be-ta'ut*
                                                    la dli shel tsfar   [12;0]
        dog inserted—head of dog, dog inserted head by-mistake
                                                    (in)to frog's jar

The manner adverbial *beta'ut* "by mistake" in the last example provides intraclause elaboration, and serves to downgrade agency, treating the dog's action as nonvolitional. Several schoolage narrators use this as a means to specify a less agentive perspective (e.g., *bli kavana* "without meaning" in (12) below).

In other words, as shown in (10) as well, early schoolage use varied linguistic devices to meet the general function of downgrading of agency in describing the dog—in-jar situation. These include intransitive verb-morphology; prepositional case-marking of the affectee role as dative; manner adverbials to describe the event as nonvolitional; and left-dislocated word-order to topicalize the dog as patient.

Elaboration is also achieved by adding predications (as discussed further in connection with perspective switching below). Examples from children aged nine and eleven are given in (12).

12. a. *kelev xipes—er—hixnis rosh ltox dli she tsfar hayta bo*   [9;5]
        dog searched—er—inserted head inside jar that frog had-been in

     b. *kelev hixnis rosh shel-o ltox dli mimenu barxa tsfar*   [9;0]
        dog inserted his head into jar from-which ran-away frog

     c. *ve kelev nixnas bli kavana la- dli she bo hayta tsfar*   [11;5]
        and dog entered without meaning (in)to jar in-which had-been frog

     d. *kelev xipes—ba-dli she bo hayta tsfar lifney mispar dakot*   [11;6]
        dog searched—in jar in which had-been frog several minutes ago

e. *ve kelev she nisa le-hariax dli, nixnas lo btox dli*   [9;6]
   and dog that tried to-smell jar, entered to-him(self) inside jar

This kind of packaging across different events by means of relative clauses was not done by any of the children up to age nine, even though Hebrew-speaking 3-year-olds can form relative clauses. Nor did the younger children coalesce different events in the same scene into a single predication, as illustrated in (13), where *yeled* "boy, child" stands for "the boy" and *magaf* "boot" stands for "(his) shoes, boots."

13.   [7b] *hem xipsu   tsfar, kelev btox dli, yeled btox magaf*
             they searched (for) frog, dog inside jar, boy inside boot

      [7f] *yeled—xipes ba-magaf, ve kelev ba-dli*
             boy searched in boot,   and dog in jar

      [9d] *az hitxilu le-xapes oto [=et tsfar] mi-kol hacdadim,*
                        btox kutonet, btox magaf, btox dli
             then (they) began searching (for) it [=frog] on-all sides,
                        inside shirt, inside boots, inside jar

      [11j] *hem xipsu be-kol, be-kol ha-xeder   kdey li-mtso et tsfar*
             they searched all over, all over the room so as to find frog

Combining events by embedding clauses as in (12), or by adding phrasal components within a single clause as in (13) occurs across the 9-and 11-year-olds, and in most 7-year-old texts, but not among the preschoolers. The ability to interweave different events in discourse within a single syntactic frame — phrasal, clausal, or sentential — is a critical feature of developing a *narrative perspective*. In the task at hand, this perspective is reflected by narrators' explicitly relating the jar to its role in preceding pictures, or by connecting the contents of this scene to the frog's disappearance earlier on.

Perspective Switching
The scene was also examined to show how initiation of the search reflects speakers' ability to switch perspective — from one protagonist to another, from agent to patient, or from punctual to durative or protracted aspect, and from one temporal or locative frame to another. Narrators could do this by switching from one protagonist to another — the boy holding up the boot and the dog stuck in the jar — and/or by shifting views on a single protagonist, for instance, from an actor-focus describing the dog looking inside or putting his head into the jar to a patient-focus that describes the dog getting or being stuck there. But speakers could also choose to categorize across a single predication: The physical situation of both boy and dog having or putting something on their head, and the mental state of looking for the frog. Continuities combined

with shifts across referents and predicates function to move a narrative forward cohesively yet flexibly. Analysis reveals a general developmental trend from this point of view: The younger children treat each frame as isolated and self-contained, a picture of a single object, state, or event; early school-age children chain from one event to the next, coordinating them along a sequential line; and more mature narrators embed two or more events within a single frame. This is illustrated by the following excerpts from two adult narratives:[10]

14. a. And [zero = he] began to search. [Zero = he] searched inside the boots, and the dog searched inside the jar, [zero = frog] may by chance have stayed inside, so that the jar remained caught [perfective] onto the dog's head, and he couldn't get free.

     b. Both of them search (for) it inside the room, when er—the dog inserts its head into the jar. The jar gets-stuck [inchoative] onto his head, and he tries to shake it off.

   The notion of "switching perspective" simply does not apply in the case of the youngest children in our sample, aged three to four; as noted, they fail to treat the different events as interrelated in any way. The only switch is in *participant reference,* going from the boy to the dog or from the dog to the boy, as follows.

15. a. and (there) came a moon, and the dog got inside the jar, and the boy put his shoe on his head.   [3;0]

     b. er . . . er . . . the boy puts his shoe on his head . . . the dog inserts its head inside the can.   [3;7]

     c. a boy and a frog. the dog er . . . took the glass. This boy he put on his Mommy's shoes.   [3;7]

     d. And the—and the dog is inside this bottle. And the boy he holds the dog.   [3;10]

These children are able to describe the contents of a picture—and they can name the relevant participants and the objects depicted there distinctively. In contrast, a couple of the older 4-year-olds, do show some initial *chaining* of events as sequentially following upon one another, for instance:

---

[10]The examples in this section are given in English translation, since the kind of thematic organization they reflect relies less on language-particular devices than clause-internal verb-argument configurations discussed in the preceding section.

16. a. After that, in the morning when the boy and the dog got up, the dog
         went into the jar of the frog.   [4;8]

     b. And the frog went outside, and . . . the dog it went onto his [=the
         dog's] head, and he fell from the window   [4;9]

But the 4-year-olds, too, fail to switch perspective from one event to
another in this scene or from this scene to an event which precedes or follows
it.[11] This more flexible orientation on a scene is found only among children
from age five, and it shows the following developmental patterning. The
five-year-olds manifest *protagonist switching* from reference to the boy and
dog together, to the boy or the dog alone—typically in the form of a
grammatical shift from plural to singular, marked on the verb as well as on
nouns and adjectives in Hebrew (examples in (16) below). The younger
schoolchildren (7- to 8-year-olds) shift from *agent to patient* for the same
protagonist, as an early means of making aspectual distinctions to mark the
inception, continuation, and/or endstate of a given situation. The older
speakers manifest a variety of shifts in perspective. For instance, many of the
nine-year olds express *temporal-aspectual switching* quite explicitly, by retrospective reference to the jar as the place where the frog had been, or by talking
about the dog as still remaining inside the jar. And from this phase on,

---

[11]The single exception is one child aged 4;3, who with many repairs and backtrackings refers
to the dog's interaction with the jar in several ways, with both intransitive *nixnas* "go in(to), enter"
and transitive *hixnis* "put-in(to), cause-to-enter":

Picture 3a: *hakelev nixnas letox hacincenet*	The-dog goes into the-jar
ve mexapes . . . hayeled mexapes	and searches . . . the boy searches
im ze betox hamagaf.	if it's inside the boot.
Picture 3b: *KAN hayeled kore latsfardea*	HERE the boy calls the frog
ve hakelev nixnas letox . . . hakufsa	and the dog goes into . . . the-can
shel hatsfardea.	of the frog.
Picture 4a: *KAN hakelev melakek oto*	HERE the-dog licks him [=the boy]
ve gam . . . ve KAN hu maxnis et harosh shelo hakelev	
and also . . . and here he *inserts/put in* his head the-dog	

Repeated use of deictic *kan* "here" shows the child moving from picture to picture in the book,
not from one event to the next in the story. And even though he uses different forms of the verb
k-n-s *go/get/put in*—they do not serve genuine perspective switching across events. Picture 4a,
where the child talks about the dog inserting its head in the jar, in fact depicts a situation that
requires a *stative* predicate for the dog's head still being inside the jar, the dog being stuck there.
Compare these two adult versions: *kelev nafal kshe rosh-o natun btox dli* "the dog fell with
his-head *situated* inside the jar," and *be-od rosh-o takua btox ha-dli* "with his-head still *stuck*
inside the jar." This 4-year-old, in contrast, knows both the transitive and intransitive of this
motion verb, but does not alternate them to switch perspective. Similarly, in describing another
scene, where the boy who is sprawled on the ground with an owl gazing down at him from the hole
into which he had been peering, Hebrew-speaking 4- and 5-year-olds often said things like *hayeled
nafal ki hayanshuf hipil oto* "the-boy *fell* because the-owl *made-fall* him = pushed him down"
(Slobin, 1987b).

speakers use numerous linguistic devices for this purpose—they subordinate background events in relative clauses, they leftdislocate nominals in order to establish them as topics, and they front oblique objects to achieve a switch in focus—illustrated by excerpts from the 6th-grade narratives in (17) below.

Shifting from plural to singular was used by 3 of the 10 5-year-olds who mentioned this scene, but by none of the younger children. As illustrated in (17), the suffix -*u* or -*im* in the Hebrew verb-forms is the plural marker for past and present tense respectively.

17. a. So they searched [=*xips-u*] very hard inside the hat and maybe in the jar, and they did not find [=*mac'-u*], and . . . the dog er got inside [=*nixnas*] the jar with its head   [5;8]

    b. They look [*mistakl-im*] in their shoes, and they do not find [*moc'-im*] and afterwards the dog gets-stuck [=*nitka*] . . .   [5;9]

The excerpts in (17) illustrate another shift made by three of the 5-year-olds, by three 7-year-olds, and by a couple of older children (one in the 9-year-old group, one of the 11-year-olds). They relate to the *consequence* of an activity—here, the fact that they looked but "did not find (the frog)." None of the younger children add a comment on what happens once the dog is inside the jar. There is also a difference in the way speakers relate to the follow-up events. Adults typically do so by explicit mention of the *aspectual protractedness,* of the resultant state, for example, (a) *fell outside with the jar on his head,* (b) *with the dog still caught inside the jar, [20d] with his head situated inside the jar,* (c) *while his head is stuck in the jar,* (d) *the jar remained stuck on the dog's head and he couldn't get free;* while (e) one adult mentioned the dog's *trying to shake off the jar.* Several older children (four 9-year-olds and two 11-year-olds) also elaborate on the event in *irrealis modality:* Like the last adult mentioned, they switch from an active to a stative perspective, in terms such as the dog's "wanting, trying, not managing, being unable to get out of the jar."

Another kind of switch is shown by half of the 9-year-olds (but by none of the younger children), who mention that the dog got inside the jar "where the frog had been" or "from which the frog had escaped" (examples are given in (12) above). This requires a shift in participant perspective—the dog is in the jar where the frog used to be—and in temporal perspective—the frog's being in the jar is retrospective to the dog's entry into the jar. This is achieved through relativization, with a syntactic shift from the main clause object—the jar—to subordinate clause subject—the frog.

This kind of switching back and forth across protagonists, and across different components of the same and of different events is clearly shown in the following three excerpts translated from sixth-grade narratives:

18. a. They search + Plur in the boots, and the dog gets into the — sticks his
        head into the jar and checks whether the frog is there, and it — and it
        isn't   [11;5]

     b. The boy searched all over the house, among his clothes, his shoes, he
        turned the house upside down. The dog searched — in the vase that the
        frog had been in a few minutes earlier, and discovered that it — wasn't
        (there), but when (he) wanted to get his get out of the vase, he
        couldn't   [11;6]

     c. And . . . (they) begin [*matxil-im*] to search all over. The boy
        gets-dressed [*mitlabesh*] and (they) decide [*maxlit-im*] to go outside.
        The dog gets in [*nixnas*] . . . the head of the dog, he inserted [*hixnis*]
        it by mistake into the jar of the frog, where the frog lived, and (they)
        begin [*matxil-im*] . . .   [12;0]

Perspective switching of this kind within a particular scene requires skilled
deployment of syntactic devices for cohesiveness — including coordination and
subordination as well as use of anaphoric pronouns and subject ellipsis. The
third example in (18) also illustrates use of left-dislocation and temporal
shifting to past tense in talking about a punctual event and its precedent within
a generally present-tense narrative. And these examples, together with those
noted for the adults earlier, show how a wide range of different structural and
lexical devices combine with different facets of the scene — aspectual, temporal, locative, causal — to determine how speakers describe the same event from
varying perspectives.

Discussion

These findings for how Hebrew-speaking children describe a single scene in a
picturebook story are discussed below in relation to the following broader
issues: The cognitive and linguistic demands of the task; the nature of
developing narrative skills compared with other discourse modes; the interaction between form and function in this development; and cross-linguistic
compared with language-particular facets of developing abilities at expressing
perspectives on events.

The task presented to the children, where they were shown the contents of
the entire booklet, and then asked to themselves "tell the story" while looking
at the pictures, provided heavy scaffolding for content. That is, children did
not have to recall or reconstruct events which they had experienced or been
told about, they could simply describe the contents of each picture in turn. But
they did have to demonstrate understanding of visual (specifically, black-
and-white pictorial) cues; to make inferences, for instance, that the boy and/or
dog were looking for something; and to relate one picture to the next, for
example, to note that they were looking for a pet frog that was no longer in the

jar where it had been held. Children from the youngest age examined (3;0) were able to describe the contents of this, as of other pictures in the booklet, quite adequately. They were less adept at making inferences and at relating one picture to the next — as shown by the findings for reference to the search-motif. These results are closely consistent with those of Karmiloff-Smith (1981, 1983) even though the storybook used here depicts a much longer and more complicated chain of events than the pictured sequences in the tasks she assigned to English and French-speaking children. They are also supported by findings on a partly comparable task performed by German children when retelling the contents of this booklet after hearing the story from their mothers (Bamberg, 1987). And they are in line with findings for veridical storytelling based on personal experiences told by children of similar ages (e.g., Peterson & McCabe, 1983).

Karmiloff-Smith's perceptive account of children's developing discourse abilities has shown that younger, preschool children, still at the "procedural phrase," will opt for a predominantly protagonist-oriented perspective. They will produce utterances which are syntactically well-formed and lexically felicitous, but they cannot as yet integrate an overall discourse — whether at the macrolevel of the entire narrative or at the microlevel such as the dog-in-jar scene — as a single organizational unit. Young schoolage children — most of the 7- and all the 9-year-olds in the Hebrew sample — treat the scene analyzed here as a coherent, well-motivated whole, but only from age 9 up do the narratives become felicitously subordinated to an overarching discourse theme, incorporated at both the local and the global level. Only at around age 9 to 10 are children able to integrate what Karmiloff-Smith has termed both "bottom-up" and "top-down" processing in narrative discourse as in other, nonlinguistic tasks.

The present study, like the others noted above and like my earlier analysis of the overall structure of these Hebrew texts (Berman, 1988), focuses on the special demands of narrative discourse. This is relevant to the general concern of this chapter from the following point of view. As I had assumed, children as young as age 3 can talk about the same situation — the dog inside a jar — in different ways. A pilot study in which subjects were prompted to elaborate on the contents of the pictures by questions such as "Why did he do it?" and "How do you think the dog got into the jar?" suggests that 3-year-olds can also establish links between events when they are explicitly required to do so. But it takes time for children to develop the special perspective of the narrative mode of discourse, which in this case means using the contents of a picturebook to tell a story that is sequentially and causally related within a single thematic frame.

Knowledge of the narrative mode depends in part on cultural norms, where schoolage children have themselves read stories beginning with "once upon a time . . ." and ending with "so in the end . . ." and they know what is expected of them when an investigator, like their classteacher, instructs them "Now you tell me a story." But it also has to do with cognitive maturation, and the ability to recount sequences of events without the mediation of explicit linguistic input. Preschool-age children *are* able to express richer and more flexible shifts in perspective, but in other discourse modes, not in the context of extended narrative. The scaffolding provided by interlocutor questions, queries, denials, challenges, and other discourse prompts in the course of *conversational* interchange leads children from an early age to shift from one perspective to another as part of the give-and-take of verbal interaction. The conversations of Hebrew-speaking 4-year-olds show, for instance, that they can alternate flexibly and skillfully between a personalized and a more impersonal description of events through switches from first and second to third person, from singular to plural, from past perfective to present tense or irrealis mood, from definite to indefinite reference, and so on. (Berman, 1987c, 1990).

It might be argued that the differences observed between preschool and schoolage descriptions of a scene are strictly "cognitive" rather than linguistic, particularly since preschool narratives based on this picture booklet differ along similar lines from those of 9-year-olds in other languages as well (Bamberg, 1987; Berman & Slobin, 1987; Slobin, 1986). But this is begging the issue, since development of a *narrative perspective* obviously relies on knowledge which is anchored in language. The explanation seems, instead, to lie in the relation between linguistic forms and the *functions* which they serve (in the broad sense of "function" noted in fn. 1 above). With development, both (a) the range of forms used to meet a particular function, and (b) the range of functions met by a particular form are extended and enriched.

For example, the array of forms illustrated in (18) above for the oldest children in the sample include: anaphorical pronouns, locative phrases, sentential coordination, relative clauses, and left-dislocations. These constructions all occur in the speech of Hebrew-speaking preschoolers (Berman, 1985). But they are not used by the younger children telling this story for the purpose of maintaining the flow of their narrative by shifting perspectives from agent to patient, from activity to event, and from inception to endstate. Rather, with age the function of shifting perspective on a situation is met by an increasing diversity of linguistic forms. For instance, in this scene it was shown that the function of lowering transitivity can be achieved by lexical choice of Aktionsart, by morphological modification of verb transitivity and voice, by reorganization of argument arrays at the clause level, by coordinating and subordinating across clauses, or by any or all of these together.

In just the same way, diverse forms of noun modification can serve the function of *object-specification*. Children start out by defining objects deictically, using words like *this* or *that,* subsequently also the equivalent of *my, mine* to specify the objects of their reference. As they mature cognitively, and are able to define entities in a context-free way, relying on purely linguistic rather than situational cues, they also acquire a wider range of devices for this function—adjectives, prepositional phrases, and genitives for instance—so that *this book* and *my book* can now alternate with *the little book, mommy's book, the book with pictures.* Somewhat later, children learn to construct propositionally complex nominals of different kinds, enabling them to further vary perspective in identifying or attributing properties to a given object — for example, *my favorite animal book, the book I got for my birthday from uncle Tim.* The distinction between a participant-neutral, impersonal or generic statement compared with a personalized, context-specific perspective is likewise achieved by a combination of factors: Use of plural versus singular; specified versus nonspecified subjects; definite versus nonspecific referents; use of deictic first and second person as against anaphoric third-person reference; and choice of specific versus irrealis tense-mood forms (Berman, 1987c). Details of developmental patterning will clearly depend to some extent on the particular language being acquired. (This is shown for relative clauses by Demuth 1983, Slobin 1986a, and for noun compounding by Berman 1987a, Clark & Berman 1987.) But in any language, an entire range of superficially unrelated forms are deployed in conjunction in presenting a particular perspective. Once cognitive maturation enables the speaker to adopt a certain stance, he or she will deploy diverse linguistic devices for this purpose.

As for a particular form acquiring more elaborated functions, it is well established that in the course of development, "old forms are used to perform new functions." This was suggested at the outset of the chapter with respect to progressive marking in English. It is also clearly demonstrated by changes in use of the coordinating conjunction *ve* — "and" in these Hebrew narratives (Geva, 1989). Likewise, the Hebrew form *benatayim* "meanwhile, in the meantime" is used as a rather vacuous discourse marker in a 3-year-old narrative, whereas in the older children's stories, as in the adults', it serves as a favored marker of simultaneity (5/12 5-year-olds, 9 of the sevens, 11 of the nines, and 8 of the adult Hebrew narratives use it in this way); in contrast, German narrators occasionally use *in der Zwischenzeit,* while English speakers hardly ever use *meanwhile, meantime* for this purpose (von Stutterheim, 1987). Similarly, an inchoative middle-voice or passive form (e.g., English *get-stuck, be-caught*) is used increasingly with age by English and by Hebrew-speakers, but not in the German narratives, to express a patient-perspective with respect to the dog-in-jar or boy-on-antlers (Berman & Slobin, 1987).

This suggests another facet of developing form-function relations. It is not always obvious which particular forms will be marshalled to meet a given function, nor what function will be met by certain forms — within a language and across different languages. Another example is Hebrew narrators' reliance on the form *pit'om* "suddenly, all of a sudden" to mark discourse boundaries when switching to a new topic (e.g., the appearance of some new creature in the forest). This form was used in this way by many children aged 5, 7, and 9 — 80 times in two-thirds (23/36) of their narratives — but by few of the younger children — 9 tokens in one-third (8/24) 3- and 4-year-old narratives; while the adults used it only 9 times in all, compared with an average of nearly 27 per group at age 5, 7, and 9). In other words, forms which appear referentially equivalent may have different discourse functions in different languages and at different phases of development. This is revealed by the way the terms for *meantime* and *suddenly* are used by the Hebrew but not the English narrators in this task, and by the fact that Hebrew and English speakers but not the Germans use passive and middle voice for lowering transitivity.

The last question to be addressed is the fact that the database for the present study was from Hebrew. Studies of the same task in other languages show that the general trends noted for different developmental phases are shared across learners of different languages — both with regard to overall organization of narratives at the macro level, and with respect to specific functions such as switching participant-perspective or making retrospective comments (Berman & Slobin, 1987; Slobin, 1986b, 1987a, b). Nonetheless, the particular language being acquired will affect what facets of a given perspective may be favored by speakers, and how they choose to express it. For instance, the rich system of Hebrew inflection is exploited by the 3-year-olds in this study to distinguish between participants by marking them as singular or plural, masculine or feminine; and Hebrew derivational verb-morphology allows the older children to switch to an undergoer focus by means of an intransitive accomplishment verb rather than its active, transitive counterpart favored at an earlier phase. On the other hand, lack of a distinct neuter gender for inanimate objects denies Hebrew speakers one way of distinguishing the boy, dog, and frog from the boot and the jar. Nor do they have a way to mark perspective-switching by grammatical verb-inflection as in English and Spanish (see fn. 2). Besides, even when forms *are* available in a language, they may not be highly favored for a particular function. For instance, English and Hebrew speakers rely on distinctions of grammatical voice more than was found for the Germans, even though German grammar does have a passive construction. These findings together suggest that, on the one hand, children acquiring different languages will with age learn to perform the same range of general discourse functions on the basis of both greater cognitive maturation and broadened expressive abilities. On the other hand, however, as they mature, speakers will tend increasingly to favor the perspectives most obviously promoted by the grammar of their native tongue, as their use of language becomes more and more strongly Hebrew, or English, Spanish, or Turkish in flavor and propensity.

The point of view I have tried to present is developmental rather than endstate in focus. This means that the child needs to abandon earlier strategies, to move away from encoding along lines of what has been termed in quite different frameworks the constraints imposed by the principle of mutual exclusivity (Chapter 3), one-to-one mapping (Slobin, 1973), or the uniqueness principle (Wexler & Culicover, 1980) in order to select alternative formulations of a particular conceptual content. This is consistent with earlier work of mine, where I have argued that children must go beyond structure-dependent knowledge of morphosyntax, moving from clause-internal phrase-structure to interclause connectivity and on to thematically motivated discourse cohesion. In the present context, this means that the development of thematic structure at the global level of narrative impinges on the expressive options selected in describing a particular event.

As analyzed here in relation to how children express perspectives on a scene in a picturebook story, the development of language use represents a complex interaction between: (a) increased efficiency at meeting the demands of *on-line processing*, which enables speakers to plan and organize their linguistic output hierarchically, in terms of higher-level thematic structures; (b) *conceptual maturation* required for speakers to infer interrelations between events and to embed description of an event in a network of causal, temporal, and other associated circumstances in order to express more elaborately varied perspectives on a situation; and (c) cumulative *linguistic knowledge* underlying speakers' ability to deploy the devices available in and favored by their language flexibly and so to adopt broad discourse perspectives such as the storytelling mode, on the one hand, and to express specific context-bound distinctions such as a more or less agentive or a more or less personalized perspective on a situation, on the other. It is a formidable but challenging task for developmental psycholinguistics to spell out the role of each factor in the child's emergent knowledge of language structure and of language use.

References

Ariel, M. (1991). *Accessing NP antecedents* (Croom Helm Linguistics Series). London: Routledge & Kegan-Paul.

Bamberg, M. (1987). *The acquisition of narratives*. Berlin: Mouton de Gruyter.

Berman, R. A. (1979). Form and function: Passives, middles, and impersonals in Modern Hebrew. *Berkeley Linguistic Society, 5,* 1–27.

Berman, R. A. (1982). Dative marking of the affectee role. *Hebrew Annual Review, 6,* 35–59.

Berman, R. A. (1985). Acquisition of Hebrew. I In D. I. Slobin (Ed.), *Crosslinguistic study of language acquisition*. Hillsdale, NJ: Erlbaum.

Berman, R. A. (1987a). A developmental route: Learning about the form and use of complex nominals in Hebrew. *Linguistics, 27*.

Berman, R. A. (1987b). Productivity in the lexicon: New-word formation in Modern Hebrew. *Folia Linguistica 21,* 425–461.

Berman, R. A. (1987c, December). *Changing predicates, changing perspectives*. Paper prepared for the Fifth Annual Tel-Aviv University on Human Language and Development, Tel-Aviv University, Israel.

Berman, R. A. (1988). On the ability to relate events in narrative. *Discourse Processes, 11*(4), 469–497.

Berman, R. A. (1990). On acquiring an (S)VO language: Subjectless constructions in children's Hebrew. *Linguistics, 24,* 1035–1087.

Berman, R. A., & Slobin, D. I. (1987). *Five ways of learning how to talk about events: A crosslinguistic study of narrative development* (Berkeley Cognitive Science Report No. 46). Berkeley: University of California, Berkeley.

Budwig, N. (1985). I, me, my and "name": Children's early systematizations of forms, meanings, and functions in talk about the self. *Papers and Reports on Child Language Development, 24,* 30–37.

Chung, S., & Timberlake, A. (1985). Tense, aspect, and mood. In T. Shopen (Ed.), *Language typology and syntactic description, Vol III: Grammatical categories and the lexicon* (pp. 202–208.) Cambridge: Cambridge University Press.

Clark, E. V. (1978). Discovering what words can do. *Chicago Linguistic Society: Papers from Parasession on the Lexicon,* pp. 34–57.

Clark, E. V., & Berman, R. A. (1987). Types of linguistic knowledge: Interpreting and producing compound nouns. *Journal of Child Language, 14,* 3.

Crain, S., & Nakayama, M. (1987). Structure-dependence in grammar formation. *Language, 63,* 522–543.

Demuth, K. (1983). *Aspects of Sesotho language acquisition.* Unpublished doctoral dissertation, Indiana University, Bloomington, IN.

Dowty, D. (1979). *Word meaning and Montague grammar.* Dordrecht: Reidel.

Foley, W., & Van Valin, R. (1984). *Functional syntax and universal grammar.* Cambridge: Cambridge University Press.

Foley, W., & Van Valin, R. (1985). Information packaging in the clause. In T. Shopen (Ed.), *Language typology and syntactic description, Volume I: Clause structure* (pp. 282–380). Cambridge: Cambridge University Press.

Gee-Gerhardt, J., & Savasir, I. (1985). On the use of *will* and *gonna:* Toward a description of activity-types for child language. *Discourse Processes, 8,* 143–175.

Gerhardt, J. (1988). From discourse to semantics: The development of verb morphology and forms of self-reference in two-year old speech. *JCL, 15,* 337–396.

Geva, R. (1989). *Form and function in the developmental patterning of conjoined constructions in children's narratives.* Tel Aviv University, Master's thesis [in Hebrew], Tel Aviv, Israel.

Giora, R. (1985). *Informational function of the linear ordering of texts.* Tel Aviv University doctoral dissertation, Tel Aviv, Israel.

Goldsmith, J., & Woisetschlaeger, E. (1982). The logic of the English progressive. *Linguistic Inquiry, 13,* 79–89.

Hamburger, H., & Crain, S. (1985). Relative acquisition. In S. Kuczaj (Ed.) *Language development, Vol 1: Syntax and semantics* (pp. 245–274). Hillsdale, NJ: Erlbaum.

Hopper, P. (1979). Aspect and foregrounding in discourse. In T. Givon (Ed.), *Syntax and semantics Vol 12: Discourse and syntax.* New York: Academic Press.

Jackendoff, R. (1987). The status of thematic relations in linguistic theory. *Linguistic Inquiry, 18,* 369–411.

Karmiloff-Smith, A. (1981). The grammatical marking of thematic structure in the development of language production. In W. Deutsch (Ed.), *The child's construction of language.* London: Academic Press.

Karmiloff-Smith, A. (1983). Language development as a problem-solving process. Keynote address. *Papers and Reports on Child Language Development, 22,* 1–23.

Levin, B. (1986). Lexical semantics in review: An introduction. In B. Levin (Ed.), *Lexical Semantics in Review* (Lexical Project Working Papers). Cambridge, MA: MIT Center for Cognitive Science.

Naigles, L., Hirsh-Pasek, K., Golinkoff, R., Gleitman, L. R., & Gleitman, H. (1987, October). *From linguistic form to meaning: Evidence for syntactic bootstrapping by two-year olds.* Paper presented at the Boston Child Language Conference, Boston, MA.

Nichols, J. (1984). Functional theories of grammar. *Annual Review of Anthropology, 13,* 97–117.

Peterson, C., & McCabe, A. (1983). *Developmental psycholinguistics: Three ways of looking at a child's narrative.* New York: Plenum Press.

Reinhart, T. (1982). Principles of gestalt perception in the temporal organization of narrative texts. *Synopsis, 4* (Tel Aviv, Israel).

Silverstein, M. (1987). The three faces of "function": Preliminaries to a psychology of language.

In M. Hickmann (Ed.), *Social and functional approaches to language and thought* (pp. 17–38). New York: Academic.

Slobin, D. I. (1973). Cognitive prerequisites for the development of grammar. In C. A. Ferguson & D. I. Slobin (Eds.), *Studies of child language development*. New York: Holt, Rinehart, Winston.

Slobin, D. I. (1985). Crosslinguistic evidence for the language-making capacity. In D. I. Slobin (Ed.), *Crosslinguistic study of language acquisition* (Vol. 2, pp. 1157–1256). Hillsdale, NJ: Erlbaum.

Slobin, D. I. (1986a). The acquisition and use of relative clauses in Turkic and Indo-European languages. In D. I. Slobin & K. Zimmer (Eds.), *Studies in turkic linguistics* (pp. 273–294). Amsterdam: John Benjamins.

Slobin, D. I. (1986b, October). *The development from child speaker to native speaker.* Paper presented to Chicago Symposium on Culture and Human Development, *Chicago, IL.*

Slobin, D. I. (1987a, January 17–18). *Frequency reflects function.* Paper presented at Conference on the Interaction of Form and Function in Language, University of California at Davis.

Slobin, D. I. (1987b). Thinking for speaking. In J. Aske, N. Beery, L. Michaelis, & H. Filip (Eds.), *Proceedings of the Thirteenth Annual Meeting of the Berkeley Linguistics Society* (Parasession on Grammar and Cognition), pp. 434–445.

Smith, C. S. (1983). A theory of aspectual choice. *Language, 59,* 479–501.

Smith, C. S., & Weist, R. (1987). On the temporal contour of a child's language: A reply to Rispoli & Bloom. *Journal of Child Language 14,* 383–86.

Talmy, L. (1978). Figure and ground in complex sentences. In J. Greenberg (Ed.), *Universals of human language, Vol 4: Syntax.* Stanford: Stanford University Press.

Talmy, L. (1985). Lexicaliziation patterns: semantic structure in lexical forms. In T. Shopen (Ed.), *Language typology and syntactic description, Vol. 3: Grammatical categories and the lexicon.* Cambridge: Cambridge University Press.

Tomlin, R. S. (Ed.). (1987). *Coherence and grounding in discourse.* Amsterdam: John Benjamins.

Van Valin, R. (1987). The unaccusative hypothesis versus lexical semantics: Syntactic vs. semantic approaches to verb classification. In *Proceedings of NELS 17.* Amherst: University of Massachusetts, GLSA.

Van Valin, R. (1989). *Functionalist linguistic theory and language acquisition.* Unpublished manuscript, University of California at Davis.

Vendler, Z. (1967). *Philosophy in linguistics.* Ithaca, NY: Cornell University Press.

Von Stutterheim, C. (1987). *Simultaneity in discourse.* Unpublished manuscript, Heidelberg.

Wallace, S. (1982). Figure and ground: The interrelationships of linguistic categories. In P. Hopper (Ed.), *Tense-aspect: Between semantics and pragmatics.* Amsterdam: John Benjamins.

Wexler, K., & Culicover, P. (1980). *Formal principles of language acquisition.* Cambridge, MA: MIT Press.

8

If De Saussure Was Right, Could Whorf Have Been Wrong?*

Izchak M. Schlesinger

Hebrew University, Jerusalem

This chapter reconsiders the age-old problem of the influence of language on thought from a developmental perspective. A theory of language acquisition is outlined and its relationship with linguistic relativism is discussed. Some studies are reported that provide evidence for the acquisition theory and for a modified relativistic thesis.

Linguistic Relativism and Radical Conventionalism

One of the most intriguing problems in cognitive psychology is that of the influence of language on cognition. This issue has come to the attention of psychologists mainly through the writings of Whorf (1956), but his ideas have been around — in a less extreme formulation — at least since the 18th-century scholar Herder wrote about the origin and functions of language (Heintel, 1964).

Whorf, it will be remembered, argued that the structure of a language imposes its categorization on its speakers' thinking and affects the way they conceive of reality. To give just one example out of the many presented by Whorf, in English (and many other languages) lightning is referred to by a noun, whereas in other languages — Hopi, for example — lightning is referred to by a verb. Now, nouns and verbs differ in what I will call here their *structural import,* namely, the cognitive distinction that seems to be implied by a linguistic categorization. The structural import of a noun is "thingness," whereas that of a verb is action. Whorf argues that this structural import has

---

* I am indebted to Yonata Levy for discussions which helped sharpen the presentation of theoretical issues in this chapter, and to Naomi Goldblum, Theo Herrmann, and Mordechai Rimor for helpful comments. The experiment in Study 1 was carried out and the data analyzed by Jorge Vulej, that in Study 3 and that on the instrumental by Alon Halter. Partial support for the research reported here was provided by a research grant from the Israel Academy of Sciences and by the Center for Human Development, The Hebrew University, Jerusalem. Some of the research was carried out while I was Fellow of the Institute for Advanced Research, The Hebrew University, Jerusalem.

a cognitive effect: The linguistic coding affects the way the phenomenon of lightning is conceived of by the speakers of the language. Speakers of English, and of other languages in which *lightning* is a noun, will tend to view lightning as thinglike, as a sort of object, whereas speakers of languages like Hopi and Rumanian, which refer to *lightning* with a verb, will tend to conceive of it as more actionlike, as a sort of event (Whorf, 1956). In Whorf's extreme formulation, different languages implicate different world views. This approach has been called *linguistic relativism.*

The thesis that linguistic coding may dictate our way of thinking has met with no little opposition. An extreme version of the anti-Whorfian view looks on language as no more than a tool for communication (and, possibly, also for thinking) which subserves these processes without influencing them in any way. According to this approach, though speakers may become aware of the structural import of a linguistic construction, it has no further influence on their cognitive processes. The word *lightning* may suggests thingness, but on this view this is merely a sort of dead metaphor: One is not taken in by its literal meaning. Linguistic constructions are counters; they are determined by convention, and one counter is as good as any other. We may know whose face it is that appears on a money bill, but our spending behavior will not be influenced by this knowledge; a dollar is a dollar. I will call this view *radical conventionalism.*

There have been many attempts to put hypotheses based on Whorf's views to an empirical test, but with very few exceptions (see further on) the results have been inconclusive; see Brown (1976, 1986) for critical reviews of some of this research. Current methodological wisdom decrees that a hypothesis that has repeatedly failed in obtaining empirical confirmation should be abandoned. But the striking fact about Whorf's ideas is that, in spite of the relative lack of success in substantiating it, his thesis refuses to die. Time and again psychologists and philosophers discuss it or attempt to muster evidence for it. Only recently another such attempt has been made by Bloom (1981), but the interpretation of his findings has been contested and this research is still controversial (see Au, 1983, 1984; Bloom, 1984; Brown, 1986). However, some support for a weaker, developmental version of the Whorfian hypothesis comes from a study by Guiora, Beit-Halachmi, Fried, and Yoder (1983) showing effects of language structure on the rate of cognitive development in a certain circumscribed area. They predicted that children acquiring languages in which there are gender categories would develop gender identity earlier than those learning a language which makes no such distinction, and they report positive results.

Why should people cling with such tenacity to a thesis with such a relatively poor empirical record? Perhaps there is a deep-seated intuition that Whorf has succeeded in getting a glimpse of an important truth. Perhaps also many people want it to be true; Relativism—whether in morals, or in other domains—is often found to have a singular appeal.[1] As the philosopher Max Black (1969) has put it: "As we stumble toward a single world order, there is all the more nostalgic attraction in crying 'vive les differences' " (p. 35).

Be that as it may, at least one prominent scholar, Roger Brown (1986), who years ago set out to put the Whorfian thesis to an empirical test, now sees the available evidence as pointing toward cognitive universalism rather than linguistic relativism. But I suspect that Whorfian notions will not be gotten rid of so easily. The trouble with Whorfianism, as Black (1969) has pointed out, is that it is vaguely formulated, so that "an enterprising Ph.D. candidate would have no trouble in producing at least 108 versions of Whorfianism" (p. 30). But this is also part of the secret of its longevity. Some of the 108 versions are likely to be laid to rest, but others will eventually rise again and may gain credence.

In the following I intend to do my share and contribute another version — or set of versions — to Black's 108. Data will be marshalled that suggest that radical conventionalism must be abandoned and that support a certain weak version of linguistic relativism. First, I try to show what light can be thrown on this issue from a developmental perspective. I elaborate on the Saussurean conception of the relationship between language acquisition and cognition, and then go on to cite some studies of adult functioning predicted by a related theory of language acquisition.

The Saussurean View of Language Development

De Saussure (1916/1959) discusses the role of language vis-á-vis thought on the one hand and sound on the other. He rejects the view that the role of language is merely to serve as a "means for expressing ideas" (p. 112). Rather, language serves to give structure to thought.

This claim of de Saussure might be construed as pertaining to the use of language by an individual. It seems to me, however, that he is concerned here primarily with the function of language in the mental development of the child acquiring it. This transpires in the same passage, where De Saussure states: "There are no preexisting ideas, and nothing is distinct before the appearance of language" (p. 112). The reference to preexisting ideas indicates that de Saussure is talking here about ontogenetic development, and the phrase "before the appearance of language" seems to refer to the prelinguistic stage in the child. The function of language, according to him, is "to serve as an [intermediary] between thought and sound, under conditions that of necessity bring about the reciprocal delimitation of units" (p. 112),[2] that is, the

---

[1] The opponents of the linguistic relativism thesis may be just as much personally involved, setting great store by the autonomy of their intellectual life and resenting its being imposed on by language or any other social institution.

[2] The English translation here has "link" for the French "intermediaire," but "intermediary" seems to capture more of the intended meaning.

categorization of the linguistic sound stream through language and the categorization of thought by means of language. The latter, it will be recalled, was insisted on by Whorf in respect to adult mental life.

De Saussure's view, as construed here, is by no means generally accepted. It has often been claimed that the child develops categories before the advent of language and then learns for each such category which linguistic label is appropriate for it. I have previously argued that there is little empirical evidence for this claim (Schlesinger, 1982, 1988). Attempts to produce such evidence have since been made by Roberts and Horowitz (1986) and by Mervis (1985). Golinkoff (1981) has provided evidence that prelinguistic children distinguish between categories that form the basis of early grammar, the actor and the patient of the action. As discussed elsewhere (Schlesinger, 1988), her results leave open the question of the nature and scope of these categories. The issue of prelinguistic categories is thus still open, and de Saussure is worth listening to.

The Saussurean developmental thesis has been fleshed out in Schlesinger's (1982) language acquisition theory. A concept, according to this theory, need not have been formed by the child before she has acquired the relevant word for it. Instead, the child may learn the concept in the process of learning the correct use of the word.

Likewise, the theory does not assume that linguistic categories are available to the child before the advent of language. It has been shown that relational categories, like Agent and Action, which operate in the child's linguistic system, can be acquired through observing how experience is structured by the input language (Schlesinger, 1988). The child's first relational categories are semantic. But as is well known, the adult grammatical system operates with formal categories, like subject and object, and these overlap only partially with semantic categories like Agent and Patient. The subjects of *hold, like,* and *see,* for instance, are certainly not Agents in the usual sense of this term. How do the child's early semantic categories develop into formal ones? To account for this, a process of *semantic assimilation* has been proposed: The child's semantic categories are extended gradually on the basis of both formal and semantic similarities perceived by the child.

To illustrate, take the formation of the syntactic category subject. It is hypothesized that this category develops out of the early semantic category Agent. Suppose the child encounters sentences with the verb *hold*. From the situation in which these occur she gradually gets a hold on the kinds of situations that the word is used to refer to; the child does not have to be credited with any prelinguistic category that enables her to learn the meaning of this word. Further, she learns that *hold* is used in the same way as words designating actions—that is, it appears in the same word order and with the same inflections—and that the word for the "holder" is used like those for agents of actions. For instance, *Mommy holds the baby* has the same structure as *Mommy feeds the baby*. In addition to this formal similarity, the child may take semantic similarity into account: her attention is drawn to some commonality between the process of holding and prototypical actions like feeding, kissing, and coddling. The word *hold* is thus assimilated into the category of action words. In the same manner other static verbs may be assimilated into this category. As semantic assimilation proceeds, the child's pristine action category gradually develops into the verb category of the mature adult system, and concomitantly the early agent develops into the subject of adult grammar.

In a similar manner, the agent is the origin of subjects expressing any one of a variety of other roles: the Instrumental *(The car hit the tree.)*, the Experiencer *(John likes the car.)*, the Thing Located *(The road runs alongside the river.)*, and so on. The subjects of a wide variety of verbs which are not action verbs have been shown to be similar in some feature or other to agents (Schlesinger, 1988).

As stated, this account of the development of categories is in the Saussurean spirit. It does not presuppose categories that antedate language acquisition, but rather assumes that in the formation of linguistic categories language is the driving force.[3]

Implications for Cognitive Functioning

The language acquisition theory outlined in the preceding section may have certain implications for adult cognitive functioning. According to the theory, a process of semantic assimilation gradually expands the child's semantic categories into formal ones. Now, the semantic origin of the latter may be expected to leave its mark on them. Furthermore, conceptual categories of the adult may be affected, as will be shown presently. These effects will be formulated here as two hypotheses.

> *Hypothesis I.* The nature of linguistic categories. Structural import influences the way linguistic constructions are conceived of: Categories in the mature grammatical system will be regarded in terms of the semantic categories they originate in.

The subject, for example, may be regarded by adult speakers as an agent of sorts, even when — "objectively" speaking — it expresses the roles of Experiencer, Instrumental, and so on. In other words, adult linguistic categories retain something of the "flavor" of the semantic core out of which they developed.[4]

---

[3] Note that this theory need assume neither prelinguistic (innate) grammatical nor prelinguistic cognitive (semantic) categories. A caveat is in order here. The theory does not claim that *all* linguistic categories are cognitively based; this would be patently false, since there are grammatical categories that have no semantic basis whatsoever. For a full discussion of this issue see Schlesinger (1988).

[4] De Saussure's insistence on the arbitrariness of the linguistic sign may not seem to square well

Strictly speaking, Hypothesis I is not a corollary of the semantic assimilation hypothesis. Conceivably, the categories of grammar may eventually lose their semantic "flavor" and be regarded in purely formal terms. An empirical disconfirmation of Hypothesis I would therefore not refute our acquisition theory. But should the hypothesis be borne out, this would constitute some support for the acquisition theory that led to its formulation. Further on I report on an empirical test of the hypothesis.

The second hypothesis is in line with de Saussure's statement, quoted above, about the "reciprocal delimitation of units" of thought and language. In a way, it is the converse of Hypothesis I.

Hypothesis II. The nature of conceptual categories. Adult cognition operates with categories that conform largely to the linguistic categories of the native language.

For instance, in adult cognition, the agent will include all that the grammar of the native language treats as an agent, that is, most subjects. This seems to follow from our theory that the child's conceptual categories are gradually shaped in accordance with the linguistic categories of her language. Speakers of different languages will therefore operate with different conceptual categories, which is precisely what Whorf claimed.

Note, however, that such a relativistic view does not follow necessarily from the semantic assimilation hypothesis. Conceivably, there may be a bifurcation in the development of a semantic category. The category is formed and shaped in accordance with a linguistic category for the purpose of using language, and for this purpose only; and at the same time a corresponding cognitive category develops independently of language and its categories. The subject may be a purely linguistic category that does not subserve any other cognitive tasks. Rather, it continues to exist side by side with independently developed conceptual categories—such as the agent, action, or whatever they are—and it is only these that are called on in cognitive processes other than linguistic ones. The answer to the question posed in the title of this chapter is therefore: Whorf *could* be wrong, even though de Saussure (as I have reason to believe) is right.

Hypothesis II, then, is not implicated by Hypothesis I, because it is based on the additional assumption that linguistic and cognitive functioning are both based on a single set of categories. In the following I propose an additional hypothesis, that does not make this assumption. This is a conservative version of the Whorfian thesis. According to previous versions of linguistic relativism, the structural import of various linguistic categories and constructions of a given language influences the speakers' cognitions. My modified version does

---

with the present proposal of the cognitive effects of structural import. But de Saussure was talking of the arbitrariness of words and there is no indication in his writings that he took the principle of arbitrariness to apply also to the grammatical level.

not assume such far-reaching effects but opts for a more limited influence on the way messages are construed:

> *Hypothesis III.* The communicative effect of linguistic categorization.
> Structural import has an effect on communication; it may influence the way the hearer construes the message, and in choosing a linguistic structure the speaker will take the possibility of such an influence into account.

It should be clear that in this hypothesis the consequences of Hypothesis I are spelled out. If grammatical categories are regarded in semantic terms, as claimed by the latter, this may be expected to have an effect on the speaker's and hearer's behavior in communication.

Given that languages differ in their categorization of experience, Hypothesis II is a relativistic thesis. It is contrary to radical conventionalism, which claims that structural import is disregarded in communication, and that it is the message that counts, not the way it is encoded.

The three studies to be reported in the next section were designed to test Hypotheses I and III. The findings were in accord with these hypotheses, and thus also provide indirect support for the hypothesized semantic assimilation process on the basis of which they were formulated.

Studies of the Communicative Effects of Structural Import

Study 1. The Role of Participants

According to the semantic assimilation hypothesis the subject category develops out of the agent category and retains some of its "flavor." From Hypothesis I we may predict therefore that the sentence subject will be perceived even by adults as having some of the characteristics of the agent.

Consider the following two sentences:

> The officer leads the band.
> The band follows the officer.

Both sentences may be used to describe the same event. They express the same, or nearly the same, content, but differ in formal structure: the subject of the first sentence appears as object in the second and the subject of the second sentence is the object in the first one.

Let us ask now: Which is the agent in each of these sentences? Since both describe the same event, there should not be any difference in respect to the ascription of agency to the participants. "Objectively" speaking, either the officer is the agent or the band, or both: but no matter who the agent is, it has to be the same in both sentences.

However, Hypothesis I predicts that for each of the above sentences the subject will be regarded as being more agentlike than the object. In the first sentence more agency will be attributed to the officer than to the band, whereas in the second sentence the reverse will be the case.

To tap the tendency to view the subject as agentlike it was decided to ask about the degree of control exercised by the "participant" designated by the subject. Control is a feature of the Agent: The agent is normally in control of the action ascribed to him. In a sentence describing a situation involving two "participants" — that is, the one indicated by the subject and the one indicated by the object of the sentence — each of the two may exercise a certain amount of control over the situation. It was predicted that for such sentences speakers of the language would accord more control to the subject than to the object.

The first study was conducted with pairs of converse (or nearly converse) verbs, like the pair *lead-follow,* in the above example. Two parallel forms — Form I and Form II — were prepared, with one verb of a pair appearing in a sentence in Form I and the other verb in Form II. It was thought that in judging sentences describing concrete participants, like *band* and *officer* in the above examples, respondents might be influenced by their conception of the particular persons involved (e.g., officers may be judged to be more in control than ordinary mortals). Accordingly it was decided to refer to the participants as *A* and *B*. Thus, each of the two parallel forms contained one of the following sentences:

A leads B.
A follows B.

Each of the two forms was responded to by 10 native English speakers, who were asked to rate the amount of control each participant has over the situation on a 9-point scale from 1 (little control) to 9 (much control). The hypothesis was that the sentence subject would be accorded more control than the object.

A parallel study with Hebrew sentences was also conducted. This included translations of 7 of the 9 sentence pairs of the English study (the other two were not translatable in a straight-forward manner), and an additional sentence pair that could not be easily translated into English, involving two Hebrew verbs meaning "enthuse (over or because of)," and "enthuse" used causatively. The Hebrew study also comprised two parallel forms. 35 University students served as subjects. About half the sample were given one of the two forms first and the other one after about two weeks, and for the other half the order of forms was reversed. Thus each respondent served as his or her own control.

Differences between degree of control accorded to A and degree of control accorded to B were tested for each sentence separately by a matched t-test (one-tailed, since the direction of the difference was hypothesized; see above).

Table 8.1 presents the mean ratings of control in the English study. In the Hebrew study, the direction of the difference between A and B was the same

Table 8.1. Mean degree of Control accorded to the subjects (A) and the object (B)

	A	B		A	B
(a)					
A troubles B	6.9	3.9[a],[b]	A worries about B	5.3	3.0[b]
A leads B[c]	5.3	3.2[a]	A follows B[c]	6.4	5.7
A sells someth. to B	6.9	4.7[b]	A buys someth. from B	7.4	5.7
A lends someth. to B	6.7	5.5[b]	A borrows someth. from B	7.1	6.2
(b)					
A teaches someth. to B	7.4	2.9[a],[b]	A learns someth. from B	5.7	5.8
A chases B	7.8	3.2[a],[b]	A flees from B	5.8	5.6
A pleases B[c]	6.7	4.7[a]	A likes B[c]	5.3	5.4
(c)					
A gives someth. to B	7.6	4.6[a],[b]	A receives someth. from B	2.0	8.0[a],[b]
A frightens B	7.9	1.7[a],[b]	A fears B	3.3	6.6[a],[b]

Notes:
[a] $p < .05$
[b] $p < .05$ in Hebrew study
[c] not included in Hebrew study

as in the English study for all sentences included (except in one case, mentioned below).

An examination of the table shows that the sentences are a mixed bag, some clearly bearing out our prediction, others not. Whether sentence structure has the predicted effect seems to depend in part on the semantics of the verb. For the purpose of discussing the results, the sentences are presented in the table as falling into three groups, (a), (b), and (c).

Group (a). Results for sentence pairs in this group bear out our predictions that more control would be accorded to the sentence subject than to the object, and that this would be the case irrespective of the manner of encoding the event referred to (that is, for *lead* as well as for *follow,* etc.). While not all the differences were significant, the fact that they were replicated in the Hebrew study, sometimes attaining statistical significance, shows that the findings are reliable.[5]

Group (b). The sentence pairs in this group present a somewhat different picture. Only one sentence of a given pair showed the predicted results—significantly higher ratings of control of A than of control of B—while for the other sentence of each pair there was only a very small and statistically nonsignificant difference (in two of the sentences the difference was in the

---

[5] The same pattern of results was obtained for the one sentence pair in the Hebrew study which was not included in the English study.

direction opposite to the predicted one, and in the third—*flees from*—the English and the Hebrew studies yielded results in opposite directions).

Still, in all the sentence pairs the difference between A and B in rated control was very much larger in that sentence where it was in the predicted direction than in the other sentence, where it was not. Matched t-tests were carried out comparing differences in rated control in one sentence with those in the complementary sentence. In the English study, the difference between control of A and control of B was significantly larger for *teach* than for *learn*. For the two other pairs the differences failed to reach significance (perhaps because of the small sample size). In the Hebrew study, the difference was significant not only for *teach* and *learn*, but also for *chase* and *flee* (the third pair was not included in the Hebrew study). These data thus provide some limited support for our hypothesis.

The results for groups (a) and (b), then, are in line with Hypothesis I. Although *buy* and *sell, lead* and *follow*, and so on pertain to the same situation, the sentence subject in each instance is conceived of as agent-like. But the picture becomes more complicated when we look at group (c).

Group (c). In the sentence pairs of this group the subjects were not judged as being more agentlike than the objects. This shows that linguistic form does not always determine which part of the sentence is conceived of as agent.

The finding on Group (c) points to a certain limitation in the effects of semantic assimilation. While the semantic origin of the subject category may affect the way the subject is conceived of by the adult language user, this effect may be overridden by our knowledge of the situation.

Note now that the situation of the respondent in this study parallels that of the addressee or hearer in the communicative situation. The results show that in construing sentences presented to him by the investigator (the "speaker") he is influenced by their structural import. Do the findings, then, confirm also Hypothesis III, which pertains to the communicative effects of structural import? In a way they do, but here an important qualification has to be made. Note that for each pair of verbs the speaker had two about equally accessible ways of expression at his disposal. He could use the verb *sell*, or else, when this conveys the wrong impression about relative amount of control in the buyer and seller, he could opt for *buy*. The hearer knows that the language makes such options available to the speaker, and therefore ascribes to him a certain intention corresponding to the choice he actually made. As we all know, different stylistic variations have different communicative effects. What the present study does not tell us is whether the sentence subject is conceived of as a sort of agent even where no simple alternative formulation is available. Perhaps the hearer in these cases somehow take into consideration that the speaker does not have much of a choice, and therefore disregards the structural import of the message.

Put differently, the above study provides evidence for the communicative effects of *language use*. Whorf, by contrast, was concerned with the cognitive effects of the *language system:* The presence or absence of certain linguistic categories and distinctions in a particular language, rather than the use made by the speaker of a language of the alternative ways of expression available within the system. It remains to be seen, therefore, whether Hypothesis III can be corroborated as far as the language system is concerned. This issue is addressed in the next study.

Study 2. Experiencer and Stimulus

The verbs used in Study 1 are exceptional in that they are converses of each other: *Please* is the converse of *like, chase* of *flee,* and so on. But language is frugal; there are few such converses. Most verbs denoting mental states and processes, like *admire, abhor,* and *detest,* for instance, have no converses, and hence do not permit alternative formulations as easily. Would the hearer impute agency to the subjects of these verbs even though no simple alternative formulation is available to the speaker?

The results of the study investigating this question are to be reported at length elsewhere (Schlesinger, in preparation) and will be summarized here only briefly. The subject of a sentence with a mental verb was judged as having more control of the situation and more intention than the object, and this was true regardless of whether the subject referred to the experiencer (as in *A admires B*) or to the stimulus of the experience (as in *A impresses B*). The findings for control were also replicated in a study with Hebrew sentences.

It might be argued that relative position was a confounding variable in this study: Perhaps it is the first noun phrase in the sentence that is accorded more control and the subject in these sentences happened to appear in first position. However, the above results were replicated for various sentence forms, such as:

> A admires B.
> B is admired by A.
> It is B whom A admires.
> It is A who admires B.

In each case it was the deep structure subject (the one who "did" the admiring) that was accorded more control and intention. The results are thus not accounted for by relative position in the sentence or by focus (although the former factor has been shown to interact with that of grammatical role). The study has also been replicated with sentences including proper names instead of "A" and "B."

As in Study I, there were a few verbs in this study the subjects of which were accorded more control than the object; for example, *dread,* and some were accorded more intention. But the great majority of verbs conformed to the predicted pattern. In the present study we also included sentences with subjects that denote the stimulus (the source of the experience) — for example, sentences with *astonish, provoke,* and *fascinate* — and as predicted, more control and intention were attributed to the stimulus subject than to the object.

The results of the present study, like those of Study 1, are in agreement with Hypothesis I. The message conveyed by the subject in adult use betrays the origin of this syntactic category in the semantic agent category. Furthermore, the findings provide evidence for Hypothesis III which pertains to the communicative effect of structural import. The message conveyed to the hearer reflects the fact that a given verb takes the experiencer, rather than the stimulus, as subject. Unlike the effects observed in the previous study, those of the present one are due to the language system, which affords the speaker with only one way of expression.

At this point an adherent of radical conventionalism might voice some objections. First, it might be argued that the finding that the hearer judges the subject of experience verbs to have more control and intention should not be put down to the influence of linguistic form, but rather may reflect something about the situation described by these verbs. The experience of admiring, so the argument might run, is such that the admirer has more control and intention than the one who is admired. And in general, experiences described by verbs with subjects referring to the experiencer are such that the experiencers are in control and have more intention. By contrast, the one who provokes has more control and intention than the one who is provoked, and likewise for all verbs that take the noun denoting the stimulus as subject. Language, on this account, does not affect the way reality is conceived of by the hearer; it merely reflects reality.[6]

That this alternative explanation is quite implausible can be seen from crosslinguistic comparisons. It is not the case that all languages code a given experience in the same way. *The actor pleased the audience* translates in Hebrew into a sentence in which *the audience,* rather than *the actor,* is the subject (and *the actor* — an indirect object). The English verb *dislike* takes the experiencer as subject, whereas the Spanish verb *desagradar,* which can be used for describing the same state of affairs, takes the experiencer as object. (*A dislikes B = B desagrada A*); and similarly for the English-Spanish pair *loathe* and *repugnar* (Epstein, unpublished paper). The Japanese equivalent to the English sentence *John sees the appletree* has *appletree* as subject. There are languages where the experiencer of some or of all mental verbs is expressed as the dative (Blansitt, 1978; Tsunoda, 1985). To the extent that our results are generalizable to other languages, we may expect to find the experiences in

---

[6] Note that this objection is relevant only to the issue of linguistic relativism vs. radical conventialism. It does not affect the support provided by the findings for Hypothesis I, because even if it were true that the our findings merely show something about the reality described by these sentences, the fact remains that this reality is reflected by the sentence structure — that is, that the subject is used for the participant who is more agentlike — which goes to show that the subject retains something of the "flavor" of the sentence category it originates in.

question to be conceived of differently as far as control and intention are concerned.

Even within a language the way a given experience is coded may undergo historical change. Some English verbs that currently take the experiencer as subject once had two uses, and could also take the stimulus as subject. Thus, *enjoy* once meant also give pleasure to, and *dread* to inspire fear. Conversely, the verb *delight* which in present-day English means to cause pleasure, once had the additional meaning of rejoicing, experiencing pleasure. Similarly, *please,* once also meant to be pleased, and still does so today in phrases like *as you please, where he pleases.* One would hardly opt for the entirely ad hoc explanation that words for which such changes have been recorded have undergone corresponding changes of meaning so that they now refer to somewhat different experiences. It appears, therefore, that these verbs once could convey different messages to the hearer in respect to the degree of control exercised by the persons referred to in the sentence and their intention. This is in line with the our interpretation of the results, rather than with the suggested alternative one.

Another possible objection to my interpretation of the findings of this study is that they may be due to an experimental artifact. Results obtained with questionnaires, it might be argued, may not generalizable to the communicative situation. (This possibility has been suggested to me by Yonata Levy.) By asking about the degree of control exercised by the participants, attention is drawn to the structural import. On hearing somebody talk, by contrast, one may very well be completely unaware of this structural import.

It seems implausible, however, that a sharp distinction can be maintained between the experimental situation in which the subject is made aware of the semantics of the experiencer and "real-life" situations, in which he is, purportedly, quite unaware of the same. Given that the structural import of the message *may* come to our attention (as shown in the present study) it is a reasonable conjecture that in at least some "real-life" situations one also becomes aware of it, while perhaps in others little or no attention is paid to this aspect of the message.

Further corroboration for Hypothesis III comes from the following study, to which none of the preceding objections applies.

Study 3. The Instrumental

While the two previous studies were based on judgments concerning the meaning components of sentences, this study used judgments of acceptability. A sentence may be unacceptable because it infringes a rule of grammar; such sentences do not concern us here. As will be shown in the following, a sentence that does not run afoul of any formal rule of grammar may be unacceptable due to its structural import. In other words, because they are aware of their structural import, speakers avoid using such sentences and people judge them as unacceptable.

In English, and in many other languages, the instrument of an action may appear as sentence subject. We may say, for instance:

The crane picked up the large box.
   This soap cleans tar stains.

There is, thus, a rule of English that permits the Instrumental to appear as surface subject. As we will see presently, the instrument in sentences like these figures as an agent.

There are certain constraints on this rule, however, which apparently cannot be formulated in syntactic terms. In the following sentence pairs, for instance, the second sentence sounds odd or is even downright unacceptable, while the first one is definitely better:

The crane picked up the large box.
The fork picked up the potato.

The alarm clock woke him.
The knife cut the cake.

The pen scribbled on the page.
The pen wrote the letter.

The janitor's key opened the door.
The janitor's key opened the door without delay.

It has been shown that these constraints are accounted for by postulating that when the instrument is in subject position it is conceived of as a sort of Agent (Schlesinger, 1982, 1985). Complicated mechanisms that operate without constant intervention of a human agent (the crane and the alarm clock in the above examples) are more eligible to agenthood than more simply constructed implements; and deliberate actions, like writing, are less tolerant of inanimate "agents" than more routine processes. Due to the structural import of this construction, speakers will refrain from formulating sentences like the second in each of the above pairs. And if those sentences sound odd, this is because hearers are aware of the structural import of the subject position and feel that something has gone wrong, namely, too much agency has been ascribed to an inanimate object. According to radical conventionalism the speaker pays no heed to structural import and there would be nothing to prevent him from availing himself of the syntactic rule that permits putting the instrument into subject position. This study, then, corroborates Hypothesis III.

The findings are clearly also in line with Hypothesis I which claims that mature categories retain something of the semantic "flavor" of the categories they originated in, for example, the subject in the agent. This study provides linguistic evidence for the instrument-subject being conceived of as an agent of sorts.

Experimental evidence has also been obtained for the above interpretation. A list of 22 sentences was prepared in which an inanimate instrument appeared in subject position. This list was presented to respondents, who were asked to indicate for each sentence to what extent it was acceptable. In addition to this questionnaire, which I will call here the S-form (subject-form), a parallel form, the W-form (with-form) was constructed by changing the sentences of the S-form into sentences in which the instrument appeared in a *with*-phrase, and for which a subject was arbitrarily supplied. For example:

S-form: The pen wrote the letter.
   W-form: The boy wrote the letter with the pen.

The W-form was given to respondents, who were asked to indicate for each sentence to what extent the instrument can be viewed as carrying out the action described in the sentence. If our above explanation is correct, one would expect the ratings on the two forms to correlate, that is, the greater the tendency of respondents to regard the instrument as carrying out the action, the more acceptable will the corresponding S-sentence be.

Acceptability judgments were obtained for two versions of the S-form, differing in the instructions given to the Ss. In one of the forms, S_1, respondents were asked to what extent the sentence was "formulated appropriately." In the other form, S_2, they were asked whether the sentence would be appropriate in everyday discourse under ordinary circumstances. (The latter variant was decided on because I had previously noted that some subjects tend to put up even with quite bizarre sentences and to justify this by suggesting circumstances in which the sentence might be acceptable. Actually the ratings on the two S-forms correlated highly: .90, Spearman rank-order correlation).

In each of the three forms ratings were made on a 9-point scale. Each of the forms was filled out by 20 Ss.

The Spearman rank order correlation between ratings on the S_1-form and the W-form was .71 and that between the ratings of the S_2-form and the W-form was .74. The results thus provide support for the explanation proposed above.

Where was Whorf Right?

The three studies reported in the foregoing show that structural import has communicative effects and that linguistic categories bear the imprint of the semantic assimilation process through which they were formed. Linguistic expressions and constructions, then, are not just counters, as radical conventionalism has it; they encapsulate meanings of their own, which may leak out and affect the speaker.

We may now ask whether the effects of native language on cognition are limited to the communicative situation, or extend, instead, to other aspects of our mental life. For instance, does the fact that our language permits treating instruments like agents have some subtle effect on the way we tend to conceive of inanimate tools or machines? Could it be, for instance, that our language predisposes us to blame machines for their shortcomings and tools for their "misdemeanors"? Or does the fact that experiencers often function linguistically like agents contribute to the view that we are responsible to some extent for our feelings and mental states, that we have some control over them? Would the command to love our neighbor sound stranger to ears of those reared in a language that deals differently with mental state verbs?

Those who are sceptical of relativistic claims will insist that there is no empirical evidence for such pervasive effects. They may accept the evidence for Hypothesis I, pertaining to the manner we conceive of linguistic categories, and for Hypothesis III, pertaining to the communicative effect of structural import, and remain persuaded that outside of the communicative situation knowledge of the world is of overriding importance and the linguistic coding system is not "taken seriously," as it were.

This approach, I submit, is based on certain tacit epistemological assumptions. These are, stated crudely, that there is only one way in which the world around us may be conceived of. If, by contrast, it is assumed that our view of the world is to some extent mediated by cultural factors, the older generation transmitting its world view to the younger, then language clearly has a major role to play. And here the conjecture becomes plausible (though, unfortunately, pertinent evidence is still scarce) that the structural import of the linguistic system may have some influence extending beyond the communicative situation. It may be the vehicle of inculcating in the child a certain categorization of reality, which she then continues to deploy in adult life.

References

Au, T. K. (1983). Chinese and English counterfactuals: The Sapir-Whorf hypothesis revisited. *Cognition, 15,* 155–187.

Au, T. K. (1984). Counterfactuals: In reply to Alfred Bloom. *Cognition, 17,* 289–302.

Black, M. (1969). Some troubles with Whorfianism. In S. Hook (Ed.), *Language and philosophy: A symposium* (pp. 30–35). New York: New York University Press.

Blansitt, E. L., Jr. (1978). Stimulus as a semantic role. In W. Abraham (Ed.), *Valence, semantic case, and grammatical relations.* Amsterdam: John Benjamins.

Bloom, A. (1981). *The linguistic shaping of thought: A study of the impact of language on thinking in China and the West.* Hillsdale, NJ: Erlbaum.

Bloom, A. (1984). Caution—The words you use may affect what you say: A response to Au. *Cognition, 17,* 257–287.

Brown, R. (1976). Reference: In memorial tribute to Eric Lenneberg. *Cognition, 4,* 125–153.

Brown, R. (1986). Linguistic relativity. In S. H. Hulse & B. F. Green (Eds.), *One hundred years of psychological research in America: G. Stanley Hall and the Johns Hopkins tradition* (pp. 241–276). Baltimore: Johns Hopkins Press.

Epstein, L. (1988). *The "irreversibility" of Spanish experience verbs.* Unpublished paper, Department of Psychology, The Hebrew University, Jerusalem, Israel.

Golinkoff, R. (1981). The case for semantic relations: Evidence from the verbal and non-verbal domains. *Journal of Child Language, 3,* 413–438.

Guiora, A. Z., Beit-Halachmi, B., Fried, R., & Yoder, C. (1983). Language environment and gender identity attainment. *Language Learning, 32,* 289–304.

Heintel, E. (Ed.). (1964). *Johann Gottfried Herder: Sprachphilosophische Schriften.* Hamburg: Meiner.

Mervis, C. B. (1985). On the existence of prelinguistic categories: A case study. *Infant Behavior and Development, 8,* 293–300.

Roberts, K., & Horowitz, F. D. (1986). Basic level categorization in seven- and nine-month-old infants. *Journal of Child Language, 13,* 191–208.

Saussure, F. de. (1959). *Course in general linguistics.* New York: Philosophical Library. (Original work published 1916)

Schlesinger, I. M. (1982). *Steps to language: Toward a theory of language acquisition.* Hillsdale, NJ: Erlbaum.

Schlesinger, I. M. (1985). *Instruments as agents* (Working Paper No. 15) Jerusalem, Israel: The Goldie Rotman Center for Cognitive Science in Education, The Hebrew University.

Schlesinger, I. M. (1988). The origin of relational categories. In Y. Levy, I. M. Schlesinger, & M. D. S. Braine (Eds.), *Categories and strategies in language acquisition theory* (pp. 121–178). Hillsdale, NJ: Erlbaum.

Schlesinger, I. M. (in preparation). *The experiencer as an agent.*

Tsunoda, T. (1985). Remarks on transitivity. *Journal of Linguistics, 21,* 385–396.

Whorf, B. L. (1956). *Language, thought and reality.* Cambridge, MA: MIT Press.

Author Index

A

Abelson, R. P., 50, *60*
Acredolo, L. P., 105, *138*
Amidon, A., 157, *170*
Anglin, J. M., 41, *58*
Anisfeld, M., 36, *58*
Ariel, M., 173, *199*
Aronoff, M., 130, *138*
Au, T. K., 203, *217*

B

Backscheider, A., 71, *86*
Baduini, C., 8, *16,* 74, 84, *86*
Baillargeon, R., 63, *86*
Baker, E., 97, *103*
Bamberg, M., 183, 195, 196, *199*
Barrett, M. D., 33, 49, 50, 51, 53, *58,* 59
Bartlett, E., 32, *58, 102*
Bates, E., 2, 3, 4, *15,* 51, 52, *58*
Bauer, P. J., 70, 71, *86*
Beit-Halachmi, B., 203, *218*
Bellugi, U., *170*
Benigni, L., 2, 3, *15*
Berman, R. A., 173, 175, 178, 183, 185, 188, 195, 196, 197, 198, *199, 200*
Billman, D., 108, *138*
Black, M., 204, *217*
Blansitt, E. L., 213, *217*
Bloom, A., 203, *217*
Bloom, L., 2, 3, *16,* 36, 51, 52, *58,* 90, *102,* 105, *139*
Bolinger, D., 73, *86*
Borer, H., 12, *16,* 108, 130, 131, *139,* 142, 166, 168, *170*
Bornstein, M., 28, *31*
Bowerman, M., 2, 3, 11, *16,* 33, 40, 47, 49, *58, 89, 102,* 108, 109, 111, 119, 130, 132, 133, *139*

Boyes-Braem, P., 64, *87*
Braine, M. D. S., 108, *139*
Braunwald, S. R., 36, 37, 49, *58*
Bretherton, I., 2, 3, *15*
Brookes, S., 53, *59*
Broughton, J., 2, 3, *16*
Brown, R., 89, 94, 97, 104, 105, *139,* 203, 204, *217*
Bruner, J., 61, *86*
Budwig, N., 174, 175, *200*

C

Callahan, M. A., 63, *86*
Camaioni, L., 2, 3, *15*
Campbell, R. N., 1, *16*
Carey, P., 157, *170*
Carey, S., 9, *17,* 32, 36, 53, 54, *58, 60,* 61, 63, 83, 84, *86, 87,* 88, 93, *102*
Cauley, K., 110, *139*
Chien, Y., 142, *171*
Chomsky, N., 30, *31,* 129, *139,* 142, 152, *170*
Chung, S., 174, *200*
Clark, E. V., 44, 47, 55, *58,* 72, 73, 74, *86,* 88, 91, *103,* 106, *139,* 150, 157, 164, *170,* 187, 197, *200*
Corrigan, R. A., *16*
Corrigan, R. L., 2, 3, *16,* 36, 52, *58*
Crain, S., 146, 149, 150, 152, 155, 158, 162, 163, 165, 166, 168, *170, 171,* 173, 175, *200*
Cromer, R. F., 2, *16*
Culicover, P., 198, *201*

D

DeGaspe-Beaubien, F., 110, *139*
Demuth, K., 173, 175, 197, *200*
De Saussure, F., 14, *16,* 204, *218*
Dickinson, D. K., 98, *103*